MARRIAGE BONDS
of
FRANKLIN COUNTY, VIRGINIA
1786-1858

BY
MARSHALL WINGFIELD

Memphis, Tenn.

1939

Notice

In many older books, foxing (or discoloration) occurs and, in some instances, print lightens with wear and age. Reprinted books, such as this, often duplicate these flaws, notwithstanding efforts to reduce or eliminate them. The pages of this reprint have been digitally enhanced and, where possible, the flaws eliminated in order to provide clarity of content and a pleasant reading experience.

First Published by :
West Tennessee Historical Society
Memphis
1939

Reprinted by:

Janaway Publishing, Inc.
732 Kelsey Ct.
Santa Maria, California 93454
(805) 925-1038
www.janawaygenealogy.com

2009, 2011

ISBN: 9781596411883

Made in the United States of America

DEDICATION

To

JUNIUS BLAIR FISHBURN

philanthropist, banker, publisher and native son of Franklin County, whose sturdiness, self-reliance and success will yield inspiration for other sons of Franklin long after he has been gathered unto his fathers

OTHER BOOKS BY MARSHALL WINGFIELD

A HISTORY OF CAROLINE COUNTY, VIRGINIA, published 1924 by Trevvett, Christian and Co., Richmond, Va. 544 pages, 79 illustrations.

FORCES OF DESTINY, published 1932 by Fleming H. Revell Co., New York, 220 pages.

TRANSLATING CHRISTMAS AND OTHER POEMS, published 1933 by Gregsonia Press, Cincinnati, Ohio.

NOTES OF A PILGRIM, published 1935 by Tubb Printing Co., Amory, Miss.

NOSTALGIA AND OTHER POEMS, published 1937 by Advertiser Publishing Co. Amory, Miss. 104 pages.

HILLS OF HOME, published by A. R. Taylor Co., Memphis, Tennessee, 110 pages.

A HISTORY OF HENRY COUNTY VIRGINIA (with J. P. A. Hill), published 1925 by the Bulletin Publishing Co., Martinsville, Va.

A HISTORY OF FRANKLIN COUNTY VIRGINIA (in printing), J. P. Bell Co., Lynchburg, Va.

THE SOUTHERN LITERARY SCENE (in manuscript).

WINGFIELD'S WORKS

FOREWORD

The transcribing of these marriage bonds was begun several years ago, with the intention of including them in my HISTORY OF FRANKLIN COUNTY VIRGINIA, but as the pages grew, it became apparent that their inclusion would make the volume too bulky. The value of the bonds as genealogical material, and the time and money I had spent in transcribing them, made publication seem a necessity. Hence this book.

I do not expect to recover the monetary outlay incident to the transcribing, to say nothing of the cost of printing and binding, but I shall have the reward of knowing that I have made available some of the most valuable genealogical material in this country.

The descendants of the couples listed herein, are to be found in all Southern and most Western States. I have many genealogical notes respecting them. Other notes are solicited. Many of these couples left Franklin County with the wagon trains that moved westward at the opening of the Nineteenth Century. Where did they settle? Who are their descendants? The children and grandchildren of other couples joined in later migrations as "westward the course of empire took its way." Who and where are their kindred? When sufficient answers to these questions are in hand, they will be given to the public in another volume.

It will be noted that but few bonds are listed for the years 1850-1858. These bonds are lost and there is but little room to hope that they will ever be found.

For the sake of brevity only Christian names of parents are given, save when full names make for clarity.

Gratitude is hereby expressed to Mrs. Blanche Garrett White who sat at the typewriter through many a summer day and wrote down these names as I unfolded and deciphered the brittle and time-yellowed papers; to Miss Doris Garrett (a sister of Mrs. White) who, years later, re-checked the names; and last, but by no means least, to my wife, Marie Gregson Wingfield, who arranged the names in alphabetical order, typed them, discovered the parentage of many of the couples and, carrying on a vast correspondence incident thereto, aided in locating bonds that had been removed from the Clerk's Office and re-arranged and re-typed the manuscript as new material came in. But for modesty, her name would appear on the title page.

Marshall Wingfield
Watkins and Eastmoreland
Memphis, Tennessee

INTRODUCTION

It is interesting to note, in connection with the Marriage Bonds of Franklin County, the following Statutes governing marriage in colonial Virginia.

In February 1631 it was enacted that , "No minister shall celebrate matrimony between any persons without a facultie or lycense graunted by the Governor, except the baynes of matrimony have been first published three several Sundays or holy days in the time of devyne service in the parish churches where the sayd persons dwell accordinge to the booke of common prayer . . . . In every parish church within this colony shall be kept by the minister a book wherein shall be written the day and year of every Christeninge, weddings, and buriall." Hening, I, p. 156-58.

1705 it was enacted that: "No minister or ministers shall celebrate the rites of matrimony between any persons, or join them together as man and wife, without lawful license, or thrice publication of the bans according as the rubric in the common prayer book prescribes, which enjoins that if the persons to be married, dwell in several parishes, the banns shall be published in both parishes; and that the curate of the one parish shall not solemnize the matrimony until he have a certificate from the curate of the other parish that the banns have been thrice published and no objection made against the parties joining together."

"That all licenses for marriage shall be issued by the clerk of the court of that county where the feme shall have her usual residence, and by him only, and in such manner, and under such rules and directions as are herein mentioned and set down: (that is to say,) he shall take a bond to our soverign lady the Queen, her heirs and successors, with good surety, the penalty of fifty pounds, current money of Virginia, under conditions that there is no lawful cause to obstruct the marriage for which the license shall be desired; and each clerk failing herein, shall forfeit and pay pay fifty pound current money of Virginia; and if either of the persons intended to be married shall be under the age of one and twenty years, and not theretofore married, the consent of the parent or guardian of every such person under the age of one and twenty years shall be personally given before the said clerk, or signified under the hand and seal of the said parent or guardian, and attested by two witnesses."

An Act of 1705, (Hening, Vol. 3, page 441, chapter 48, section 8) provided for the following fees in connection with marriages: "And be it also enacted by the authority aforesaid, and it is hereby enacted, That the fees upon the said marriages, be as follows, viz. To the Governor or Commander in Chief for the Time being, for each license or marriage, twenty shillings, or two hundred pounds of tobacco. To the Clerk of the County Court, issuing the same, five shillings or fifty pounds of tobacco. To the minister, if by license, twenty shillings or two hundred pounds of tobacco; if by banns, five shillings or fifty pounds of tobacco. To the minister, or reader, for publishing banns and certifying the same, if required, one shilling and sixpence, or fifteen pounds of tobacco. And that these, and every of these said fees, if not in ready money, shall be paid at time of year, in tobacco, of the growth of the parish where the feme lives; and upon refusal of payment, be leviable by distress, by such officer, or person, and in such manner as directed for clerks fees."

"And be is further enacted, by the authority aforesaid, "That from and after the said twentieth day of April, the minister of every parish within this Colony, shall keep a fair and exact register of all the births and deaths of the persons within his parish, of which notice shall have been given to him; according to the direction of this act; as also of all persons which shall be baptised by him; And the clerk of every parish Church or chappel, whereof there shall be no minister, shall keep a fair and exact register of all the births and deaths of the persons within the parish or place whereof he shall be clerk, of which he shall have had notice, in manner as is above directed: In which said register shall be expressed and distinguished, the names of the persons which shall be born free, and of their parents, and the names of the persons which shall be baptised, and the names of the master or owner of the slaves which shall be born and whether such slaves be male or female; and also the names of all persons dying, together with the names of the master or owner of the persons dying in slavery; a fair and true copy of which register signed by the minister or clerk keeping the same, shall, on the twentieth day of April, and on the twentieth day of October, in every year, by hime be returned to the office of the secretary of this dominion; For the keeping and returning of which said register, as above directed, there shall be satisfied and paid to the minister or clerk respectively keeping the same, three pounds of tobacco for every person so registered; The fee for registering of the births and christenings of all free persons, shall be paid by the parents of such child; and the fee for registering the births of all slaves, shall be paid by the owner of such slaves; and the fee for registering the death of all free persons, shall be paid by the person who shall give notice of such death; and the fee for registering the death of all slaves shall be paid by the owner of such slaves: All which fees for registering, shall and are hereby declared to be distrainable. And if any minister or clerk shall neglect or refuse to keep or return such register, in manner before in this act appointed, every minister or clerk so refusing or neglecting to keep or return such register, shall forfeit and pay two hundred pounds of tobacco for every month he shall refuse or neglect to keep or return the same."

In 1748 it was enacted that "No minister shall celebrate the rights of matrimony between any persons . . . . without lawful license, or thrice publication of banns according to the rubric in the book of common prayer . . . . And if any minister shall celebrate the rights of matrimony . . . . without such license, or publication of banns, as by this act required, he shall for every such offense be imprisoned one whole year, without bail or mainprise, and shall also forfeit and pay five hundred pounds current money."

The General Assembly of 1780 passed an Act: "For encouraging marriages and for removing doubts concerning the validity of marriages celebrated by ministers other than those of the Church of England. Be it enacted by the General Assembly that it shall and may be lawful for any minister of any society or congregation of Christians, and for the society of Christians called Quakers and Menonists, to celebrate the rites of matrimony, and to join together as man and wife, those who may apply to them agreeable to the rules and usages of the respective societies to which the parties to be married respectively belong, and such marriages as well as those heretofore celebrated by dissenting ministers, shall be, and they are hereby declared good and valid in law. Provided always, and it is the true intent and meaning of this Act, that nothing herein before contained shall extend or be construed to extend to confirm any marriages heretofore celebrated, or hereafter to be celebrated between parties within the degrees of affinity or consanquinity forbidden by law. Provided also, that no persons except the people called Quakers and Menonists, shall hereafter be joined together as man and wife, without lawful license first had, or thrice publication of banns in the respective parishes, or congregations where the parties to be married may severally reside, agreeable to the direction of an Act of Assembly passed in the year one thousand seven hundred and forty eight, entitled, 'An Act concerning marriages.' Provided, That the license so obtained may be directed to any regular minister that the parties to be married may require. Every minister of any society or congregation, not of the Church of England, offending against the directions of the said Act concerning marriages, shall be subject to the same pains and penalties in case of omission or neglect as by the said recited Act are imposed upon ministers of the Church of England.

"And be it further enacted, That instead of the fees prescribed by the said recited Act, the several ministers may demand and receive for the celebration of every marriage, twenty-five pounds of tobacco, and no more, to be paid in current money at the rate which shall be settled by the grand jury at the term of the general court next preceding such marriages.

"And that a register of all marriages may be preserved, Be it enacted, That a certificate of every marriage hereafter to be solemnized signed by the minister celebrating the same, or in the case of Quakers, by the Clerk of the meeting, shall be by such minister or clerk, as the case may be, transmitted to the clerk of the county wherein the marriage is solemnized, within three months thereafter, to be entered upon record by such clerk, in a book to be by him kept for that purpose, which shall be evidence of such marriage. The clerk shall be entitled to receive and demand of the party to be married, ten pounds of tobacco for recording such certificate. And be it further enacted, That every minister or clerk of a Quaker's or Menonist's meeting, as the case may be, failing to transmit such certificate to the clerk of the court in due time, shall forfeit and pay the sum of five hundred pounds, to be recovered with costs of suit by the informer in any court of record. This Act shall commence and be in force from and after the first day of January in the year of our Lord one thousand seven hundred and eighty one.

"For carrying this act into execution, Be it further enacted, That the courts of the different counties shall and are hereby authorized, on recommendation from the elders of the several religious sects, to grant license to dissenting ministers of the gospel, not exceeding the number of four of each sect in any one county, to join together in holy matrimony any persons within their counties only; which license shall be signed by the judge or elder magistrate under his hand and seal." (Hening Vol. 10, pp. 361-363.)

The following interesting facts may be deduced from the foregoing Statutes: Ministers of the Established church were at liberty to celebrate marriages under the authority of both banns and license. Banns constituted a legal substitute for a license. Marriages under licenses were recorded in the office of the County Clerk; those under banns in the Parish Register. Hence all Colonial marriages were not evidenced by Marriage Bonds filed with the County Clerk. The marriage fee under banns was just one fourth as much as the fee under license, hence it is reasonable to suppose that many couples were married by banns. Not many copies of the Parish Registers were delivered "to the office of the secretary of this dominion" as the law required, hence genealogists much face the fact that many of the records of Colonial marriages are irrevocably lost.

It should also be noted that a Marriage Bond was not something given by the prospective groom to the prospective bride or her parents. Landon C. Bell, in his SUNLIGHT ON THE SOUTHSIDE, points out the fact that even so eminent a biographer as Burton J. Hendricks labored under this delusion, stating in his THE TRAINING OF AN AMERICAN, that "the first existing bit of family history (Page family) is the record of the marriage bonds given by Lewis Page to Sallie Justice." Had Mr. Hendricks been familiar with the nature of a marriage bond he would have said that Lewis Page gave a bond to the State as a prerequisite to securing a license to marry Sallie Justice.

It will also be noted from the foregoing Statutes that Colonial laws discriminated against dissenting ministers. In MEMORIALS OF METHODISM IN VIRGINIA, (p. 105) we read that: "Methodists claimed that their ministers were in every essential qualification for the administration of Christian ordinances, the equals of the parish ministers, and yet there was not a preacher from Asbury down who could administer the Holy Sacrament, celebrate the rites of matrimony or baptize a child. These rites they were compelled to seek at the hands of the Established Clergy." In the closing years of the Establishment dissenting ministers began to celebrate marriages without the warrant of civil law. Such instances of "presumption" were sharply rebuked by the parish priests. Such marriages were regarded by most people as irregular, and by strict Churchmen as illegal and adulterous. The Act of 1780 removed all doubts as to the validity of these marriages and, at the same time, provided that each religious "sect" might have four recognized marrying ministers in each county. This Act was later amended so that every recognized minister of every denomination might perform marriage ceremonies upon compliance with certain simple requirements of law.

Quakers, Menonists and Dunkards were not required to procure a license, publish banns or give bonds, though most of the members of them conformed to the legal requirements which were binding on others.

The regular form of a marriage bond was as follows: "Know all men by these presents, That we (usually filled in with name of groom and one other man), are held and firmly bound unto the Commonwealth of Virginia (bonds sometime given to the Governor) in the just and full sum of One Hundred and Fifty Dollars, the true payment whereof, well and truly to be made, we bind ourselves, our heirs, executors and administrators, jointly and severally, firmly by these presents. Sealed with our seals, and dated this............day of.............

"The conditions of the above obligation is such, That whereas the above bound..., hath obtained from the Clerk of the County Court of Franklin, a license for his intermarriage with................................., of said county. Now if there shall be no lawful cause to obstruct said marriage, then the above obligation to be void, else to remain in full force and virtue.

(Signatures of Bondsmen) "

The foregoing form was change on April 7, 1858, and no marriage bonds were given after this law became effective. The new form was as follows:

"Certificate to Obtain a Marriage License

Having applied to the Clerk of the........................Court of........................for a Marriage License, and being requested, I make the following Certificate as required by the Act of the General Assembly, passed April 7th, 1858.

Date of marriage..
Place of marriage..
Full names of parties married..
Age of husband..
Age of wife..

Condition of husband (widowed or single) ....
Condition of wife (widowed or single) ....
Place of husband's birth ....
Place of wife's birth ....
Place of husband's residence ....
Place of wife's residence ....
Names of husband's parents ....
Names of wife's parents ....
Occupation of husband ....

   Given under my hand this......day of......................, 18.....
   ....(Name of husband)

"Within two months after the marriage shall have taken place, the Minister solemnizing the same must certify the fact to the Clerk of the Court."

On March 15, 1861, an Act was passed requiring that Certificate to obtain a Marriage License, and Certificate of Minister solemnizing same, be annexed to the license itself.

MARRIAGE BONDS OF FRANKLIN COUNTY VIRGINIA 1786-1858

KEY: s, son; ss, stepson; gs, grandson; dau, daughter; sdau, stepdaughter; gdau, granddaughter; g, guardian; bro, brother; sis, sister; wid, widow; u, uncle; au, aunt; c, cousin; w, wife; h, husband; m, married; mhr, mother; smhr, stepmother; gmhr, grandmother; fr, father; sfr, stepfather; gfr, grandfather; ps, parents; gps, grandparents; dcd, deceased; sur, surety. Numbers at end of entries refer to officiating ministers who are listed and numbered at back of the volume.

Abshire, Abraham and Phebe Wright, Feb. 3, 1814. Sur. Geo. Wright, Jr. 130.

Abshire, Abraham and Hannah Nafe, Feb. 1, 1827. 18.

Abshire, Abraham and Susannah Vinson, Jan. 14, 1801. Sur. Wm. Brown. 21.

Abshire, Ambrose and Charlotte Wright, Jan. 17, 1827. Sur. Geo. Wright, Sr. 48.

Abshire, Ammon and Cinthy Wright, May 11, 1840. Sur. Geo. Wright. 18.

Abshire, Andrew and Calley Payne, May 25, 1819. Sur. Mark Payne. 98.

Abshire, Edward and Dinah Short, dau. Winny, Nov. 17, 1790. Sur. John Abshire. 52.

Abshire, Geo. and Lucinda Angel, Jan. 11, 1836. Sur. Joshua Angel.

Abshire, Isaac and Joanna Wright, Apr. 3, 1809. Sur. James Wray. 96.

Abshire, Jabez L. and Susan D. Turner, Dec. 22, 1852. 96.

Abshire, James and Elizabeth Overholts, Mar. 6, 1804. Sur. Wm. Brown.

Abshire, James and Elizabeth Teel, May 1, 1848. Sur. Wm. Teel. 18.

Abshire, John and Elizabeth Binnion, Sept. 21, 1796. Sur. Wm. Poteet.

Abshire, John and Rhoda M. Bond, Sept. 29, 1826. Sur. Clabon Bond.

Abshire, John and Sarah Ann Mitchell, dau. James P. and Penelope, Oct. 2, 1843.

Abshire, Nelson and Polly Wright, Jan. 7, 1822. Sur. John Wright. 48.

Abshire, Peter and Nelly Doran, dau. Mary and Harthum, Aug. 19, 1787. Sur. Peter Doran and Abraham Abshire. 52.

Abshire, Randolph and Mary A. Angel, dau. Wm., Sept. 28, 1840. Sur. Joshua Angel.

Abshire, Wm. s. Nelson and Sally R. A. F. Lyon, dau. John B., Nov. 1, 1850. Sur. D. D. Farbes. 86.

Adams, Creed H. and Elizabeth Mooring, (Morrison), Nov. 6, 1834. Sur. Meade Morrison.

Adams, Creed H. and Anna Beckelhimer, Nov. 5, 1858.

Adams, Elisha and Elizabeth Newton, June 14, 1798. Sur. H. Nele. 72.

Adams, Elisha and Jane Purtle, July 25, 1817. Sur. Amos Harrison. 130.

Adams, James and Elizabeth Broaddy, Mar. 1, 1824. Sur. Robert Innes.

Adams, James and Elizabeth Thompson, Aug. 9, 1834. Sur. Thos. Thompson.

Adams, John and Catherine H. Johnson, June 24, 1839.

Adams, John and Sally Crawford, May 6, 1839. Sur. David Good. 132.

Adams, Joshua and Elizabeth Ingram, dau. James, Nov. 18, 1850. Sur. Isaac Ingram.

Adams, Martin and Polly Adkins, Nov. 12, 1809. 122.

Adams, Moza and Alsey Ann Johnson, Dec. 2, 1852. 68.

Adams, Reed and Susan Campbell, dau. Lucy, Feb. 7, 1843. Sur. Wm. Campbell.

Adams, Sneed T. and Cynthia W. Angle, Jan. 8, 1842. Sur. Peter Campbell.

Adams, Spencer, s. Absalom, and Elizabeth Bowles, dau. Wm. and Sally, Sept. 8, 1819. Sur. Peter Boles. 98.

Adkins, John and Elizabeth Adkins, dau. David, April 24, 1788. Sur. John Fuson.

Adkins, John and Susannah Meador, Oct. 6, 1830. Sur. Stephen Booth. 48.

Adkins, Joseph and Elizabeth Galaspie, dau. Evan, Nov. 25, 1833. Sur. Evan Galaspy. 48.

Adkins, Spencer and Nancy Standley, March 1813. 44.

Adkins, Wm. C. and Oma Ann Willis, July 29, 1858.

Adkins, Wm. and Lucy Bozwell, Oct. 10, 1841. Sur. David Moore. 39.

Adney, Daniel and Anna Coger, Feb. 13, 1798. 89.

Adney, John Thos. and Barbara Leseuer, dau. Elizabeth, Jan. 11, 1797. Sur. Samuel Reedy.

Adney, Thos. and Polly Rose, dau. Gabriel, Feb. 19, 1803. Sur. Gabriel Rose.

Agee, Ephraim and Elizabeth Dunn, dau. Thomas, April. 6, 1801. Sur. James L. Hale. 141.

Agee, Isaac and Joannah Key, dau. George, July 6, 1822. Sur. Geo. T. Key.

Agee, James O. and Sarah Ann Maxey, dau. James, Oct. 4, 1847. Sur. Wm. Craghead.

Agee, Jesse and Elizabeth Childress, Mar. 3, 1788. Sur. Philip Raley. 37.

Agee, Levi and Sally Maxcy, Sept. 23, 1811. Sur. Jeremiah Maxcy. 15.

Agee, Reason G. and Judith M. Maxey, dau. James and Sarah, Dec. 5, 1836. Sur. Levi Maxcy. 3

Agee, Wm., s. Joshua, and Nancy W. Robertson, Dec. 12, 1844. Sur. John Robertson.

Akers, Daniel and Rebecka Webster, dau. Luke and Sarah, Dec. 2, 1800. Sur. Blackburn Akers. 21.

Akers, Edward G. and Lucy Webster, Feb. 6, 1839. Sur. John B. Webster.

Akers, Eli and Amanda J. Akers, Feb. 3, 1845 Sur. Richard F. Darnell. 18.

Akers, Fleming and Nancy Akers, dau. Samuel, Oct. 3, 1825. Sur. Joseph Burnett.

Akers, Henry and Sarah Wimmer, dau. John and Hannah, Mar. 24, 1823. Sur. John E. McCrery.

Akers, James and Lucy Webster, dau. Luke and Sarah, Jan. 2, 1792. Sur. Wm. Akers. 52.

Akers, James and Susannah Smith, Jan. 29, 1811. Sur. James Smith. 122.

Akers, James and Nancy Webster, Apr. 22, 1815. Sur. Joel Akers. 130.

Akers, James H. and Lucy Ann Brown, dau. Martha H., Apr. 24, 1832. Sur. Nathaniel Brown. 46.

Akers, James and Sarah Angel, Oct. 28, 1840. Sur. Joshua Angel.

Akers, James and Paulina Howell, Feb. 16, 1829. Sur. Moses Howell. 26.

Akers, Joel Jr. and Mary T. Angle, Jan. 27, 1849. Sur. A. T. Angel. 18.

Akers, Joel and Elizabeth Clack, July 24, 1821. Sur. Michael Clack. 130.

Akers, John and Sarah Brown, Aug. 8, 1793. 52.

Akers, Luke and Jane Webster, Jan. 12, 1824. Sur. Daniel Webster. 130.

Akers, Madison and Sarah Lynch, Dec. 13, 1849. 18.

Akers, Nathaniel and Elizabeth Akers, Oct. 7, 1806. Sur. John Akers. 130.

Akers, Nathaniel S. and Elizabeth Boon, Dec. 29, 1845. Sur. Stephen Boon. 18.

Akers, Nathaniel and Mahala F. Turner, Feb. 4, 1851. 134.

Akers, Samuel and Sarah Highly, Aug. 2, 1802. Sur. James Highly. 72.

Akers, Steven and Rachael Coxel, Apr. 3, 1820. Sur. — — Ferguson.

Akers, Wm. and Livinia Capper, Apr. 23, 1821. Sur. Jacob Hartsel. 130.

Akers, Wm. and Nancy White, Dec. 24, 1807, 130.

Akers, Wm. H. and Elizabeth Akers, Jan. 26, 1846. Sur. James Akers. 134.

Akers, Wm. and Jincey Haynes, dau. Drewry, Aug. 26, 1834. Sur. Thos. Saul. 145.

Albright, Wm. and Jane Meador, dau. Jehu, Oct. 23, 1821. Sur. Abel Meador.

Albright, Wm. and Sarah Nimmo, dau. Robert, Feb. 14, 1832. Sur. Thos. Mimmo. 140.

Aldrich, Joseph L. and Mary M. Webster, Feb. 25, 1850. Sur. H. H. Webster. 68.

Aldridge, John F. and Lucy Akers, Aug. 31, 1835. Sur. James Akers. 60.

Aldridge, John and Charlotte Mills, dau. Nancy Whorley, Feb. 5, 1833. Sur. John F. Aldridge. 48.

Aldridge, Madison M. and Mary Gibson, Apr. 27, 1837. Sur. Absalom Gibson.

Aldridge, Stanton R. and Mary Jane Williams, Jan. 24, 1848. Sur. Robert Williams. 60.

Alleck, Daniel and Elizabeth Bowman, Aug. 17, 1797. Sur. Lawrence Bowsman. 52.

Alleck, David and Hannah Shueman, dau. Mary, Mar. 25, 1797. Sur. John Shueman.

Aliff, James and Kitty Gibson, dau. Absalom, June 22, 1850. Sur. Miles Gibson. 68.

Aliff, John B. and Sarah J. Puckett, Feb. 24, 1847. Sur. Joel J. Childress. 96.

Allaway, Abner and Polly Kent, Nov. 10, 1805. Sur. Peter Bernard.

Allen, Andrew and Lavina Roberts, Mar. 1, 1823. Sur. Wm. Allen.

Allen, Daniel and Zina Moore, Nov. 9, 1846. Sur. John Moore. 60.

Allen, James and Mary Beasley, Aug. 5, 1819. Sur. Mary Beasley.

Allen, James and Amelia Ferguson, Jan. 19, 1818. Sur. John Ferguson.

Allen, Jeremiah and Frances Payne, Apr. 6, 1812. Sur. Flail Payne.

Allen, John and Lucy David, Feb. 4, 1794. 141.

Allen, John W. and Nancy Dillon, May 1, 1819. Sur. Wm. Pasley. 130.

Allen, John P. and Teresse Bradley, Feb. 29, 1848. Sur. W. C. Mitchell. 86.

Allen, Mathew R. and Margaret E. Meador, Sept. 21, 1858.

Allen, Preston and Lucy Boyd, dau. Hugh, Jan. 5, 1827. Sur. Andrew Boyd. 61.

Allen, Reynolds and Phoebe Perdue, Jan. 11, 1820. Sur. John Plyborne. 130.

Allen, Stephen and Sally Radford, dau. James, Sept. 10, 1792. Sur. John Waid.

Allen, Thos. and Mary Craghead, dau. John, Dec. 6, 1790. Sur. John Craghead.

Allen, Wm. Jr., s. William Sr. and Susannah Smith, dau. Daniel, Mar. 10, 1812. Sur. Samuel Williams.

Allen, Wm. Sr. and Clary Pearson, Feb. 11, 1812. Sur. John Bozwell.

Allen, Wm. and Mary Atkins, Nov. 20, 1851. 60.

Allie, David and Charity Bybee, Dec. 4, 1786. Sur. Nicholas Alley and Thos. Arthur.

Allie, John and Mildred Lawrence, Jan. 1, 1787, Sur. Nicholas Alley. 66.

Allie, Wm. and Suckey Bibsy, Nov. 10, 1802. Sur. Sherod Bibry.

Allman, Sebastian and Sally Webb, Aug. 25, 1797. Sur. Samuel Webb.

Almond, John, s. Mary, and Elizabeth Trent, Jan. 5, 1833. Sur. Benj. Trent. 48.

Almond, Phillip and Polly Dillion, Mar. 3, 1811. Sur. Alexander Lane.

Altice, Abraham and Elizabeth Reid (Reed) June 2, 1806. Sur. John Altic

Altice, Jacob and Elizabeth Sink, Dec. 22, 1803. Sur. Abraham Sink.

Altice, Joseph and Susannah Bowsman, Mar. 16, 1807. Sur. Adam Bousman.

Altice, Peter and Barbara Beckner, May 6, 1816. Sur. Jacob Beckner. 130.

Altice, Solomon and Elizabeth Michael, Mar. 11, 1806. Sur. Jacob Michael.

Altice, Wm. and Catherine H. Johnson, June 24, 1839. Sur. Henry B. Johnson. 132.

Altick, Abraham and Catherine Kinsie, Nov. 7, 1848. Sur. David Kinsie. 11.

Altick, Christopher and Tabitha Laprade, Aug. 21, 1848. Sur. Andrew Laprade. 18.

Altick, Christopher and Hannah Beckner, July 19, 1813. Sur. Jacob Beckner. 130.

Altick, Daniel and Elizabeth Altick, Aug. 17, 1797. Sur. Lawrence Bousman. 89.

Altick, David and Polly Snidor, dau. John, Apr. 3, 1837. Sur. Otey Sink.

Altick, David and Foley Snider, Dec. 28, 1840. 18.

Altick, Geo. and Omey F. Starkey, June 12, 1851. 19.

Altick, John and Malinda Hutts, Nov. 1, 1819. Sur. Leonard Hutts.

Altick, Jonathan and Polly Sink, Jan. 31, 1843. Sur. Henry Sink. 18.

Altick, Joseph and Anna Rankins, July 24, 1839. Sur. George W. Mills, 18.

Altick, Leonard and Sarah Jane Saul, Dec. 1, 1840.

Altick, Michael and Sarah J. Turner, dau. Elizabeth, Nov. 8, 1847. Sur. James A. Turner.

Altick, Samuel and Mary Ann Goode, Dec. 19, 1832. Sur. David Goode, Jr. 48.

Altize, Joseph and Mary Boyle, Nov. 10, 1835. 18.

Amos, James and Rachael Warren, dau. Elijah, Nov. 25, 1818. Sur. Winnford Warren.

Amos, John and Anne Payne, dau. Isham, Dec. 5, 1833. Sur. Wilson Amos. 140.

Amos, Joseph and Nancy Williams, Nov. 1, 1842. Sur. Daniel Williams.

Amos, Meredith and Mary Meador, dau. Geo., Oct. 14, 1841. Sur. Wm. C. A. Meador. 86.

Amos, Spencer and Nancy Payne, dau. Silas, Oct. 5, 1839. Sur. Silas Payne. 86.

Amos, Wm. and Martha Barton, dau. Elisha, May 26, 1841. Sur. John Barton. 18.

Amos, Wm. and Henny Boswell, Nov. 5, 1804. Sur. Wm. Boswell.

Amos, Wm. and Sally Payne, Mar. 25, 1836 Sur. Joseph Payne.

Amos, Wm. F. and America B. Gregory, dau. Wm. H., Jan. 4, 1848. Sur. Wm. H. Gregory, Jr.

Amos, Wilson and Elizabeth Adams, Mar. 6, 1812. Sur. John Adams.

Anderson, Geo. and Millia Jones, — 1787. 66.

Anderson, James, s. Jesse and Polly, and Caroline B. Gilliam, dau. Arch and Nancy, Oct 20, 1853. 91.

Anderson, James B. and Sarah Ann Hunt, dau. Riley H., Oct 18, 1848. Sur. Riley H. Hunt. 11.

Anderson, James C. and Zillah P. Sutherland, dau. Polly, Oct. 7, 1845. Sur. Samuel S. Bryant.

Anderson, Joel C. and Betty C. Allen, Nov. 4, 1850. Sur. Jeremiah Allen.

Anderson, Joseph and Nancy Coleman, Dec. 31, 1813. Sur. Thos. Arrington.

Anderson, Nelson and Selina Taylor, Feb. 7, 1825. Sur. Wm. Childers. 48.

Anderson, Otey, s. John, and Ann Stearman, dau. Nancy, Nov. 12, 1827. Sur. A. G. Vannesson. 140.

Angel, James and Patty Simmons, dau. Joseph, Oct. 20, 1800. Sur. Joseph Simmons.
Angel, Joshua and America Quigley, dau. Elizabeth, Feb. 1, 1841. 18.
Angel, Wm. Jr. and Jane S. McGuffin, Dec. 16, 1831. Sur. Joseph McGuffin. 48.
Angle, Daniel and Gilda Wood, Apr. 26, 1828. Sur. Thos. Wood. 48.
Angle, Daniel and Elizabeth Perdue, Jan. 11, 1844. 18.
Angle, Daniel and Dianna Hughes, June 22, 1822. Sur. Elijah Hughes.
Angle, Edwin W. and Mary Elizabeth Beckner, dau. Lidia, Mar. 1, 1847. 18.
Angle, Henry and Sally Robertson, Feb. 22, 1812. Sur. Thos. Robertson. 130.
Angle, Henry J. and Lucy Wood, Apr. 4, 1825. Sur. Thos. Wood. 48.
Angle, Jacob and Caty Snidor, Sept. 27, 1803. Sur. John Snidor. 72.
Angle, John and Fanny Rudy, Apr. 3, 1798. Sur. Daniel Rudy. 89.
Angle, John and Mary J. Creasy, Dec. 16, 1852. 18.
Angle, Nathaniel and Sarah F. Wills, Nov. 18, 1852. 18.
Angle, Peter and Nancy Zeigler, Feb. 11, 1818. Sur. John H. Stewart.
Angle, Peter and Frances Beckner, Oct. 1, 1832. Sur. Stephen Sink.
Angle, (Angel) Taylor A. and Lioney Dodd, Apr. 19, 1827. Sur. John Dodd.
Angle, Thos. and Dolly Weaver, Dec. 24, 1834.
Anglin, Robt. and Clarissa Bottom, dau. James, Jan. 28, 1830. Sur. Greenberry Nichols.
Archer, Chapman and Suffy Beckelhimer, dau. John, July 16, 1802. Sur. Edmund Richards. 72.
Argabright, Geo. Washington and Elizabeth Shilling, Apr. 7, 1846. Sur. J. K. Shilling.

Argabright, Wm. D. and Catherine Wimmer, dau. John and Elizabeth, Dec. 14, 1850. 96.

Armstrong, Thos. and Mary Allen Bowles, Dec. 28, 1786. Sur. Wm. Drake.

Armstrong, Thos. and Jane Duvall, June 21, 1797. Sur. Samuel Duvall. 21.

Armstrong, Wm. and Alianna Hill, dau. Thos., Dec. 26, 1792. Sur. Thos. Jones. 52.

Arnold, John and Rebecca Willis, Mar. 8, 1808. Sur. Wm. Thompson. 117.

Arrington, Absalom, s. John, and Jane Cockran, dau. Isham, Sept. 22, 1817. Sur. Isham Cockran. 61.

Arrington, Arthur and Eleanor Ward, July 28, 1832. Sur. David Durham. 98.

Arrington, Chas. C. and Nancy Brooks, dau. Levi, Mar. 22, 1830. Sur. Thos. Hamlin. 48.

Arrington, Isham, s. Anderson, and Mary Via, dau. Absalom, Oct. 3, 1844. Sur. Anderson Via.

Arrington, Lewis and Sally Edwards, dau. Brice, Mar. 31, 1823. Sur. Isham Cockran. 61.

Arrington, Marvel M. and Elizabeth Amos, Dec. 21, 1846. Sur. James Amos. 137.

Arrington, Robt. and Pamelia Ashworth, May 3, 1838. Sur. Ransom Law.

Arrington, Samuel, s. John, and Nancy Griffith, dau. Daniel, Nov. 4, 1824. Sur. Absalom Arrington.

Arrington, Samuel and Evelina Phelps, dau. Polly, Sept. 24, 1828. Sur. Zadock Bernard.

Arrington, Samuel and Elizabeth Greer, Dec. 20, 1800. Sur. John Coleman. 21.

Arrington, Thos. and Milly Coleman, Sept. 27, 1791. Sur. James Coleman.

Arrington, Thos. and Sally McGuire, Sept. 5, 1815. Sur. Jubal Harris.

Arthur, Barnabas and Jane Wright, Oct. 6, 1823. Sur. J. G. Wright. 48.

Arthur, Carey and Lucy West, g. Joseph Greer, Apr. 5, 1815. Sur. Thos. Heptinstall.

Arthur, Jefferson and Christina Angle, Sept. 19, 1831. Sur. John Angle.

Arthur, John and Mary M. Griffin, Mar. 26, 1849. Sur. Greenberry Griffin. 96.

Arthur, John and Elizabeth Greer, dau. Nathan, Mar. 18, 1809. Sur. Stephen Dudley. 8.

Arthur, John and Barbary Richard, May 8, 1818. Sur. Andrew Thompson. 130.

Arthur, Jonn Jr. and Charlotte Smith, Sept. 7, 1818. Sur. John Fisher. 130.

Arthur, Lewis and Lucy Dillion, June 24, 1819. Sur. John Dillon. 130.

Arthur, Shelby and Rebecca Naff, Apr. 25, 1858. Sur. Jonathan Naff. 18.

Arthur, Thos. and Nancy Webster, Dec. 21, 1802. 106.

Arthur, Wm. and Polly Southerland, Dec. 24, 1807. Sur. Willie Young.

Asbury, Geo. Jr. and Catherine Ferguson, Aug. 25, 1827. Sur. Eli Ferguson Jr. 140.

Asbury, Joel and Elizabeth Ferguson, Aug. 2, 1847. Sur. Joseph B. Meador.

Ascue, John Jr. s. John Sr., and Rachael Brogan, dau. Robt. May 5, 1824. Sur. Samuel H. Ferguson.

Ascue, Lewis and Peggy Jones, dau. John L., Oct. 6, 1828. Sur. Samuel Radford.

Ascue, Phillip and Ruth Vandover, Jan. 3, 1804. Sur. George Vanover.

Ascue, Wm. and Docia Allen, Feb. 17, 1817. Sur. Wm. Allen.

Askue, Christopher and Hannah Vanover, Jan. 31, 1805. 122.

Ashinghurst, John and Lucy A. Hill, June 12, 1827. Sur. Zadock Bernard. 48.

Ashlin, Chesley and Phoebe James, Dec. 30, 1822. Sur. Catlett James.

Ashworth, Chas. and Sarah Chandler, dau. Jerusha, Aug. 20, 1834. Sur. Stephen Chandler. 12.

Ashworth, Henry and Jane W. Bond, Dec. 2, 1822. Sur. Claiborne Bond.

Ashworth, John and Jane White, June 27, 1836. Sur. Wm. White.

Ashworth, Parks and Jane Hall, Apr. 1, 1822. Sur. Wm. Hutcherson.

Ashworth, Samuel and Joanna Hiett, dau. Nancy Williams, Dec. 2, 1830. Sur. Moses Hiett. 48.

Ashworth, Stephen and Lucy Law, Mar. 10, 1811. Sur. John B. Callicott.

Ashworth, Wm. C. and Catherine Wingo, Apr. 23, 1831. Sur. Thos. Hamlin.

Atkins, Henry and Susanna Bradshaw, May 29, 1790. 52.

Atkins, Jacob and Phebe Bradshaw, dau. Susannah, Mar. 28, 1791. Sur. Chas. Bradshaw. 52.

Atkins, James and Polly Kennett, Oct. 25, 1825 Sur. Singleton Kasey.

Atkins, Littleberry and Nancy Atkins, dau. Mary, May 29, 1790. Sur. Jacob Atkins. 52.

Atkins, Pleasant and Polly Freeman, Feb. 28, 1825. Sur. Jabez Snow.

Atkinson, Chas. and Rebecka Haislip, (Haslip), Aug. 7, 1799. Sur. Henry Hazlip.

Atwood, Joseph and Polly McGuffin, Jan. 18, 1826. Sur. Robt. M. Beard.

Austin, Daniel S. and Letitia A. Bird, Oct. 4, 1858.

Austin, James J. and Charlotte Fisher, Oct. 7, 1858.

Austin, John M. and Frances A. Holloway, Dec. 3, 1842. Sur. Hugh Holloway.

Austin, Wm. and Lucy Ann Willis, July 7, 1845. Sur. Miles Austin, 132.

Ayres, Marshall and Rebecca Callicote, Jan. 11, 1838. Sur. Leroy B. Law.

Babcock, Christopher and Julia Hendrick, dau. Bernard G., July 15, 1833. Sur. Tracy Good.

Baber, Hairston L. and Emily Chewning, Oct. 15, 1849. Sur. Clemons Oyler.

Bailey, Chas. C. and Martha H. Rowland, Mar. 26, 1818. Sur. Wm. I. Walker. 124.

Bailey, James and Elizabeth Wright, dau. Elizabeth, Dec. 11, 1798. Sur. Benj. Belcher. 89.

Baker, Edward and Susannah Mullins, Apr. 24, 1793. Sur. Wm. Mullins.

Baker, German and Mildred James, dau. Spencer, Oct. 26, 1808. Sur. Braxton James. 44.

Baker, Peter and Ann Lazenby, dau. Elizabeth, Apr. 1, 1805.

Baker, Pleasant and Phebe J. Meador, Dec. 16, 1843. Sur. Joel Meador.

Baker, Wm. and Jane Payne, dau. Fannie, Dec. 2, 1822. Sur. Wm. Hatcher.

Bakleheimer, John and Nancy Hutts, Apr. 24, 1835. Sur. John Bowman.

Ball, John and Annah Shockley, dau. David, Dec. 22, 1800. Sur. David Shockley. 37.

Ball, Joseph and Elizabeth Phillips, dau. James, May 7, 1804. Sur. Jesse Chappel.

Ball, Joseph and Elizabeth Perdue, Sept. 15, 1804. Sur. Meshack Perdue.

Ballard, Aaron and Nancy Pearson, Jan. 2, 1832. Sur. Peyton Pearson. 132.

Ballard, Chas. and Mary Craghead, Aug. 6, 1787. Sur. Nathan Swanson. 52.

Ballard, James and Rachael Howser, June 26, 1787. Sur. Jasper Howzer.

Ballard, Micajah Stone and Nancy Boulton, Mar. 6, 1809. Sur. David Clarkson. 8.

Bandy, Carey and Frances Woods, dau. Peter, Nov. 14, 1791. Sur. James Chafin. 131.

Bandy, John C. s. Richard, and Sarah F. Wood, Mar. 3, 1845. Sur. Solomon Wright.

Bandy, Richard and Peggy Wright, Jan. 13, 1823. Sur. Solomon Wright. 130.

Banks, James and Lydia C. Short, dau. Reuben, Oct. 9, 1817. Sur. John Short. 61.

Banks, John and Agnes Marcum, Dec. 19, 1789. Sur. Thos. Marcum. 37.

Banks, Samuel and Elizabeth Marcum, Apr. 3, 1786. Sur. Thos. Markham and Phebe Love. 66.

Banks, Thos. and Elizabeth Cannaday, May 20, 1847. Sur. James Cannaday. 60.

Banks, Wm. and Elizabeth Harris, Jan. 10, 1793. 52.

Barbour, James M. and Cecily Belcher, Dec. 14, 1850.

Barbour, Jeremiah and Margaret P. Mattox, Dec. 16, 1851. 18.

Barbour, Joseph and Celia Jones, dau. Eady Martin, Mar. 1, 1830. Sur. John Nowlin. 61.

Barbour, Wm. and Cynthia Mathews, dau. John, Jan. 23, 1844. Sur. Wm. Mathews.

Barger, David and Anne Sutherland, dau. Fanny, Nov. 14. Sur. Philemon Sutherland. 57.

Barker, Wm. and Sally Hobbs, Oct. 24, 1817. Sur. Wm. McCormack.

Barnes, Austin and Polly Hall, Mar. 7, 1840. Sur. Edward Hall. 132.

Barnes, Austin and Elizabeth Stanley, Mar. 7, 1826. Sur. Davis Leever. 129.

Barnes, James and Permelia Jones, Aug. 6, 1798. Sur. Alexander Lair. 72.

Barnes, Shadrach and Sina Sowder, Nov. 28, 1843. Sur. Carey Gray. 68.

Barnes, Tuishitha and Nancy Highly, dau. Wm., Dec. 18, 1797. Sur. Thos. Highley. 21.

Barnhart, Abraham and Elizabeth Naff, Oct 21, 1818. Sur. Geo. Knave, 130.

Barnhart, Benj. and Nancy Wanger, Jan. 10, 1832. 18.

Barnhart, Daniel and Eve Bowman, July 30, 1812. 130.
Barnhart, Daniel and Elizabeth Naff, (Nave) dau. Jacob. Feb. 12, 1788. Sur. Thos. Hill 52.
Barnhart, Daniel and Anna Wenger, Jan. 16, 1840. 18.
Barnhart, Geo. and Mary Flora, Dec. 13, 1858.
Barnhart, John and Fanny Bowman, Dec. 26, 1808. Sur. Peter Bowman. 130.
Barnhart, John and Fanny Peters, May 4, 1837. 18.
Barnhart, Jonathan and Susannah Peters, July 3, 1832. 18.
Barrett, Geo. and Nancy McComack, Nov. 3, 1803. Sur. Micajah McCormack.
Barrett, Wm. and Mary Craig, Oct. 29, 1801. Sur. Thos. Craig.
Barrow, John D. s. Jessie, and Elizabeth Belcher, dau. Isham, Sept. 1, 1841. Sur. Robt. Prunty. 39.
Barratt, John and Elizabeth Brammer, Oct. 27, 1810. Sur. John Brammer
Barte, Geo. and Elizabeth Highley, Nov. 8, 1796. Sur. Wm. Highly and Benj. White.
Bartlett, James and Susannah P. Short, dau. Reuben, Apr. 5. 1813. Sur. John Massey.
Bartlett, Reuben S. and Mary Snuffer, Sept. 21, 1841. Sur. John Snuffer. 60.
Bartlett, Thos. and Labrine Hill, dau. Thos., Nov. 19, 1816. Sur. J. U. Hill. 130.
Barton, Anderson, s. David and Nancy Showalter, dau. Abraham, Mar. 1, 1823. Sur. James Barton.
Barton, James and Susannah Martin, July 23, 1819. Sur. Wm. Martin. 98.
Barton, John and Jane Campbell, Aug. 31, 1836. Sur. Jeremiah Campbell.
Barton, John F. and Frances Roberson, Dec. 22, 1853. 60.
Barton, Joshua and Jane Hale, Jan. 11, 1800. Sur. Thos. Hale.
Barton, Jubal and Mary E. Hix, Nov. 23, 1841. Sur. Wm. Hix.
Barton, Matthews B. and Minerva Hopkins, Oct. 7, 1844. Sur. Geo. W. Hopkins. 16.

Barton, Swinfield and Ruth Hill, dau. Swinfield, Nov. 24, 1806. Sur. Wilson Hill.

Barte, John and Dicey Kirby, Sept. 4, 1787. Sur. Francis Kirby. 37.

Basham, Banks and Elizabeth Heptinstall, May 5, 1810.

Basham, John and Frankey Meadors, Jan. 2, 1804. Sur. Jesse Meadors.

Basham, John and Lucy Ann Palmer, g. Pleasant Brown, Apr. 6, 1846. Sur. Joseph W. Palmer.

Basham, John and Margaret Basham, Sept. 30, 1834. Sur. Millender Basham.

Basham, Jonathan and Kittinah Payne, dau. Joseph, Oct. 17, 1837. Sur. Paschal Meador.

Basham, Jonathan and Delilah Payne, June 8, 1818. Sur. James P. Preston.

Basham, Millinder and Chenessee Payne, dau. Joseph, Feb. 5, 1838. Sur. Silas Payne.

Basham, Silvester and Jane E. Hill, dau. Julia, Mar. 13, 1848. Sur. Wm. Ridgeway. 111.

Basham, Uriah and Rhoda Simmons, dau. Chas., May 28, 1801. Sur. Thos. Simmons.

Basham, Wm. C. and Rocksey Ann Hudson, July 3, 1858.

Basham, Wm. and Ama Meador, dau. Jesse, Dec. 4, 1797 Sur. Jesse Meador.

Bass, John and Barsheba Eldridge, Apr. 4, 1825. Sur. Freeland Farmer. 81.

Bassett, Patrick A. and Mary Catherine Powell, dau. Wm. H., Dec. 18, 1835.

Bates, Daniel and Lydia Bradshaw, Aug. 22, 1793. 52.

Bates, Wm. and Elizabeth Harris, dau. John, Jan. 7, 1793. Sur. Jonas Turner. 52.

Batsche, Frederick and Mary Bland, Feb. 28, 1844. 18.

Batsche, Henry and Martha C. Keen, dau. Thos., Jan. 17, 1842. Sur. Wm. L. Stockton.

Bays, John P. and Letitia English, Jan. 26, 1825. Sur. James English.

Bays, (Baze) Amos and Polly Vance, dau. Jacob, Oct. 25, 1824. Sur. Edward Miles.

Beach, Wm. B. and Elizabeth T. Brown, June 17, 1833. Sur. Reuben Brown. 53.

Beard, Abner, s. Robt. M. and Nancy, and Martha Hale, dau. W. N., Oct. 12, 1853. 134.

Beard, Edward and Elizabeth Nowell, Sept. 24, 1823. Sur. John P. Palmer.

Beard, John and Sally Beckner, Jan. 7, 1822. Sur. Jonathan Beckner. 130.

Beard, Jonathan and Mary Ann Wray, Jan. 1, 1844. Sur. Chesley Wray. 18.

Beard, Robt. and Nancy C. Webb, dau. Sarah, Oct. 14, 1809. Sur. Geo. Walker.

Beck, Edward aad Nanny Oldakers, Sept. 2, 1799. Sur. Jacob Oldakers. 89.

Beck, John and Franky Oldakers, May 4, 1801. Sur. Jacob Oldakers.

Beck, Joseph and Isabella Buckhannan, dau. Jeremiah, Jan. 31, 1791. Sur. Jeremiah Buckhannan. 52.

Beck, Moses and Anne Richards, Aug. 25, 1791. Sur. Isaac Lemons. 52.

Becker, John B. and Martha L. Roberson, Nov. 17, 1853. 60.

Becker, Lewis and Martha C. Batsche, dau. Thos. L. Keen, Feb. 15, 1848. Sur. Zachariah W. Dewitt. 132

Beckett, Richard and Mary Mavity, dau. Wm., Apr. 14, 1810. Sur. Jesse Mavity. 122.

Beckner, Abner and Martha F. Angle, Sept. 9, 1845. Sur. Daniel Angle. 18.

Beckner, Alfred and Sarah F. J. Hughes, Oct. 15, 1846. Sur. Elijah Hughes. 18.

Beckner, Jacob and Elizabeth Rupe, Dec. 17, 1817. Sur. John Rupe. 98.

Beckner, Jacob and Catherine Board, Oct. 23, 1844. Sur. Henry Board, 18.
Beckner, Joel and Elizabeth Angle, dau. Daniel, Dec. 16, 1850. 97.
Beckner, John and Pamelia Guthry, Sept. 27, 1836. Sur. Buford Guthry.
Beckner, Jonathan and Polly Sink, Nov. 5, 1810. Sur. Stephen Sink.
Beckner, Samuel and Margaret Rupe, Mar. 16, 1812. Sur. John Rupe.
Beheler, Geo. and Mary Doss, Jan. 8, 1794. 52.
Beheler, Jacob and Susanna Doss, Nov. 19, 1807. Sur. Geo. Beheler. 8.
Beheler, John and Lydia Coleman, Dec. 12, 1816. Sur. John Coleman.
Belcher, Benj. E. and Jane Hunt, Apr. 2, 1849. Sur. Chas. Hunt. 80.
Belcher, Elias and Nancy Belcher, Apr. 1, 1833. Sur. Isham Belcher.
Belcher, Francis and Charlotte Dunn, Aug. 1, 1809. Sur. Thos. Dunn.
Belcher, Geo. and Mary Pinckard, Jan. 16, 1832. Sur. Benj. F. Pinkard.
Belcher, Harrison C. and Susan E. Hunt, Dec. 15, 1842. Sur. Daniel B. Hunt. 132.
Belcher, Henry S. and Sally Bernard, Oct. 9, 1835. Sur. Benj. Bernard.
Belcher, Isham Jr., and Melissa Belcher, Feb. 5, 1849. Sur. Benj. F. Cooper.
Belcher, Isham and Patsy Mitchell, Jan. 4, 1836. Sur. Henry Mitchell.
Belcher, Isham and Patsy Hodges, Jan. 3, 1791. Sur. Isham Hodges.
Belcher, Matthew C. and Martha Zeigler, dau. John, Nov. 5, 1842. Sur. John Zeigler.

Belcher, Wm. and Sally Kingery, dau. Peter, Oct. 4, 1809. Sur. Abraham Picklesymer. 117.
Belcher, Wm. and Patty Hartwell, dau. John, Aug. 31, 1809. Sur. John Hartwell. 8.
Belcher, Wm. and Celia White, dau. Polly, Mar. 4, 1822. Sur. Isham Belcher.
Belcher, Wm. I. and Sally Bernard, Oct. 9, 1835.
Bell, Geo. and Rachael Goudy, Dec. 7, 1800. Sur. Wm. Edmunds.
Bell, James and Franky Meador, dau. John, Jan. 31. 1798. Sur. Peter Holland.
Bell, James H. and Nancy Brown, Feb. 26, 1828. Sur. John M. Bell. 48.
Bell, John and Sally Stanley, July 5, 1813. Sur. Obediah Stover.
Bell, John M. and Polly Brown, Feb. 11, 1823. Sur. John Bird.
Bell, John M. and Ann Bird, May 23, 1839.
Bell, Peter H. and Ella Cassell, Feb. 24, 1852. 75.
Bell, Wm. and Lucy Law, May 6, 1805. Sur. Henry Law. 8.
Bell, Wm. J. and Jane McCall, Feb. 19, 1827. Sur. Robt. H. McCall. 48.
Benman, (Bunnion) Isaac and Elizabeth Poteet, dau. Wm. Apr. 13, 1789. Sur. Gilbert Stephens. 77.
Bennett, Cyrus D. and Martha E. Ashworth, Dec. 20, 1858.
Bennett, John R. and Ellen C. Bennett, Nov. 15, 1853. 80.
Bennett, Preston and Polly Belcher, dau. Prudence, Apr. 24, 1829. Sur. Wm. S. Neblett.
Bennett, Richard C. and Pamelia Glass, July 14, 1847. Sur. Jacob G. Mackenheimer.
Bennett, Willis H. and Martha White, dau. Polly, Nov. 21, 1829. Sur. Samuel Cook.
Bernard, (Barnard) Benj. and Sarah Betz, Sept. 1, 1806. Sur. Conrad Betz. 117.
Bernard, Benj. A. and Judith E. Hutcherson, dau. Wm., Dec. 9, 1843. Sur. Wm. Brown.
Bernard, Creed and Martha E. Houseman, July 28, 1858.

Bernard, John and Judith Kitchin, Dec. 5, 1818. Sur. Zadock Bernard.

Bernard, Robt. and Sarah Scott, Jan. 6, 1823. Sur. Wm. Luke.

Bernard, Wm. and Hope Ann Powell, dau. Robt., Jan. 5, 1835. Sur. Chas. P. Powell.

Bernard, Zadock and Mary Kitchen, Nov. 24, 1819. Sur. Samuel Allman.

Best, Banks and Elizabeth Heptinstall, Mar. 5, 1810. Sur. Caleb Heptinstall.

Best, John and Lydia Meador, May 19, 1801. Sur. Joel Meador. 106.

Betz, Abraham and Sally Ramsey, Mar. 4, 1816. Sur. Pleasant Blankenship.

Betz, Benj. and Frances Ann Sink, dau. Ann, Aug. 10, 1829. Sur. Jesse Harper. 48.

Betz, John and Catherine Ikenberry, Sept. 3, 1821. Sur. John Ikenberry.

Betz, John F. and Julia Ann Blankenship, Aug. 20, 1846. Sur. John R. Divers.

Beverly, Herod and Lucy Freeman, (Negroes, freed slaves of John Early, dec'd) Feb. 23, 1808. Sur. Samuel _____ 117.

Billups, Edward and Susannah Webster, dau. Samuel, Dec. 18, 1798. Sur. James Webster. 52.

Billups, Richard and Margaret Webster, dau. Luke and Sarah, Dec. 30, 1799. Sur. Henry Webster.

Billups, Thos. and Sally Webster, Nov. 28, 1793. 52.

Binnion, Job or John and Milly DeHaven, Jan. 23, 1804. Sur. Abraham DeHaven.

Binnion, John and Sally Wheeler, 1795. 37.

Binnion, John and Sarah Cockran, (Cothran) Feb. 8, 1796. Sur. Jesse Prunty.

Binnion, (Bunnion) Peyton and Drewailler Law, Jan. 15, 1819. Sur. Butler Law.

Birchfield, James R. and Mary A. Fishburne, Dec. 14, 1858.

Bird, Abner and Jane Jamison, dau. Thos., Mar. 7, 1791.

Bird, Benj. and Levicy Akers, June 17, 1848. Sur. Adam R. Webster
Bird, Benj. and Susan Caine. Apr. 4, 1831. Sur. Drury O. Howell. 48.
Bird, Benj. and Nancy Hunt, dau. Stephen and Katharine, Nov. 18, 1844. Sur. Riley H. Hunt. 133.
Bird, Benj. K. s. Wm., and Ester Hunt, Dec. 16, 1833. Sur. Obediah Hunt. 48.
Bird, Benj. T. and Irene M. Oxley, Nov. 19, 1834. Sur. John Oxley.
Bird, Daniel M. and Susan Lloyd, Mar. 1, 1850. Sur. Samuel Hall. 80.
Bird, James and Fanny Mason, Sept. 3, 1787. Sur. Robt. Mason.
Bird, James L. and Julia Perdue, Oct. 4, 1858.
Bird, John and Mary Davis, dau. Williamson, Nov. 22, 1798.
Bird, John and Nancy Alias, Mar. 23, 1811. Sur. John Ader.
Bird, John and Asenath Beckner, Dec. 1, 1828. Sur. Jonathan Beckner. 26.
Bird, John and Phebe Oxley, Sept. 26, 1835. Sur. Samuel Oxley. 3.
Bird, John R. and Susan Jenkins, dau. Henry, Mar. 15, 1845. Sur. Sanford H. Oxley.
Bird, Obediah W. and Matilda F. Hutts, Sept. 15, 1858.
Bird, Samuel and Polly Jackes (Jakes), Dec. 30, 1807. Sur. James Jacks.
Bird, Stephen M. and Malinda A. Hunt, dau. Obadiah, Dec. 17, 1842. Sur. Wm. M. Bird.
Bird, Thos. and Susannah Brody, Apr. 29, 1806. Sur. John Broady.
Bird, Thos. A. and Emily J. Oxley, dau. Samuel, Nov. 12, 1842. Sur. Jenkins M. Oxley. 132.
Bird, Wm. and Hannah Thornton, Mar. 24, 1803. 72.
Bird, Wm. and Asenath Sink, dau. John, Sept. 25, 1828. Sur. John Sink. 48.

Bird, Wm. Jr., and Malinda Cain, dau. Selby Howel, Dec. 4, 1837. Sur. Benj. Bird.

Bird, Wm. M. and Catherine Hunt, Jan. 17, 1838. Sur. Obadiah Hunt.

Bird, Vincent M. and Sally R. Bradley, Dec. 17, 1839. Sur. Wm. Bradley.

Bishop, Chas. M. and Polly Pedigo, Jan. 4, 1836. Sur. Josiah R. Willis.

Bishop, John D. and Judith Walker, Feb. 5, 1831. Sur. John Walker.

Bishop, Joseph and Elizabeth Johnson Bishop, Dec. 21, 1805. Sur. Isaac Bishop.

Bishop, Joseph and Elizabeth Bishop, Jan. 25, 1818. Sur. Peter C. Stockton.

Bishop, Landon and Polly Haislip, Aug. 26, 1808. Sur. John Kidd. 8.

Bishop, Wm. and Lucy Thompson, Apr. 16, 1814. Sur. Edmund C. Bishop.

Blankenship, Andrew and Rhoda Baker, Apr. 6, 1829. Sur. David Durham. 140.

Blankenship, Barnett and Barsheba Meador, dau. Jesse, Oct. 15, 1792. Sur. Hezekiah Blankenship. 23.

Blankenship, Hezekiah and Rhoda Meador, dau. Joel, Feb. 28, 1791. Sur. Elijah Blankenship.

Blankenship, Jesse and Sarah Butler, Jan. 28, 1817. Sur. Isham M. Ferguson.

Blankenship, Jesse and Mary Shumaker, Mar. 29, 1851. 18.

Blankenship, John and Mary Webb, Aug. 21, 1818. Sur. Martin Dillion.

Blankenship, John and Patty Blankenship, July 31, 1794. 41.

Blankenship, John and Rhoda Blankenship, Aug. 29, 1798. Sur. Isham Blankenship. 141.

Blankenship, Lewis and Frances Hambrick, Jan. 6, 1845. Sur. Joel Chitwood. 18.

Blankenship, Lewis and Fanny Blankenship, Jan. 11, 1826. Sur. Wm. Rutledge. 48.

Blankenship, Lewis W. and Elizabeth Mitchell, dau. Wm., Jan. 4, 1832. Sur. Thos. Mitchell.

Blankenship, Obediah and M. Boitnott, Oct. 14, 1850. Sur. David Boitnott. 11.

Blankenship, Peter and Jane Hook, dau. Patty, Nov. 2, 1842. Sur. Wm. Patterson.

Blankenship, Peter and Elizabeth Brown, dau. Marmaduke, Jan. 5, 1829. Sur. Henry Dillion, Jr. 48.

Blankenship, Pleasant and Rhoda Stewart, dau. Wm., Mar. 7, 1808. Sur. Robt. Stewart.

Blankenship, Presley and Franky Ross, dau. Mounring, Dec. 24, 1891. Sur. Elisha Blankenship.

Blankenship, Shadrach and Edey Perdue, June 2, 1792. Sur. Wm. Chitwood. 23.

Blankenship, Smith and Jemima Charlton, Dec. 2, 1794. Sur. Alex Ferguson.

Blankenship, Smith and Elizabeth Beckner, Mar. 5, 1825. Sur. Osborn Branch. 48.

Blankenship, Thos. and Polly Hughes, Feb. 28, 1827. Sur. Daniel Layman. 48.

Blaydes, Geo. S. and Nancy Epperson, dau. John, June 6, 1791. Sur. Benj. Booth.

Board, Christopher and Susannah Phelps, dau. Polly, June 7, 1819. Sur. Moses Ferguson.

Board, Francis and Anny Greer, dau. Joseph, Feb. 17, 1813. Sur. Elisha Greer.

Board, Henry and Nancy Myers, g. Alexander Ferguson, Dec. 25, 1813. Sur. Thos. Ferguson, Jr. 130.

Board, James and Mary Ferguson, Oct. 16, 1793. 41.

Board, Jefferson and Sally Harrison, dau. Milly, Oct. 3, 1826. Sur. John D. Taylor. 48.

Board, Micajah and Judith Arrington, Jan. 17, 1807. Sur. Daniel Arrington.

Board, Samuel H. and Inda M. Meador, Dec. 13, 1858.

Board, Wm. and Gilly Ann Beckner, dau. Lydia, Aug. 5, 1850. Sur. Edwin W. Angle. 18.

Board, Willison and Hetty Reynolds, g. J. Woods, Sept. 23, 1828. Sur. Robt. T. Woods. 26.

Bocock, John and Lucy Hughes, dau. Nancy, by her 1st husband, Dec. 29, 1800. Sur. Wm. Bocock. 37.

Bocock, Matthew and Miley Dawson, Apr. 19, 1810. Sur. Thos. Dawson. 8.

Bocock, Wm. and Cally Rody, ..., 1800. 37.

Boggs, Andrew and Sarah (Sabra) Booth, Jan. 19, 1843. Joseph D. Meador.

Boggs, Robt. and Alice Adkins, June 22, 1843. Sur. Hay Turnbull.

Bohannon, James and Harriet Hughes, Apr. 29, 1833. Sur. Wm. Crump.

Boitnott, David and Elizabeth Donahue, June 30, 1841. Sur. Wm. Donahow. 18.

Boitnott, Ferdinand and Ellender Beckner, Feb. 20, 1839. Sur. Jacob Beckner. 18.

Boitnott, Geo. and Polly Hambrick, Feb. 1, 1830. Sur. Samuel Ophenchane. 48.

Boitnott, Henry and Adaline Goode, Apr. 1, 1850. Sur. David Boitnott.

Boitnott, Peter and Julia Sink, June 21, 1836. Sur. Peter Fisher, Jr. 68.

Boles, (Bowles) Zachariah and Teanor Abshire, dau. Abraham, Dec. 12, 1849. Sur. Abraham Abshire. 11.

Bolling, Joseph and Rebecca Maddox, dau. Nathan, Mar. ...., 1795. Sur. Jordan Kemp. 82.

Bolling, Joseph and Rebecca Davis, Feb. 1, 1796. Sur. Samuel Davis.

Bond, Benj. and Thea Ross, Apr. 15, 1803.

Bonds, Jeremiah and Elizabeth Martin, May 16, 1812.

Bonds, Robt. and Sally Ann Starkey, dau. Joshua, Oct. 12, 1796. Sur. Samuel Osburn. 82.

Bonds, Wm. M. and Elvira F. Perdue, July 1, 1847. Sur. Obadiah Perdue. 84.

Bondurant, Jacob P. and Susan A. C. Neil,   , 1851. 132.

Bondurant, Joel and Sally Wheat, July 11, 1800. Sur. Guy Smith. 72.
Bondurant, John and Nancy Finney, g. Peter, Nov. 4, 1828. Sur. Peter Finney.
Bondurant, Joseph and Sally Hunt, Mar. 16, 1829. Sur. Daniel B. Hunt.
Bondurant, Thos. and Jane B. Neblett, dau. Wm., Oct. 29, 1823. Sur. John Neblett.
Boone, Abraham and Susannah Kelley, Dec. 31, 1806. Sur. Wm. Kelly. 130.
Boone, Abraham and Nancy Gearhart, Dec. 13, 1817. Sur. Hiram Geerhart. 130.
Boone, Andrew W. and Lucy A. Fralin, Dec. 4, 1848. Sur. Jacob Frailin. 18.
Boone, Benj. and Susan Oyler, Nov. 7, 1848. Sur. Daniel Oyler. 18.
Boone, Cormick and Emily Rupe, Nov. 6, 1837.
Boone, Daniel and Martha A. Turner, Feb. 12, 1852. 18.
Boone, Fleming and Susannah Kingery, Feb. 24, 1829. Sur. Otey Kinsey. 26.
Boone, Isaac and Clarissy Kinsey, May 5, 1817. Sur. Jacob Kinsey.
Boone, Isaac H. and Mary L. Wade, Sept. 28, 1845. Sur. Isaac Wade.
Boone, Jacob Jr. and Rachael Kessler, Aug. 31. 1807. Sur. Wm. Greer. 130.
Boone, Jacob and Barbara Kesler, Dec. 17, 1832. Sur. Peter Kesler. 48.
Boone, John and Martha Turner, dau. Richard Greer, Oct. 22, 1832. Sur. Bartley Turner. 48.
Boone, John and Susan Fowler, ...,1811. 130.
Boone, Joseph and Keziah Wray, Oct. 2, 1843. Sur. Chesley Wray. 18.
Boon, Ludwick and Emily Ross, Nov. 6, 1837. Sur. Sutherlin Ross.

Boone, Peter and Catherine Willis, June 27, 1817. Sur. Joseph H. Townes. 130.

Boone, Stephen and Mahala Oyler, Nov. 9, 1846. Sur. Valentine Oyler. 18.

Booth, Benj. and Elizabeth Divers, Dec. 16, 1795. Sur. John Divers.

Booth, Christopher and Mary L. Hancock, Sept. 3, 1832. Sur. Benj. Hancock.

Booth, Edward C. and Nancy F. Griffith, Mar. 2, 1852. 18.

Booth, Isaac and Mary Ferguson, Oct. 8, 1810. Sur. Robt. Guilliams. 122.

Booth, Isaac and Doshia Radford, dau. James, Oct. 30, 1843. Sur. Geo. Radford. 121. Note: Both from Montgomery Co.

Booth, James and Frances Ferguson, dau. Wm., Apr. 16, 1805. Sur. James Dixon. 122.

Booth, James C. and Laurette Hutts, dau. Sally, Apr. 19, 1850. Sur. John H. Booth. 19.

Booth, John and Elizabeth Craghead, dau. John Sr., Feb. 26, 1832. Sur. Chas. P. Craghead.

Booth, John H. s. Richard, and Nancy G. Bradley, dau. Elibabeth, Dec. 17, 1839. Sur. Wm. Bradley. 86.

Booth, Josiah and Minerva A. Simpson, dau. Thos., Dec. 31, 1849. Sur. Green B. Forbes. 86.

Booth, Peter and Fanny Smith, Dec. 29, 1812. Sur. Wm. Smith. 15.

Booth, Peter and Nancy Blades, Aug. 24, 1808. Sur. Francis Blades.

Booth, Richard and Agnes Lee, Mar. 10, 1819. Sur. Drury Holland.

Booth, Richard and Susannah Johnson, dau. Michie, June 24, 1808. Sur. Michie Johnson. 130.

Booth, Samuel and Sallie Johnson, Sept. 17, 1851. 18.

Booth, Stephen and Polly Conway, dau. Ester, Sept. 15, 1826. Sur. Weatherston S. Greer.

Booth, Stephen and Penelope Guthrey, Sept. 15, 1786. Sur. David Guthry.
Booth, Wm. and Mary Smith, Mar. 5, 1832. Sur. Henry Smith. 3.
Booth, Wm. C. and Mary Long, g. Nancy Booth, Dec. 31, 1841. Sur. Geo. R. Booth. 39.
Boswell, Creed T. and Elizabeth Moore, Dec. 7, 1846. Sur. John N. Moore.
Bozwell, Mark and Jane Moore, dau. James, June 26, 1833. Sur. David Moore.
Bottom, James and Mary Rives, dau. Frederick, Nov. 9, 1808. Sur. Lansford Brizendine. 8.
Bottom, James and Hannah A. Mason, Aug. 7, 1847. Sur. Nathan Mason. 132.
Bottom, Miles and Jane Choice, June 3, 1823. Sur. John Doughton.
Boulton, (Bowlton) Matthew and Mary Penyman (Perryman), Mar. 22, 1788. 37.
Bousman, Philip, s. James, and Elizabeth Poteet, Apr. 24, 1847. Sur. Wm. Poteet. 18.
Bousman, Geo. and Rebecca Dillion, June 21, 1833. Sur. John Plyborn.
Bowen, Matthias and Polly Webster, Aug. 2, 1858.
Bower, Christopher and Susan Snuffer, July 24, 1843. Sur. John Snuffer. 108.
Bower, Philip and Catherine Snuffer, Mar. 6, 1843. Sur. John Snuffer. 108.
Bowles, Butler and Levicy E. Woods, dau. Frances, Jan. 14, 1846. 134.
Bowles, David and Elizabeth Clower, May 20, 1803. Sur. John Clower. 72.
Bowles, Geo. W. and Anny Bram, (Brown), Feb. 1, 1853. 68.
Bowles, Geo. W. and Frances Moore, May 15, 1847. Sur. Steward Tinsley. 68.
Bowles, Jubal and Omey Young, Jan. 28, 1840. Sur. Geo. Standley.

Bowles, Jacob and Polly Wright, dau. Geo. Sr., Aug. 21, 1827. Sur. Luke Wright.
Bowles, Jeremiah and Elizabeth Martin, May 16, 1812. Sur. Hugh Martin.
Bowles, Jeremiah and Mary Ann Walden, dau. Wm., Dec. 5, 1838. Sur. Fleming Graham. 132.
Bowles, Wm. and Nancy Bolling, Dec. 27, 1800. Sur. John Bowles. 72.
Bowles, (Boles) Joseph and Elizabeth Frasier, Oct. 5, 1812. Sur. Geo. Turner.
Bowles, Martin, s. Ben and Elizabeth, and Susan Trent, dau. Jacob and Polly, Aug. 24, 1853. 18.
Bowles, Peter S. and Elizabeth Lavinder, dau. John, June 22, 1849. Sur. Wm. Willard. 18.
Bowles, Robt. and Frances Brammer, Oct. 27, 1814. Sur. Jesse Mavity. 130.
Bowles, Robt. and Matilda Green, dau. Elizabeth, Feb. 6, 1850. Sur. Caleb Maxey. 68.
Bowles, Samuel H. and Martha A. Adams, Jan. 29, 1842. Sur. Swinfield Standley. 132.
Bowles, Thos. T. and Mary A. Hunter, Nov. 20, 1848. Sur. John Hunter. 132.
Bowles, Wm. and Scena Green, May 29, 1820. Sur. John Gearhart.
Bowles, Wm. R. and Catherine Eller, Sept. 4, 1826. Sur. Joseph Flora. 48.
Bowles, Wm. and Sally Preston, Jan. 22, 1797. Sur. John Preston.
Bowles, Wm. and and Elender Willis, Feb. 17, 1852. 11.
Bowling, (Bolling) Gabriel and Catherine S. Lavinder, Oct. 15, 1849. Sur. Grandison B. Lesuer.
Bowling, Wm. M. and Jerusha Wingfield, dau. John, Nov. 1, 1817. Sur. Christopher Wingfield.
Bowman, Benj. and Sophia Ferguson, July 10, 1826. Sur. Standifer Ferguson. 48.
Bowman, Daniel and Catherine Naff, Nov. 14, 1817.

Bowman, Isaac and Hannah Naff, Dec. 3, 1849. Sur. Geo. Naff. 96.
Bowman, Jacob and Mary Ferough, Aug. 8, 1839. 18.
Bowman, Joel and Irene Layman, Oct. 3, 1838. Sur. John Laymon. 18.
Bowman, John F. and Elizabeth Boone, Dec. 20, 1842. Sur. Jacob Boon.
Bowman, John T. and Evaline Griffith, Sept. 21, 1845. Sur. Moses Carper. 18.
Bowman, John and Perizade Ferguson, dau. John, Feb. 11, 1813. Sur. Caleb Tate. 130.
Bowman, Joseph and Anne Altice, Mar. 22, 1827. Sur. Daniel Altic. 48.
Bowman, Peter and Mary Saunders, Sept. 3, 1804. Sur. John Sanders.
Bowsman, Abraham and Frances Lumsden, Nov. 20, 1837. Sur. Dudley Lumsden.
Bowsman, Adam and Susannah Crowl, Jan. 30, 1805. Sur. Devault Crowl.
Bowsman, Geo. and Elizabeth Pool, _____, 1794. 89.
Bowsman, John and Lucida Chitwood, dau. John, Nov. 8, 1831. Sur. Geo. Bowsman. 48.
Bowyer, (Boyer) Henry A. and Emily L. Webb, dau. Theo. F., Dec. 5, 1849. Sur. Tazewell A. Webb.
Boyd, Andrew s. Hugh, and Nancy Cockran, Dec. 1, 1817. Sur. Hugh Boyd. 60.
Boyd, Andrew s. John, and Mary Stephens, dau. Nancy Worley, June 12, 1826. Sur. Edward New. 61.
Boyd, Andrew L. and Ann Booth, Mar. 6, 1837. Sur. Benj. Booth.
Boyd, Chas. J. and Nancy E. Thomas, Aug. 2, 1858.
Boyd, Elisha and Ella Leah Cockran, Nov. 18, 1830. Sur. Isham Cockran. 61.
Boyd, Geo. and Mary Charter, dau. Margaret, Aug. 1, 1808. Sur. Anthony Simmons.

Boyd, Henry W. and Ellender Wood, June 28, 1806. Sur. John Wood. 122.
Boyd, Hugh and Elizabeth Boyd, Apr. 20, 1814. Sur. David Via.
Boyd, Hugh and Sarah Ward, Mar. 1, 1794. 22.
Boyd, Hugh and Elizabeth Jeffers, Apr. 21, 1814. 122.
Boyd, Isaac and Sarah McGhee, Dec. 16, 1826. Sur. Angus McGhee. 61.
Boyd, Jesse and Polly George, dau. John A. Newberry, Sept. 16, 1843. Sur. John A. Newberry.
Boyd, Jesse and Milla Hurd, Dec. 21, 1813. Sur. Heron Boyd, 122.
Boyd, Newberry T. and Jane Leffue, dau. Josiah, Mar. 1, 1847. Sur. John A. Newberry. 60.
Boyd, Samuel and Ruth Griffith, dau. Daniel, Dec. 29, 1834. Sur. Jehu Griffith. 61.
Boyd, Wm. s. Wm. Sr., and Sarah Newberry, dau. Wm., Mar. 23, 1805. Sur. Levi Newberry.
Boyd, Wm. s. Wm., and Jane Stevens, Jan. 1, 1830. Sur. Andrew Boyd.
Boswell, Creed and Elizabeth Craghead, Mar. 12, 1821.
Bozwell, Creed and Elizabeth Hatcher, dau. Mary, Oct. 31, 1821. Sur. John Poindexter.
Bozwell, Gilbert and Elizabeth Mason, dau. Nathan, June 5, 1809. Sur. Wm. Bozwell. 8.
Bozwell, John and Lucy Moore, dau. James, Dec. 27, 1820. Sur. James Moore.
Bozwell, Wm. and Caty Davis, July 24, 1807. Sur. Wm. Davis. 9.
Bradley, Archibald and Lucy English, dau. James, Apr. 7, 1821. Sur. Zachariah Kennett.
Bradley, Archibald and Betsey A. Bradley, Oct. 4, 1819.
Bradley, James H. and Sarah Craghead, May 19, 1853. 75.
Bradley, John R. and Fanny A. Powell, dau. Sarah, Oct. 2, 1848. Sur. Robt. E. Powell.
Bradley, John and Sarah Payne, ..., 1851. 86.
Bradley, Philip and Elizabeth Forbes, dau. John, Oct. 17, 1817. Sur. John R. Forbes.

Bradley, Samuel and Elizabeth Bowers, June 26, 1837. Sur. Benj. Bowman.
Bradley, Wm. and Elizabeth Pasley, dau. Robt., Nov. 29, 1841. Sur. Moses G. Carper.
Bradley, Wm. and Elizabeth A. Martin, dau. Daniel, Sept. 16, 1845. Sur. James H. Bradley.
Bradshaw, Allen and Mounring Richardson, dau. Lucy, Jan. 26, 1793. Sur. Richard Richardson. 131.
Bradshaw, Chas. and Hannah Bates (Boles), Mar. 9, 1790. Sur. John Bates. 52.
Bradshaw, Moses and Sarah Bates, Mar. 15, 1798. 72.
Brammer, Hezekiah and Henley White, g. Geo. Turner, Sept. 1, 1824. Sur. Robt. Brammer.
Brammer, Jesse and Sarah Cannaday, dau. Elizabeth, Aug. 26, 1844. Sur. Isaac Y. Cannaday.
Brammer, Joel and Aimey Keys, Jan. 30, 1851. 47.
Brammer, Joel and Dorothy Kingery, dau. Thos. July 7, 1846 .Sur. Thos. Kingery. 83.
Brammer, John and Mary E. Short, dau. John Y., Sept. 23, 1844. Sur. Joshua Cannaday.
Brammer, Noah and Caty Jones, dau. John, Mar. 5, 1803. Sur. John Johns.
Brammer, Peter and Lucy Ellison, dau. Peyton, Jan. 15, 1835. Sur. Davis M. Ellyson.
Brammer, Robt. and Frances Booth, Oct. 14, 1817. Sur. Geo. Turner.
Brammer, Wm. Jr. and Molly Bowles, Nov. 6, 1813. Sur. Robt. Bowles.
Branson, (Bronson) Hezekiah and Agnes Preaddy, dau. Nancy, Sept. 3, 1789. Sur. David Thomason. 37.
Braxton, Drake and Patsy Greer, Apr. 29, 1795,
Breedlove, John and Catherine Wright, Oct. 20, 1841. Sur. Thos. Waid.
Breedlove, Pleasant E. and Hannah M. Crump, dau. Geo., Jan. 7, 1828. Sur. Wm. Crump.

Brewer, Arthur and Matilda Bennett, Dec. 7, 1829. Sur. Willis H. Bennett.
Brewer, (Brower) Hopkins and Susannah Mitchell, Mar. 2, 1835. Sur. Wm. J. Mitchell.
Brewer, James and Polly Martin, Dec. 22, 1829. Sur. Josiah R. Willis.
Brewer, Larkfield and Elizabeth A. Cooper, Oct. 14, 1833. Sur. Wm. Cooper.
Brewer, Samuel and Nancy Clardy, dau. Archibald, June 27, 1825· Sur. Arthur Brewer.
Briggs, Buford and Emaline Fray, Feb. 17, 1853. 96.
Briggs, Townley and Charity Guilliams, Feb. 7, 1798. Sur. John Guilliams. 72.
Bright, Samuel G. and Mary Jane Bernard, Apr. 17, 1851. 97.
Bristoe, Benj. and Sarah Miles, dau. Samuel, Dec. 7, 1789. Sur. David Pugh. 52.
Bristow, Wm. and Martha Beck, dau. Martha, Oct. 3, 1796. Sur. Edward Beck.
Britton, Richard and Susannah Turnbull, Feb. 9, 1804. Sur. Geo. Turnbull.
Brizendine, Henry L. and Charlotte Hawke, June 30, 1824. Sur. John Woody. 48.
Brizendine, John B. and Elizabeth Cockran, Feb. 9, 1818. Sur. Samuel Cockran.
Brizendine, John and Edy Ann Walker, Nov. 19, 1830. Sur. Henry Frailin.
Brizendine, Richard and Elizabeth Williamson, dau. James, Dec. 19, 1820. Sur. James Edwards. 48.
Broadie, Thos. and Polly Craig, dau. Wm., Oct. 19, 1811. Sur. John Craig.
Brock, Joshua and Fanny Estes, dau. Elisha and Margaret, Dec. 26, 1800. Sur. John Cooly. 37.
Brock, Jubal and Doshia Stuart, Dec. 9, 1796. Sur. David Stuart.
Brock, Lorenzo Dow and Mary Kidd, Feb. 14, 1832. Sur. Elisha Kidd.

Brock, Moses and Susannah Dyer, Mar. 5, 1793. Sur. Elijah Brock.

Brock, Zachariah and Nancy Cooley, Jan. 16, 1815. Sur. Chapman Cooley.

Brockman, Wm. and Elizabeth Henderson, dau. Wm., Feb. 15, 1813. Sur. Samuel Henderson. 130.

Broady, Wilks and Nancy Bobbitt, Oct. 7, 1822. Sur. Willis Luttrel.

Brodie, Wm. F. and Seney P. Mason, Mar. 18, 1850. Sur. Lewis Mason. 132.

Brogan, John and Letha Underwood, Nov. 3, 1829. Sur. Angus McGhee.

Brogan, Robt. and Grace Allen, Feb. 13, 1806. Sur. Joseph Underwood.

Brooks, Andrew and Mary C. Brown, dau. John, Dec. 31, 1821. Sur. Joseph Rives.

Brooks, Baker B. and Polly Koon, dau. Henry, Sept. 6, 1808. Sur. Zachariah Perdue. 130.

Brooks, Cluffee M. and Permelia Mattox, Nov. 15, 1830. Sur. Gabriel Mattox. 48.

Brooks, Cluffee M. and Sarah Dudley, Oct. 14, 1839. Sur. Sarah Dudley.

Brooks, Ewell M. and Levinia W. Gilbert, dau. Samuel, Oct. 15, 1834. Sur. Wm. W. Gilbert.

Brooks, Isaac D. and Katherine M. Dudley, dau. Martha, Oct. 10, 1839. Sur. Thos. Dudley.

Brooks, Jesse and Lydia Holland, dau. John M., Dec. 31, 1823. Sur. Peter H. Holland. 49.

Brooks, Jeremiah and Catherine McLewain (McCwain), dau. Jacob Miller, Aug. 18, 1794. Sur. Abraham Ritter. 89.

Brooks, Joel and Fanny Noell, dau. Garrett, Nov. 18, 1809. Sur. Robt. Arnold. 8.

Brooks, Robertson and Nancy Williamson, dau. James, Jan. 16, 1829. Sur. Lewis Dudley. 140.

Brooks, Pleasant D. and Frances S. Gilbert, dau. Themuel C., Apr. 24, 1833. Sur. Ewell Brooks. 48.

Brooks, Wm. and Mary Sellars, Nov. 14, 1798. Sur. Wm. Scott.
Brower, John and Rebecca Harter, Sept. 5, 1803. Sur. Christian Harter. 122.
Brower, John and Esther Rinehart, Sept. 2, 1805. Sur. Jacob Reinhart. 130.
Brown, Abraham and Betsy Harter (Horten) Nov. 3, 1800. Sur. Geo. Harter. 21.
Brown, Bird and Polly Spradling, Oct. 31, 1825. Sur. Wright Spradling.
Brown, Daniel and Elizabeth Arrington, Jan. 10, 1811. Sur. James Arrington.
Brown, Daniel and Sallie Harris, Sept. 16, 1816. Sur. Jubal Harris.
Brown, Frederick R. and Jane V. Prunty, dau. Nancy, Oct. 1, 1838. Sur. Andrew S. Brooks. 4.
Brown, Garland R. and Lucy Hensley, Feb. 25, 1824. Sur. Crowl Marcum.
Brown, Geo. W. (Capt.) and Miriam Crump, dau. Geo., Feb. 6, 1826. Sur. Wm. Crump. 48
Brown, Geo. W. and Sophia Aliff, July 24, 1853. 111.
Brown, Henry Jr. and Hannah Dillman, Aug. 4, 1800. Sur. Jacob Dillman. 21.
Brown, Jacob and Anne Rudy, July 17, 1798. Sur. Daniel Rudy.
Brown, John and Aggy Brown, Nov. 4, 1816. Sur. John Martin. 98.
Brown, John and Peggy Brown, Nov. 27, 1824. Sur. Rodham F. Brown. 130.
Brown, John and Mary Jane Meador, dau. Benj., Aug. 31, 1842. Sur. Josephus A. Meador.
Brown, John and Sarah Rives, July 8, 1793. Sur. Ashford Napier.
Brown, John S. and Mary Ann Patterson, dau. Sarah, May 29, 1838. Sur. Samuel J. Patterson. 3.
Brown, Joseph and Ann Carter, Aug. 20, 1812. 130.
Brown, Jubal and Elizabeth Pugh, Sept. 7, 1835. Sur. Richard Pugh. 68.

Brown, Marmaduke and Mary Weaver, dau. Jacob, Dec. 16, 1802. Sur. Rodham Felso Brown.
Brown, Martin and Miriam J. Doran, dau. John, Sept. 14, 1841. Sur. Jubal Brown. 18.
Brown, Nathaniel and Polly Maclewain, Nov. 27, 1812. 44.
Brown, Nathaniel and Elizabeth Akers, dau. Samuel, Mar. 5, 1832. Sur. Fleming Akers. 48.
Brown, Ruffin and Jean Jamison, Nov. 8, 1794. 120.
Brown, Reuben and Sally Corn, Nov. 12, 1829.
Brown, Reuben S. and Mary Ann Witcher, dau. Mary, June 5, 1838. Sur. Frederick R. Brown. 3.
Brown, Richard and Sally Koon, dau. Henry Sr., Nov. 12, 1829. Sur. Henry Koon Jr. 140.
Brown, Samuel and Martha Holt Thompson, dau. Thos., Apr. 19, 1804. Sur. Wm. Thompson.
Brown, Skelton and Mary Napier, dau. Ashford and Mary, Dec. 22, 1796. Sur. John Naper.
Brown, Stephen and Harriet Basham, dau. John and Catherine Wood, Nov. 17, 1828. Sur. Fleming Saunders. 140.
Brown, Thos. and Sarah Smith, Jan. 2, 1794. 52.
Brown, Wm. and Ann E. Harvey, Aug. 24, 1852. 18.
Brown, Wm., s. Daniel, and Sarah Hutts, Jan. 1, 1844. Sur. Asa. Dillion. 18.
Brown, Wm. and Lucy English, dau. Stephen D., Jan. 13, 1840. Sur. Thos. English.
Brown, Wyatt, s. Martha, and Jemima Hatcher, Oct. 26, 1835. Sur. Thos. Heptinstall. 3.
Browner, Daniel and Sally Flora, Oct. 22, 1808. Sur. Jacob Flora. 130.
Brubaker, Henry and Elizabeth Frantz, Oct. 2, 1848. Sur. Samuel Frantz. 96.
Brubaker, Joel and Mary Naff, Nov. 29, 1841. Sur. Jonathan Naff. 18.
Brubaker, John and Susannah Flora, Sept. 30, 1833. Sur. Jacob Flora. 48.

Brumley, Peter and Patsy Boyd, Sept. 13, 1837. Sur. John Scott. 68.
Brumley, Wm. and Frances Pegrum, dau. Susannah, Aug. 3, 1812. Sur. Isham Edwards.
Brummitt, Reason (Renne) and Mary Estes, Apr. 10, 1790. 37.
Bryant, Daniel and Lucy Key, Nov. 17, 1829. Sur. John Spencer. 48.
Bryant, David and Rachael Spencer, Oct. 27, 1834. Sur. Wesley Key.
Bryant, David and Elizabeth Kemplin, July 6, 1852. 68.
Bryant, Jacob and Lucy Mullins, Oct. 13, 1845. Sur. Stephen Mullins. 134.
Bryant, James and Sally Brummet, July 7, 1788. Sur. James Brumit. 37.
Bryant, John and Ruth Briant, Sept. 6, 1802. 122.
Bryant, John and Frances Atkins, Apr. 20, 1852. 60.
Bryant, Richard and Annie Young, Nov. 2, 1815. Sur. James Young.
Bryant, Samuel S. and Eliza H. Sutherland, dau. Polly, Sept. 7, 1835.
Buckanan, (Buchanan) Jeremiah and Sarah Jones, dau. Moses, Dec. 15, 1786. 66.
Buckner, John and Elizabeth R. Young, Mar. 25, 1851. 68.
Budgett, (Bridgett) Geo. and Catherine Eads, June 22, 1787. Sur. John Adkins.
Bunning, Adam and Rachael Wright, Sept. 20, 1788.
Burch, John and Sarah Huddleston, dau. Abram, July 5 1841. Sur. John C. Hutcherson.
Burdel, Wm. and Rachael Osburn, dau. John, Dec. 6, 1794. Sur. Benj. Osburn.
Burdett, John and Patsy Lucinda Craghead, Feb. 7, 1820. Sur. Isaiah Craghead.
Burgess, Armistead and Millie Smith, July 25, 1832. Sur. Bowker Preston.
Burnett, Bluford and Mary E. Bond, dau. Matilda, May 23, 1836. Sur. Hiram Hundley.

Burnett, James and Susannah Slone, dau. Malinda, Oct. 7, 1844. Sur. Anderson Starkey.
Burnett, Jeremiah and Sarah Campbell, Oct. 2, 1820.
Burnett, John and Mary Prillaman, Jan. 6, 1823. Sur. Jacob Prillaman. 61.
Burnett, Pleasant and Elizabeth Jarrett, dau. Allen, Dec. 31, 1825. Sur. Samuel Price.
Burnett, Zebedia and Martha Ann Prater, dau. Mary, Oct. 21, 1833. Sur. David Durham. 86.
Burns, Horatio and Peggy Carter, Oct. 6, 1794. 141.
Burns, Jeremiah and Elizabeth Rowland, Mar. 20, 1794. 141.
Burriss, Thos. and Catherine Booth, Aug. 19, 1832.
Burson, Silas, s. Nathan, and Charity Bird, dau. Luke, Aug. 14, 1812. Sur. Reason Garrett. 35.
Burton, Jubal and Sallie McGraw, Mar. 5, 1821. Sur. Jacob Slone. 48.
Burton, Wm. and Hannah Lykins, Dec. 14, 1797. 39.
Burwell, Armistead and Elizabeth M. B. Hix, dau. Patrick, Nov. 13, 1833. Sur. John S. Hale.
Burwell, John S. and Elizabeth M. Woods, June 2, 1806. Sur. Josiah Wood.
Bush, Griffith and Drucilla D. Brooks, Apr. 5, 1853. 18.
Butler, James and Sarah Ferguson, Apr. 27, 1811. Sur. Mitchell Ferguson.
Butts, Reginald and Celia White, Mar. 4, 1822.
Byars, David and Rachael Wimmer, Sept. 16, 1796. Sur. Jacob Wimmer.
Bybee, Allen, s. John and Betty, and Sarah Linkens (Likens), dau. Sarah, Mar. 13, 1786. Sur. Wm. Watson.
Bybee, John and Elizabeth Colley, dau. Wm., May 6, 1791. Sur. Sherwood Bybee. 52.
Bybee, Noel McCan and Mary Evans, dau. John and Betsy, Sept. 16, 1792. Sur. Thos. Evans. 52.
Byrd, John and Nancy Glass, Mar. 23, 1811.
Byrd, John and Mary Stewart, Oct. 7, 1792. Sur. James Byrd.

Byherd, (Ryherd) Jacob and Peggy Dehaven, Mar. 27, 1803. 106.

Cabaniss, Courtland and Catherine M. Powell, dau. Mary, July 15, 1839. Sur. Wm. Powell.

Cabaniss, John and Martha E. Sink, Aug. 13, 1858.

Cabaniss, Matthew and Martha Sink, dau. Anna, Aug. 15, 1844. Sur. Benj. Betz. 18.

Cahill, John C. and Nancy A. Ingram, dau. Alexander, Nov. 15, 1841. Sur. Alexander Ingram.

Cahill, Thos. and Clementine Turner, Mar. 5, 1821. Sur. Shores P. Turner.

Cain, John and Elizabeth Earhart, ..., 1819. 130.

Calhoun, Wm. and Milly Turnbull, Nov. 21, 1812. Sur. Geo. Wheeler. 130.

Callaway, Henry and Polly Guerrant, July 5, 1812. 44.

Callaway, James S. and Martha J. Reynolds, dau. Chas. B. June 20, 1814. Sur. Tazewell Taliaferro 104.

Callaway, James and Elizabeth Greer, Apr. 26, 1802. 72.

Callaway, James S' and Mary S. Saunders, Nov. 17, 1852. 47.

Callaway, John and Polly Hairston, dau. Samuel, Dec. 7, 1809. Sur. Caleb Tate.

Callaway, Peter H. and Elizabeth Tabitha Guerrant, dau. John R. Feb. 8, 1848. Sur. Geo. W. Taliaferro.

Callaway, Thos. C. and Susan Callaway, dau. Henry T., May 20, 1846. Sur. Skelton T. Helms. 134.

Callaway, Walter C. and Judith Hale, Jan. 29, 1837. Sur. Moses C. Carper.

Callicoat, Giles H. and Martha J. Metts, Jan. 10, 1846. Sur. John Metz.

Callicoat, John B. and Rebecca Dillion, dau. Samuel, Feb. 13, 1817. Sur. Richard Fields. 7.

Camp, (Kemp) Robt. and Sally Mattox (Mattocks) dau. Nathaniel, Dec. 6, 1802. Sur. Jordan Kemp.

Camp, Robt. and Milly Edmundson, dau. Richard, Oct. 2, 1786. Sur. Richard Edmondson.

Camp, Wm. and Susannah Hail, dau. Stephen, Dec. 24, 1790. Sur. Thos. Camp.

Campbell, Edgar and Susan Boone, dau. Peter, Nov. 28, 1838. Sur. Isaac Boon.

Campbell, Elijah and Cynthia Barton, Mar. 18, 1819. Sur. Jeremiah Campbell. 130.

Campbell, Jeremiah and Polly Faris, Dec. 21, 1816. Sur. Joel Fairs. 7.

Campbell, John and Martha Sandifer, Jan. 13, 1816. Sur. Wm. Parberry. 7.

Campbell, John G. and Sarah Wray, dau. Benj. Feb. 21, 1826. Sur. Jacob Slone. 48.

Campbell, John and Judy Hodges, dau. Reuben, June 28, 1843. Sur. Geo. Lumsden. 18.

Campbell, John and Nancy Dunn, dau. Dickinson, June 16, 1849. Sur. Peter Saunders. 64.

Campbell, John and Elizabeth Nowlin, May 3, 1799. Sur. Wm. Poteet. 21.

Campbell, Peter and Lucy Jarrett, Oct. 2, 1809. Sur. Young Jarrett. 7.

Campbell, Peter and Louisa M. Cooper, Aug. 30, 1845. Sur. John A. Willis. 80.

Campbell, Samuel and Ann Sink, Oct. 6, 1845. Sur. Jonathan Sink.

Campbell, Thos. and Charity Price, Feb. 16, 1804. Sur. Luke Standifer.

Campbell, Thos. and Anny Lavinder, Aug. 9, 1814. Sur. John Lavinder. 130.

Campbell, Wm. and Martha Ingram, Jan. 12, 1827. Sur. Isaiah Welch. 61.

Campbell, Wm. Jr. and Lucy A Law, dau. Daniel, Dec. 21, 1832. Sur. Amos B. Law. 12

Campbell, Wm. C. and Mary Ann Jordan, July 30, 1846. 18.

Campbell, Wm. and Mary Hale, dau. Wm., Feb. 25, 1789. Sur. John Ferguson, Jr. 52.

Campbell, Wm. and Isabella White, Dec. 31, 1852. 75.

Cannaday, Chas. and Mary Ingram, dau. Alexander, Apr. 6, 1822. Sur. James Ingram. 61.

Cannaday, Constant and Sarah Hall, Oct. 21, 1839. Sur. John Cannady.

Cannaday, David and Jane Walker, Aug. 2, 1819. Sur. Joel Walker.

Cannaday, Jacob B. and Ellender Cannaday, dau. Wm. and Elizabeth, Oct. 11, 1841. Sur. Joshua Cannaday. 60.

Cannaday, James N. and Sarah Young, dau. Peter, Feb. 22, 1813. Sur. Thos. Young. 61.

Cannaday, James H. and Sarah H. Turner, Nov. 21, 1843. Sur. Geo. Turner. 68.

Cannaday, James Jr. and Martha Turner, Apr. 2, 1838. Sur. Geo. Turner. 60.

Cannaday, John and Martha Winfree, dau. Stephen, May 11, 1812. Sur. Richard R. Winfree. 44.

Cannaday, John and Orpha Ingram, Jan. 21, 1835. Sur. Alexander Ingram.

Cannaday, Joshua, s. Wm. and Lydia Short, Jan. 21, 1839. Sur. John Y. Short.

Cannaday, Peter and Mildred Ann Turner, Mar. 4, 1836. Sur. Geo. Turner. 60.

Cannaday, Wm. and Mary Douty (Dowdy) dau. Elizabeth Dorothy Parker, May 23, 1798. Sur. Dickinson Thompson.

Canter, (Carter) Truman and Cynthia Harris, dau. John, Mar. 19, 1792. Sur. Samuel Harris.

Canterberry, Samuel and Loncey Webb, dau. Loncey, Nov. 9, 1796.

Caper, (Capper) Thos. and Elizabeth Crawn, Nov. 23, 1799. Sur. David Overholt.

Capper, Samuel and Barbara Prillaman, Feb. 11, 1806. Sur. Jacob Prillaman.

Carmichael Wm. and Elizabeth Cassell, dau. Elizabeth, Mar. 14, 1818. Sur. John Cassell.

Carper, Henry and Nancy Greer, Feb. 17, 1801. 72.

Carper, Moses G. and Catherine Tate, Nov. 27, 1834. Sur. James D. Taylor.

Carrico, Vincent and Frances Estes, dau. Frances, wid., July 5, 1791. Sur. Bottom Estes.

Carter, Dabney and Celia Brock, dau. Lucy and Joshua, Aug. 18, 1808. Sur. Zachariah Brock. 8.

Carter, Hartwell and Martha W. Terry, Apr. 28, 1842. Sur. Carter B. Terry.

Carter, Henry and Malinda Oxley, Mar. 18, 1844. Sur. Wilson Oxley. 132.

Carter, Job and Gincy Sneed, dau. John, Nov. 1, 1808. Sur. Nathaniel Brown.

Carter, John and Fanny McCutchen, dau. James, Nov. 19, 1795. Sur. Wm. Keef. 66.

Carter, John P. and America Turner, Feb. 22, 1853. 20.

Carter, Langdon C. and Emily J. Hall, Sept. 11, 1858.

Carter, Lawson and Elizabeth S. Carper, Jan. 24, 1824. Sur. Moses G. Carper. 48.

Carter, Madison D. and Paulina A. Clement, dau. Geo., Jan. 1, 1844. Sur. Wm. Martin.

Carter, Philip and Sarah Prunty, dau. James, Jan. 9, 1804. Sur. Reuben Day.

Carter, Thos. and Elizabeth Oldened, June 25, 1789. 52.

Carter, Thos. and Sarah Ann Williamson, Jan. ....., 1851. 132.

Carter, Travers and Mary Sneed, dau. Nancy and John, Nov. 24, 1804. Sur. Lewis Ross.

Carter, Walker and Frances Stegall, Jan. 31, 1803. Sur. Geo. Rives.

Carter, Wm. and Ruth Mary Huff, dau. Mary, Oct. 13, 1802. Sur. Wm. Huston. 72.

Carver, Wm. and Elizabeth Prunty, Mar. 5, 1794. Sur. James Prunty.

Cassell, John and Lucy Dent, Jan. 4, 1813. Sur. Walter McGregor.

Cassell, Nicholas and Ally Wade, dau. Braby and Mary, Feb. 6, 1840. Sur. Isaac Wade.

Cassell, Wm. M. and Mary Waid, Dec. 11, 1843. Sur. Bradley Waid. 68.

Cassetty, Thos. and Sarah Thomas, dau. Wm. and Deborah, Feb. 25, 1796. Sur. Ephrem Thomas.

Caufman, (Coffman) Benj. and Hannah Naufsinger, Oct. 15, 1798. Sur. John Nofsinger. 21.

Caylor, Jacob and Elizabeth Holdeman, dau. Christian and Elizabeth, Sept. 3, 1800. Sur. John Holdeman. 21.

Chambers, Anthony and Mary Martin, Nov. 21, 1820. 122.

Chambers, John and Agnes Moore, dau. Agnes, Dec. 10, 1799. Sur. James Garner.

Chambers, John and Elizabeth Adney, Dec. 15, 1813. Sur. Caleb Tate.

Chambers, John and Rebecca Saunders, Oct. 10, 1818. Sur. Geo. D. Saunders.

Chambers, Middleton and Nancy I. Oyler, Nov. 2, 1852. 127.

Chambers, Philip and Catherine Mitchell, Sept. 29, 1815. Sur. Wm. Mitchell.

Chambers, Samuel and Nancy Nabours, Dec. 25, 1805. Sur. Fleming Meador.

Chambers, Schuler F. and Mary A. Simpson, dau. Thos., Jan. 9, 1847. Sur. Henry C. Dillion.

Chambers, Silas W. and Irene Ferguson, Nov. 25, 1850. Sur. Alexander P. Ferguson. 18.

Chambers, Wm. and Franky Wood, Apr. 24, 1809. Sur. John Smith. 8.

Chambers, Wm. P. and Mary E. Law, Dec. 22, 1853. 80.

Chandler, Benj. and Jane Fallis, Jan. 23, 1793. Sur. James Brummet.

Chandler, Daniel and Margaret Roan, Jan. 2, 1797. Sur. John Stone.

Chandler, Moses and Elizabeth W. Hodges, dau. Robt. and Susannah, July 7, 1825. Sur. Robt. Hodges Jr.

Chandler, Shadrach and Anne Brummett, dau. James and Agnes, Oct. 8, 1789. 37.

Chandler, Stephen and Frances Sutherlin, Dec. 4, 1837. Sur. Ransom Sutherlin. 3.

Chandler, Thos. and Charity Elliott, g. Moses Clemons, Mar. 13, 1787. Sur. Daniel Brown.

Chandler, Wm. and Jane Douglass, dau. Thos. and Jean, May 21, 1788.

Chapman, Nathan and Betsy Coleman, Feb. 12, 1791. Sur. James Coleman. 50.

Charter, Jonathan and Margaret Brockman, Aug. 9, 1800. Sur. Jasper Franklin. 21.

Charters, Wm. and Jean Read, dau. Samuel, Sept. 28, 1787. Sur. Thos. Charter.

Chasteen, Barnett and Sarah Hixon, Dec. 13, 1795. Sur. Daniel Hixon. 66.

Chasteen, (Chartain) Renny and Massey Robbins, dau. Jacob and Mary, Sept. 17, 1795.

Chasteen, Robt and Maglin Moore, dau. Jane, Sept. 21, 1791. Sur. James Roberts.

Chavers, Benj. and Anna Beverly, Aug. 24, 1801. Sur. Silvester Beverly. 72.

Chavers, Ellison and Susannah Chandler, Jan. 3, 1825. Sur. Jesse Chandler. 48.

Chavis, Starling and Betsy Chandler, Jan. 14, 1830. Sur. Moses Chandler.

Cheek, Stephen and Matilda A. Booth, Dec. 21, 1850. 97.

Cheeling, Joseph and Judith Bass, Sept. 16, 1833. Sur. Dabney Bass.

Chewning, Nathaniel and Jane Smith, Mar. 21, 1848. Sur. Stephen P. Smith.

Chewning, Walter and Nancy E. Spradlin, Feb. 6, 1849. Sur. Clemons Oyler.

Childress, Abraham and Elvira Wysong, July 25, 1833. Sur. Jacob Wysong. 110.

Childress, Abram and Jane Turner, July 11, 1851. Sur. Pleasant Brown. 19.

Childress, Henry and Sally Greer, Nov. 4, 1816. Sur. Isaiah Greer. 130.

Childress, John and Sally Ferguson, dau. Nancy, Dec. 18, 1811. Sur. Eli Ferguson.
Childress, Joshua and Sarah May, Sept. 22, 1830. Sur. Hiram Hodges.
Childress, Laban and Sarah Board, (Beard), Mar. 17, 1841. Sur. Henry Beard. 18.
Childress, Laban and Polly Brown, Nov. 7, 1839. Sur. Jacob Puckett.
Childress, Thos. D. and Fannie D. James, dau. Catlett, Dec. 2, 1850. Sur. Pyrant T. James
Childress, Wm. and Tabitha Taylor, dau. Skelton, Jan. 3, 1810. Sur. Otey Taylor.
Chitwood, Edmond and Mary Seay, Oct. 18, 1832. Sur. Abram B. Seay. 48.
Chitwood, Jefferson and Lucy Lumsden, Sept. 3, 1832. Sur. Dudley Lumsden. 48.
Chitwood, Joel and Elizabeth Rigney, Oct. 20, 1815.
Chitwood, Joel and Sally Short, dau. Winaford, Jan. 6, 1800. Sur. Thos. B. Short. 21.
Chitwood, Matthias and Judith Woody, Aug. 9, 1817. Sur. Squire Chitwood. 130.
Chitwood, Randolph and Celia Dillon, Dec. 2, 1831. Sur. Wm. Harrison. 48.
Chitwood, Richard and Betsy Kitchen, Feb. 1, 1830. Sur. Chesley Kitchin. 48.
Chitwood, Squire and Mary Wray, dau. Benj., Jan. 5, 1801. Sur. Benj. Wray.
Chitwood, Wm. and Elocky Thurmond, Dec. 14, 1811. Sur. John Thurmond. 130.
Chitwood, Wm. and Nancy Seay, Mar. 6, 1837. Sur. John Seay.
Choice, Franklin and Martha Copeland, Jan. 3, 1848. Sur. Oliver B. Copeland. 80.
Choice, John H. and Elizabeth A. Arnold, July 7, 1845. Sur. Henry Stegall. 14.
Choice, John and Jenny Hagood, Feb. 1805. Sur. John Cook.

Chumley, Archibald and Mary Doss, dau. Anny, Mar. 18, 1846. Sur. Wiley Doss. 132.
Clack, (Click) John and Lydia Betz, Sept. 2, 1820. Sur. Conrade Betz.
Claiborne, Ferdinand L. and Emily L. Taliaferro, Feb. 17, 1842. Sur. Tazewell Taliaferro.
Claiborne, Wm. A. and Sarah D. Turnbull, Oct. 22, 1828. Sur. Stephen Turnbull. 48.
Clark, Christopher H. and Elizabeth Hook, Apr. 24, 1790. Sur. Stephen Smith.
Clark, John and Miriam Hale, dau. F., Oct. 26, 1833.
Clark, Robt. and Mary J. Stone, Dec. 6, 1858.
Clark, Wm. and Frances Blades, Jan. 15, 1802. Sur. Francis Blades. 106.
Clay, Ezekiel and Jincey Brizendine, dau. Joshua, Jan. 2, 1811. Sur. John Clay.
Clay, John and Elizabeth Middleton Dickinson, Mar. 27, 1801. 14.
Clay, Lemuel and Mildred Tyree, Feb. 25, 1832. Sur. John Tyree. 62.
Clay, Wm. and Lucy Reedy, Dec. 8, 1798. Sur. Richard Dale.
Clay, Wm. B. and Margaret L. Dickinson, dau. Jane, Mar. 7, 1843. Sur. Cary B. Dickinson. 104.
Claytor, Harvey and Adeline Walker, dau. Geo., Sept. 24, 1830. Sur. Geo. Walker. 48.
Clement, Geo. W. and Sally Cook, Nov. 22, 1834. Sur. Micajah W. Harris. 53.
Clement, Geo. W. and Sarah J. Clement, dau. Geo. W. Sr., Jan. 2, 1841. Sur. Ralph A. Clement.
Clement, John and Mary Frances Pollard, Jan. 22, 1852. 134.
Clement, John and Susan Altick, Dec. 22, 1845. Sur. Christopher Altick. 18.
Clement, Ralph A. and Elizabeth Ann Dickinson, Sept. 9, 1852. 80.
Clement, Wm. and Elizabeth Goard, dau. Wm., Oct. 7, 1790. Sur. Wm. Goard.
Clifton, Austin and Elizabeth Wood, Jan. 21, 1824. Sur. John Wood. 65.

Clifton, Joanathan and Polly Martin, June 8, 1827. Sur. John Cannaday. 61.

Clingenpeel, (Klingenpeel) David and Mary Fisher, Aug. 7, 1824. Sur. Jonathan Fisher. 130.

Clingenpeel, Geo. and Elizabeth Himbeck, (Hambrick), Feb. 28, 1809. Sur. Andrew Himlick. 130.

Clingenpeel, Jonathan and Milly Hambrick, Sept. 12, 1811. Sur. James Hambrick. 130.

Clingenpeel, Jospeh Jr. and Margaret Betz, Nov. 21, 1812. Sur. Joseph Clingenpeel, Sr.

Clingenpeel, Nathaniel and Fanny Brower, Aug. 19, 1814. Sur. Henry Brower. 130.

Clingenpeel, Peter and Elizabeth Goode, Apr. 1, 1822. Sur. Joseph Clingenpeel.

Clingenpeel, Samuel and Sarah Quigley, Sept. 21, 1846. Sur. Elias Quigley. 96.

Clingenpeel, Wiley and Susan Sink, dau. Anna, Jan. 16, 1838. Sur. Benj. Betz.

Clower, Jacob Jr. and Elizabeth Glasspy, Apr. 4, 1803. Sur. John Glaspy. 72.

Clower, John Jr. and Nancy Bowles, Sept. 1, 1821. Sur. Geo. Bowles

Clower, John and Rebecca Harris, May 11, 1796. Sur. Wm. Harris.

Clower, Wm. and Nancy Ullman, Mar. 21, 1827. Sur. Wm. Starkey.

Coats, Kinzey and Joany Turner, Apr. 13, 1789. Sur. James Turner. 52.

Cockran, Chas. and Ruth Radford, dau. Elender and Robt., Nov. 7, 1848. Sur. Wm. R. Radford.

Cockran, Daniel and Polly Brizendine, Sept. 1, 1817. Sur. John B. Brizendine.

Cockran, John and Susannah Lumsden, dau. John, Jan. 21, 1786. Sur. Wm. Crump.

Cockran, Peter and Sally Newberry, June 3, 1835. Sur. Thos. Newberry. 129.

Cockran, Samuel and Catherine Wright, Oct. 18, 1836. Sur. Joshua Hall. 129.
Cockran, Wm. R. and Rhoda Pasley, Nov. 2, 1812. Sur. Wm. Pasley
Cockran, Wm. and Lucy Milam, Dec. 12, 1803. Sur. Benj. Davis.
Coffman, Jacob and Catherine Rudy, ..., 1794. 89.
Coger, Wm. and Elizabeth Kingery, dau. Peter and Mary, Sept. 18, 1804. Sur. Wm. Kelly.
Coleman, Geo. and Mary E. Brodie, Nov. ___, 1853. 132.
Coleman, John and Patsy Arrington, dau. Samuel, Feb. 17, 1792. 84.
Coleman, Samuel and Priscilla Beheler, Jan. 14, 1819. Sur. Geo. Beheler.
Coleman, Shelton and Jane Cole Dent, dau. Kezia, Nov. 25, 1830. Sur. John Doughton. 132.
Coleman, Wm. and Elizabeth Woody, Apr. 22, 1814. Sur. John Woody.
Colley, John and Lucy Martin, June 27, 1822. Sur. John Martin.
Collier, James and Anna Dalton, May 16, 1814. Sur. Solomon Pasley.
Combs, Gilbert Jr. and Nancy Potter, Apr. 7, 1824. Sur. Lewis Potter.
Comer, Richard and Milley Shockley, dau. Rebeckah and Levi, Dec. 20, 1790.
Comer, Wm. B. and Elizabeth Griffith, Nov. 8, 1853. Sur. Stephen Haynes. 31.
Compton, Micajah and Naomi Davis, Dec. 29, 1828. 48.
Compton, Thos. A. and Hannah Scarborough, Oct. 24, 1842. Sur. Robt. Scarborough.
Conner, Greenville R. and Ann Prillaman, Sept. 23, 1858. Sur. Daniel Prillaman.
Conner, John M. and Margaret Ruble, dau. Owen and Margaret, Aug. 17, 1795. Sur. Francis Kirby. 52.
Conner, Jonathan and Rozina Ingram, May 1, 1835. Sur. John Conner and James Ingram.

Conoway, Edward and Elizabeth Early, Feb. 4, 1805. Sur. Jasper Franklin.

Cook, Benj. F. Jr. and Julia A. F. Mitchell, dau. Wm., Sept. 5, 1842. Sur. Benj F. Cook, Sr.

Cook, Benj. F. and Susan A. F. Meredith, dau. James, Dec. 14, 1850. Sur. John W. Meredith. 80.

Cook, Frederick A. and Mariah Wingfield, dau. Lucy, Mar. 6, 1843. Sur. James Cooper.

Cook, John and Anny Belcher, Dec. 14, 1805. Sur. Francis Belcher.

Cook, John Jr. and Mary Ann Bondurant, Aug. 22, 1844. Sur. Robt. Bondurant.

Cook, John W. and Mary E. Street, Feb. 16, 1825. Sur. Benj. F. Cook.

Cook, Joseph and Sarah Edwards, Aug. 23, 1788. Sur. Arthur Edwards.

Cook, Mordecai and Emily T. Dickinson, ..., 1851. 132.

Cool, Wm. and Martha Shelton, Oct. 13, 1844. 18.

Cooley, James and Patsy Stewart, dau. David, Oct. 4, 1786. Sur. James Haggart.

Cooly, John and Nancy Brock, dau. Joshua, Sept. 18, 1795. Sur. Jubal Brock. 37.

Coon, Frederick and Rosannah Weaver, Dec. 15, 1814. Sur. Daniel Sink. 8.

Coon, Henry and Sarah Brown, Dec. 28, 1824. Sur. Rodham Brown. 48.

Coop, David and Christina Stofer, dau. Christian, May 12, 1794. Sur. Daniel Barnhart.

Coop, John and Sarah Hall, dau. Lane, May 8, 1793. Sur. Wm. Greer. 52.

Cooper, Ambrose and Nancy S. Richardson, Dec. 24, 1846. Sur. Geo. Richardson. 19.

Cooper, Andrew and Locky Akers, Jan. 8, 1848. Sur. Stephen Akers.

Cooper, Andrew and Elizabeth Pearson, Jan. 23, 1846. Sur. Pleasant Beard. 18.

Cooper, Benj. and Rebecca Lamberth, Nov. 5, 1834. Sur. Benj. Lambert.

Cooper, Caleb and Nancy Ann Webb, dau. Reuben and Nancy, Jan. 22, 1845. Sur. Reuben Webb.

Cooper, Chas. and Jane Richardson, dau. Green and Jane, Mar. 7, 1786. Sur. Joseph Young.

Cooper, Chesley and Jane Richardson, Mar. 24, 1835. 140.

Cooper, Edward and Susannah Cornelius, dau. Susannah, Mar. 25, 1801. Sur. James Cornelius. 21.

Cooper, Francis s. Sterling, and Anna Napier, Sept. 19, 1807. Sur. Skelton Brown. 57.

Cooper, Geo. and Polly Wingfield, Sept. 23, 1824. Sur. Austin Wingfield.

Cooper, Gideon and America Law, dau. Cheadle, Apr. 5, 1824.

Cooper, Greenville P. T. and Lucinda E. Brodie, dau. Williamson, Sept. 3, 1849. Sur. Wm. F. Brodie.

Cooper, Iles and Elizabeth Gearhart, Oct. 15, 1810. Sur. John Wright. 130.

Cooper, Ike and Polly Lemon, May 18, 1812. 130.

Cooper, James H. s. Wm. and Elizabeth L Wingfield, dau. Lucy, Jan. 25, 1838. Sur. John Wingfield.

Cooper, Langston and Stiry Cooper, Jan. 4, 1813. Sur. John Pinkard.

Cooper, Reuben and Nancy Peters, Dec. 2, 1836. Sur. Zebedee Whitlock. 132.

Cooper, Sterling and Eleanor Willis, Sept. 20, 1824. Sur. Josiah R. Willis.

Cooper, Sterling and Ann E. Williams, Sept. ...., 1852. 132.

Cooper, Thos. s. John, and Nancy Cornelius, dau. Susannah, Aug. 25, 1797. Sur. James Cornelius. 21.

Cooper, Wm. and Lucy Willis, Dec. 6, 1819. Sur. David Willis.

Cooper, Wm. Jr. and Nancy Martin, dau. Sarah, Mar. 3, 1828. Sur. Samuel H. Martin.

Copeland, Oliver B. and Charity M. Cooper, dau. Geo., Oct. 16, 1848. Sur. Peter Campbell. 80.

Copeland, Wm. and Martha W. Neblett, July 8, 1827. Sur. Wm. Safford Niblett.

Core, Henry and Nancy Webster, Nov. 12, 1851. 68.

Corell, Geo. and Malinda Wimmer, dau. John, Feb. 7, 1839. Sur. Peter Guerrant, Jr. 18.

Corell, Valentine C. and Susan B. Toney, Apr. 13, 1847. Sur. James Toney. 68.

Corley, (Carley) Chatham and Delilah Basham, Dec. 27, 1804. Sur. Bartlett Basham.

Corn, Samuel and Molly Slaughter, Nov. 19, 1810. Sur. John Slaughter.

Couzens, Martin and Polly Beverly, Mar. 31, 1814. Sur. Benj. Chavis.

Cowden, James and Lucy Rives, dau. Frederick, Jan. 26, 1799. Sur. Drinkard Steagall. 21.

Cowden, Josiah and Milly Clay, Dec. 31, 1799. Sur. Wm. Clay. 141.

Cowden, Wm. and Elizabeth Keen, dau. Edw., Feb. 12, 1802. Sur. John Keen.

Cox, Daniel R. and Sally Ann Farris, dau. Valentine, Jan. 16, 1844. Sur. Moses W. Cox.

Cox, Daniel and Jemima Knowles, dau. John, Feb. 13, 1822. 61.

Cox, James and Sarah Ross, dau. Daniel, Jan. 22, 1799. Sur. James Randal.

Cox, Moses and Cynthia Peters, Nov. 26, 1837. Sur. Jordon Peters. 1.

Cox, Robt. and Cynthia Doran, Oct. 2, 1845. Sur. Geo. Doran.

Craddock, Jarmon and Frances Crews, Oct. 16, 1834. Sur. Joseph Cox. 129.

Craghead, John and Elizabeth Hale, Apr. 3, 1789. Sur. John Camp.

Craghead, John and Jane Martin, Jan. 1, 1842. Sur. Henry Law.

Craghead, John and Julia Smith, dau. Wm., Dec. 18, 1830. Sur. Wright Smith. 3.

Craghead, John and Sally Powell, Jan. 2, 1794. 141.

Craghead, John B. and Sally Hale, dau. James T., Oct. 28, 1823. Sur. James T. Hale. 48.

Craghead, Robt. and Nancy Powell, Nov. 18, 1792. Sur. Robt. Powell.

Craghead, Timothy and Mary Agee, Dec. 6, 1802. Sur. Matthew Agee. 106.

Craghead, (Craighead) Townsend and Sarah Bernard, dau. Peter, Jan. 14, 1824. Sur. Wesley Mattox.

Craghead, Wm. and Susannah Maxey, Mar. 4, 1828. Sur. James Maxey. 3.

Craghead, Wm. and Nancy Craghead, dau. John, May 13, 1822. Sur. Townsend Craghead.

Craghead, Wm. and Jean Dunn, dau. Thos., Jan. 13, 1800. Sur. Thos. Dunns. 37.

Craig, David and Maria Stockton, Oct. 13, 1818. Sur. Thos. Craig.

Craig, James, s. Henry, and Mildred Payne, dau. Shom J., Apr. 22, 1842. Sur. Wm. C. A. Meador. 86.

Craig, James W. and Mary P. Woodson, dau. Benj., May 8, 1834. Sur. James Webster.

Craig, Robt., and Ellender Gibson, dau. John, Aug. 4, 1823. Sur. James Saul.

Craig, Thos. and Lucy Bird, dau. Samuel, Aug. 17, 1789. Sur. Samuel Bird.

Craig, Thos. Jr., and Delia Cabaniss, dau. Cassimer, Aug. 16, 1827. Sur. Wm. H. Cabaniss

Craig, Wm and Elizabeth Jamison, Nov. 26, 1834. Sur. Thos. Jamison.

Craig, Wm., s. Henry and Mildred, and Nancy S. Arthur, dau. John and Charlotte, Dec. 8, 1853. 96.

Craig, Wm. M. and Martha Woodson, dau. Benj., May 14, 1839. Sur. Samuel Akers.

Craig, Wm. and Catherine Mitchell, Nov. 27, 1841. Sur. Wm. S. Mitchell. 132.

Crawford, James and Cinderella Richards, Nov. 14, 1792. Sur. Ambrose Raymore. 23.

Crawford, Russell D. and Sarah Goode, Sept. 23, 1824. Sur. David Goode.

Crawford, Wm. and Isabella McClure, dau. David, Jan. 16, 1783. Sur. Wm. Mary and Sam Henderson.

Creasy, Coonrad and Martha Ann Beckner, Dec. 8, 1852. 18.

Creasy, Jourdan and Malinda Hold, Dec. 12, 1834. Sur. John Creasy. 134.

Crews, Robertson and Eliza A. Read, Jan. 17, 1846. Sur. Wm. Beard. 20.

Crews, (Cruse) Thos. and Mary Cynthia Divers, dau. Elizabeth, Nov. 30, 1840. Sur. Richard Roberson. 86.

Crockett, Tilman and Elizabeth Dennis, Oct. 27, 1796. Sur. Thos. Highley.

Crook, David and Nancy Hutts, Nov. 27, 1822. Sur. Jacob Slone. 130.

Crook, Geo. and Mary Ann Crotty, Feb. 25, 1843. Sur. Michael Crotty.

Crook, Jacob and Lener Terah Slone, Nov. 26, 1817. Sur. Jacob Slone. 98.

Crook, Jonathan and Louisa Wood, June 20, 1842. Sur. Stephen Wood. 18.

Crook, Matthias and Polly Taylor, Oct. 7, 1822. Sur. Abraham Martin. 49.

Crotty, James T., s. Michael, and Eliza J. Meador, dau. Jonas, Aug. 1, 1842. Sur. Hubbard Meador. 45.

Crouss, (Crauss) Michael and Catherine David, Feb. 19, 1823. Sur. Daniel Laymon. 49.

Crowl, (Crowell) Dewalt, Jr. and Sally Rudy, Aug. 13, 1803. Sur. Daniel Rudy. 72.

Crowl, Henry and Elizabeth Cross, dau. Jacob, Sept. 25, 1801. Sur. Jacob Cross. 21.

Crowl, Jacob and Polly Altic, Sept. 7, 1801. Sur. John Altick. 21.

Crowl, John and Hannah McNeal, Jan. 1, 1828. 18.

Crow, (Grow) John and Nancy Thomas, Oct. 7, 1811. Sur. Aaron Hodges.

Crowell, Zenus and Nancy Bartee, dau. Wm., Oct. 16, 1786. Sur. Wm. Thompson.
Crowl, (Crowell) John and Polly Amos, Feb. 8, 1812. Sur. James Amos.
Crown, Joseph and Norah Allen, Aug. 1, 1808. Sur. James L. Hail. 8.
Crown, Nehemiah B. and Nancy Greer, Dec. 11, 1810. Sur. Joseph Crown. 8.
Crowder, Henry, s. Berry and Polly, (Roanoke Co.) and Elizabeth Evans, dau. Thos., Dec. 12, 1853. 47.
Crowder, Wm. and Sally Burton, Oct. 11, 1828. Sur. Wm. Clay.
Crowder, Wm. and Susannah Cook, dau. Izabel, Nov. 17, 1829. Sur. Thos. Saul. 132.
Crum, Abraham Jr. and Lucy E. Bird, dau. Sarah, Mar. 7, 1826. Sur. Luke Bird. 48.
Crum, Abraham and Julia Perdue, Aug. 8, 1839. 18.
Crum, Berry J. and Eve Housman, Feb. 16, 1847. Sur. Geo. Housman. 104.
Crum, John and Naomi Smith, dau. John, Jan. 15, 1816. Sur. Juny Smith.
Crum, Robt. and Sarah Perdue, Oct. 18, 1842. Sur. Coalman English.
Crump, Geo. and Dyce Haynes, July 23, 1792. Sur. Wm. Haynes.
Crump, Wm. and Gilly Law, Oct. 2, 1815. Sur. Burwell Law. 7.
Crumpecker, Owen and Alean Helm, Sept. 21, 1838. Sur. Samuel M. Helm.
Cruse, Edward and Mary J. Creasey, dau. John, Oct. 28, 1850. Sur. Littleberry Robertson. 97.
Cruse, Leniaus S. and Elizabeth Southall, dau. Turner, Dec. 9, 1846. Sur. Eli Ferguson.
Crutcher, Thos. and Caty Smith, Jan. 13, 1796. Sur. James Callaway. 93.
Cuff, Wm. and Polly Gee, Apr. 8, 1816. Sur. Henry T. Kennon. 130.

Cuff, Wm. and Rachael Monis (Moris), Feb. 16, 1797. 89.
Culp, John and Mary McGuire, May 8, 1801. Sur. John McGuire. 21.
Cumbuford, James and Rebecca Cornelius, dau. Susannah, Oct. 26, 1807. Sur. Abraham Stilley.
Cundiff, Isom and Nancy Hall, Mar. 3, 1831. Sur. John Hall. 48.
Cundiff, Meshack and Elizabeth Dale, Dec. 27, 1797. Sur. Richard Dale.
Cundiff, Wilson and Rhody Hale, Feb. 26, 1832. Sur. John Hall, Jr. 48.
Cunningham, Ambrose and Sarah Richards, dau. Jeremiah, Dec. 14, 1826. Sur. Andrew Richards. 61.
Cunningham, Fleming and Jane Lemon, Sept. 20, 1830. Sur. Isaac Lemon. 48.
Cunningham, James and Judith Sutherland, dau. Ransom, Oct. 3, 1808. Sur. Ransom Sutherland.
Cunningham, John and Elizabeth Leay, Jan. 1, 1816. Sur. John Leay.
Custer, Henry and Suckey Hambrick, Aug. 25, 1810. Sur. Joseph Himbrick. 8.
Custer, (Custard) John and Elizabeth Hudson, dau. Elizabeth, June 2, 1801. Sur. Michael Shepherd. 21.
Custer, Davis and Zaney Nowlin, dau. Elizabeth Campbell, Dec. 9, 1799. Sur. Dudley Lumsden. 21.
Custer, Hiram and Elzira Willis, Jan. 16, 1850. Sur. Hardin Willis. 11.
Custer, Hiram and Malinda Lumsden, dau. Chas., May 23, 1838. Sur. Moses G. Carper. 18.
Custer, Isaac and Polly Willis, Feb. 3, 1834. Sur. Monk Willis.
Custer, Jacob and Sally Loyd, dau. Cornelius and Henrietta, Jan. 3, 1809. Sur. Valentine Kymes.
Dabney, Garland and Polly Martin, dau. John, Jan. 11, 1799. Sur. Tyree G. Dabney.
Dale, Richard and Mary Haizlip, Jan. 31, 1837. Sur. Wm. Kirks. 3.

Dalton, Jubal L. and Margaret P. Wright, dau. Wm., Feb. 18, 1832. Sur. Wesley Wright.

Dame, John and Elizabeth Oyler, Mar. 2, 1807. Sur. John Oyler.

Dangerfield, Alexander and Clarkey Teal, dau. Jemima, Dec. 20, 1832. Sur. Terry Teel. 48.

Dangerfield, Edward and Sarah R. Hoffman, dau. John, Aug. 24, 1847. Sur. Michael Hoffman. 68.

Dangerfield, Leonard H. and Polly Kesler, dau. Luke, Oct. 29, 1829. Sur. Geo. Kesler. 26.

Daniel, Washington and Nancy Hodges, dau. Robt., Dec. 19, 1839. Sur. James Hodges.

Darnell, Richard and Susan Akers, Nov. 5, 1840. Sur. Richard M. Taliaferro.

Daughtry, Joshua and Melinda Wallis, Jan. 6, 1829. Sur. Geo. Farmer.

Davenport, John and Lucy Hall, dau. Isham, Dec. 12, 1791. Sur. Robt. Hodges.

Davenport, Wm. and Polly Trout, May 28, 1825. Sur. David Trout. 48.

David, Abraham and Rachael Edmond, Dec. 5, 1803. Sur. Wm. Edmonds.

David, Isaac and Malinda Powell, dau. Robt., Dec. 8, 1827. Sur. Joseph Edmonds.

David, John P. and Happy A. Hines, Aug. 24, 1851. 97.

David, Peter and Elizabeth Hale, Nov. 8, 1793. Sur. Elijah Hatcher.

Davis, Benj. and America Ann Hunter, Feb. 23, 1843. Sur. John Hunter. 132.

Davis, Isaac and Jean Bird, dau. John, Apr. 28, 1798. Sur. Williamson Davis.

Davis, Israel and Judith Rodgers, Oct. 9, 1804. Sur. Elija Brockman.

Davis, James and Milly James, dau. Jack, Sept. 18, 1801. Sur. Jack James.

Davis, James M., and Mary E. Ashworth, dau. Lucy, Nov. 8, 1845. Sur. John S. Hancock. 14.
Davis, Jonathan and Elizabeth K. Davis, Oct. 9, 1843. Sur. Thomas B. Davis. 132.
Davis, Jonathan and Sally Hibbs, Oct. 13, 1802. 72.
Davis, Jonathan and Sarah Parcell, July 12, 1827. Sur. Wm. Parcel. 48.
Davis, Jonathan and Nancy Turner, Dec. 18, 1831. Sur. Jacob Turner.
Davis, Joshua and Mary Dulaney, dau. Samuel and Mary, Feb. 20, 1804. Sur. Edward Abshire.
Davis, Joseph W. and Mary N. Mitchell, Oct. 7, 1839. Sur. Thomas H. Mitchell. 56.
Davis, Leftwich and Martha Belcher, Feb. 17, 1849. Sur. Nathaniel Richardson.
Davis, Middleton and Charlotte Akers, Dec. 13, 1847. Sur. Jesse Akers. 134.
Davis, Moses and Serena Hodges, Oct. 6, 1838. Sur. Chas. Kitchen.
Davis, Peter B. and Emily Wade, dau. John, May 30, 1850. Sur. James Patterson. 132.
Davis, Sampson J. and Bathsheba Turner, Oct. 10, 1836. Sur. Geo. Turner. 132.
Deering, Lewis and Patsy Bennett, Dec. 22, 1813. Sur. Thos. Huddleston. 8.
Dehaven, Abraham and Sarah M. Fowlkes, Aug. 28, 1843. Sur. Wm. M. Featherston.
Dehaven, Abraham, Jr. and Polly Chitwood, Jan. 4, 1820.
Dehaven, Isaac and Prudence Kemp, Aug. 21, 1823. Sur. Jourdan Kemp.
Delancy, (Dulany) Elijah and Marchel Griffith, dau. Jonathan and Oney, June 25, 1810. Sur. John McGuire.
Delancy, Lewis, s. Mahalah, and Barbara Hudson, dau. Wm., Dec. 17, 1838. Sur. Eli Webb. 68.
Delany, (Delaney) Samuel and Polly Griffith, Jan 14, 1805. Sur. Jonathan Griffith. 130.

Demoss, Wm. and Priscilla Greer, May 10, 1787. Sur. Granberry Greer.
Dennis, John and Ann Prillaman, dau. John, June 6, 1812. Sur. Abraham Prilliman.
Dent, John and Mary Clower, Oct. 3, 1793. 52.
Davis, Thos. and Louisa King, Jan. 5, 1807. Sur. Stephen King.
Davis, Wm. and Lucy Craig, Mar. 7, 1825. Sur. Daniel P. Hunt.
Davis, Wm. and Judith Woody, Dec. 19, 1796. Sur. John Davis.
Davis, Wm. and Jane Daniel, dau. Geo., Apr. 2, 1787. Sur. Lewis Davis.
Davis, Wm. H. and Lucy Ann Robertson, Dec. 29, 1849.
Davis, Williamson and Polly Craig, Oct. 19, 1811.
Dawson, Thos. and Fanny Martin, dau. John, Dec. 9, 1810. Sur. Mark Willis.
Dearing, John and Polly Wilkes, dau. John, Nov. 28, 1801. Sur. John Wilks.
Dearen, John A. and Evalina Belcher, Jan. 20, 1834. Sur. Stephen Preston.
Dent, Mark and Elizabeth Ferguson, dau. Wm., Oct. 17, 1805. Sur. Geo. Ferguson.
Dent, Walter Jr. and Keziah Doughton, Dec. 9, 1813. Sur. Absalom Dent. 130.
Dent, Walter Jr. and Drucilla Warner, Nov. 12, 1800. Sur. Thos. Prator.
Dent, Wm. H. and Elizabeth Fishburn, Feb. 7, 1831. Sur. Willis Tinsley. 48.
Denton, John and Elizabeth A. Dunman, Jan. 29, 1841. Sur. James W. Dunman.
Denton, Thos. and Catherine Bell (Ball), Nov. 15, 1800. 141.
Derrem, (Durham) Jesse T. and Elizabeth Patterson, Nov. 10, 1828. Sur. Martin G. Wright. 140.
Dewese, Harvey and Sarah Wimmer, June 3, 1845. Sur. John Wimmer. 68.
Dewitt, Archibald and Tiney Parker, dau. Starling, Apr. 2, 1841. Sur. Wm. P. Scott. 68.

Dewitt, Zachariah W. and Mary Ann Keen, dau. Thos. L., Jan. 7, 1846. Sur. Wm. L. Stockton. 80.

Dickenson, John and Cerena Martin, July 3, 1826. Sur. Josiah W. Dickinson.

Dickenson, Pleasant and Martha C. Brown, Nov. 2, 1814. Sur. Robert N. Dickinson.

Dickerson, Davis and Jane Martin, dau. John, Nov. 16, 1799. Sur. Garland Dabney.

Dickerson, Geo. W. and Lucy Brown, Sept. 2, 1816. Sur. Josiah Dickinson.

Dickerson, Robert N. and Cynthia N. Rives, Sept. 15, 1826. Sur. Joseph Rives.

Dickson, John J. and Nancy Hutts, Sept. 1818. Sur. Michael Hutts.

Dillard, Henry and Mary Jane Taliaferro, July 7, 1833. Sur. Richard M. Taliaferro. 29.

Dillion, Jesse and Polly Housman, Aug. 1, 1814. Sur. Peter Housman. 8.

Dillingham, Peter and Susannah Rentfro, Apr. 24, 1793. Sur. John England.

Dillon, Asa and Elizabeth Greer, dau. Elizabeth, Aug. 13, 1798. Sur. Aquilla Greer.

Dillion, Asa and Jane Saunders, dau. Jesse, Dec. 20, 1842. Sur. Bowker Saunders.

Dillion, Asa Jr. and Mahala Hutts, Dec. 12, 1836. Sur. Leonard Hutts, Jr.

Dillion, Cajah and Polly Callicote, Dec. 15, 1808. 8.

Dillon, Greer and Lucy Spradling, Dec. 29, 1819.

Dillion, Henry and Sarah Young, Nov. 6, 1794. 22.

Dillon, Henry and Joanna Parsley, Oct. 15, 1801. Sur. Robt. Parberry. 106.

Dillion, Henry and Sarah Marr (McMarr), July 3, 1826. Sur. Randolph Dillion. 48.

Dillion, Henry C. and Lucy Ann Akers, June 9, 1853. 80.

Dillion, Henry Jr. and Margaret Brown, Dec. 3, 1827. Sur. Marmaduke Brown. 48.

Dillon, James and Martha Belcher, dau. Isom, Feb. 2, 1789. Sur. Jeremiah Lumsden.

Dillion, James R. and Mary J. Smith, Dec. 3, 1849. Sur. Henry Smith, Jr. 86.

Dillion, Jesse and Mary J. Starkey, Dec. 23, 1850. Sur. Joshua Starkey. 18.

Dillion, Jesse C. and Gilly F. Dudley, dau. Nancy, Jan. 7, 1850. Sur. Jesse Dillion. 18.

Dillon, Jesse Jr. and Rebecca Plybon, Jan. 18, 1808.

Dillion, John and Mary Dillion, Jan. 15, 1836. Sur. Lewis Dillion.

Dillon, John and Susannah Woody, dau. John, Jan. 21, 1823. Sur. Henry Woody.

Dillion, Joseph and Jerusha Frazier, dau. Elizabeth Bowles, Feb. 5, 1831. Sur. Solomon King.

Dillion, Lewis and Lucy Greer, Feb. 1, 1833. Sur. Benjamin Harris. 48.

Dillion, Luellen E. and Lucinthia Saunders, Jan. 7, 1833.

Dillion, Meredith and Polly Ryherd, Feb. 17, 1806. Sur. Aaron Ryherd. 8.

Dillon, Peter and Rebecca B. Crum, Jan. 1, 1844. Sur. John Crum.

Dillion, Randolph and Charlotte Hawk, June 28, 1824. Sur. John Woody, Sr.

Dillion, Robt. P. and Martha Dillion, May 15, 1832. Sur. John Saunders. 140.

Dillion, Samuel and Margaret Kesler, Dec. 22, 1853. 80.

Dillion, Samuel Jr. and Frances Dillion, Oct. 14, 1831. Sur. Martin Dillon.

Dillion, Squire and Celia Ward, Sept. 1, 1806. Sur. Benj. Ward. 3.

Dillion, Snellin E. and Lucintha Saunders, dau. J., Jan. 7, 1833. Sur. Robt. Pasley.

Dillion, Thos. and Obedience Tyree, Apr. 27, 1820. Sur. John Tyree, Sr.

Dillion, Wm. and Polly Starkey, Apr. 3, 1809.

Dillion, Wm. Jr. and Ann Betz, Aug. 6, 1833. Sur. Joseph Payne.
Diller, (Dillen) Arthur and Jane Ross, Apr. 20, 1797. 141.
Dilmon, Jacob and Susannah Brown, Jan. 1, 1808. Sur. Henry Brown, Jr.
Dinwiddie, James and Sarah A. Holland, dau. Nancy, Oct. 2, 1850. Sur. Alexander G. Holland.
Dishon, Wm. and Susannah McIlhany, dau. Sally, Nov. 21, 1832. Sur. Thos. Fowler. 48.
Dishong, Jacob and Marey Brown, Sept. 9, 1841. 18.
Divers, Annanias and Mary Holland, Nov. 24, 1807. Sur. Thos. Holland. 8.
Divers, Aquilla and Nancy Bradley, Apr. 7, 1794. Sur. Achilles Smith. 41.
Divers, Baily and Nancy G. Divers, Nov. 3, 1835. Sur. Francis Divers. 140.
Divers, Berry and Mary A. Bradley, July 4, 1847. Sur. Peter Bradley.
Divers, Christopher and Lucy Smith, dau. John, Jan. 27, 1789. Sur. Samuel Read. 77.
Divers, Davis and Parthena Mitchell, dau. Fineses, Jan. 17, 1842. Sur. James H. Mitchel. 18.
Divers, Francis and Elizabeth Harris, Oct. 15, 1810. Sur. Samuel Harris. 8.
Divers, Geo. and Frances Robertson, dau. John, Dec. 23, 1840. Sur. Paschal Meador. 86.
Divers, Jeter and Martha Brown, Jan. 9, 1851. 18.
Divers, John and Anna Starkey, Feb. 21, 1821. Sur. Wm. Dillion.
Divers, John and Mildred Ferguson, Nov. 4, 1822. Sur. Otey Ferguson.
Divers, John R. and Nancy Betz, Dec. 12, 1845. Sur. Abraham Betz.
Divers, Moses and Matilda Hunley, Sept. 22, 1834. Sur. Archibald Hunley.

Divers, Oliver P. and Ursula Dudley, dau. Levi, Sept. 2, 1839. Sur. H. Hiett.
Divers, Otey and Terissa Ferguson, Feb. 20, 1823. Sur. Davis Ferguson. 48.
Divers, Silas G. and Louisa Divers, dau. Francis, Aug. 8, 1838. Sur. Oliver P. Divers. 86.
Divers, Stephen and Susan Perdue, Nov. 2, 1830. Sur. Jesse Perdue.
Divers, Thos. and Lydia Plyborne, Oct. 12, 1830. Sur. John Starkey. 48.
Divers, Wm. H. and Lucy Ann Robertson, dau. John, Dec. 29, 1849. Sur. James Robertson. 19.
Divers, Wm. and Fanny Blankenship, July 28, 1790.
Divers, Wm. R. and Peggy Weaver, Oct. 3, 1814. Sur. Jubal Harris. 8.
Divine, Daniel and Bridget Flood, Oct. 14, 1790.
Dixon, Edmond and Martha Jinney, Aug. 31, 1827. Sur. Moses Janny. 61.
Dixon, John and Elizabeth Watson, May 1, 1798. Sur. John Wiet. 141.
Dixon, John and Lucy Parrott, June 2, 1807. Sur. Thos. Cemp. 9.
Dobbins, Thos. and Polly Foster, dau. Geo., June 22, 1826. Sur. Isaac Shively.
Dobyns, Samuel and Mary Menefee, Dec. 7, 1846. Sur. George C. Menefee.
Dodd, Benj. and Mary Prosese, June 16, 1801. Sur. William Prosese. 21.
Dodd, Booker and Hannah Peters, dau. Jonathan, July 28, 1843. Sur. Geo. Peters. 18.
Dodd, Geo. and Lucinda Turner, dau. Wm., Jan. 20, 1816. Sur. Greenville Turner. 130.
Dodd, John and Polly Short, Mar. 26, 1806. Sur. Noah Ferguson. 130.
Dodd, Wm. and Ann E. Woodson, dau. Benj., Dec. 21, 1833. Sur. James W. Craig.
Dodson, Frederick W. and Sarah Akers, Dec. 1, 1852. 20.

Dogget, Chattin (Chasteen) and Peggy Wilks, Aug. 3, 1801. Sur. Frank Wilks. 141.

Donahoe, Geo. and Frances J. Altick, Dec. 17, 1849. Sur. Henry Altick. 11.

Donahoe, Patrick and Martha Ferguson, Nov. 7, 1796. Sur. Alexander Ferguson.

Donohew, Henry and Rebecca Peters, Feb. 24, 1836. 18.

Donahoe, John and Susannah Sink, Nov. 7, 1825. Sur. John Sink.

Doran, Cana and Elizabeth Minter, 1811. 130.

Doran, John and Fanny McCormack, Apr. 16, 1804. Sur. Micajah McCormack.

Doran, Jubal A. and Martha Bailey, June 19, 1851. Sur. John Bowman.

Dorerty, James and Elizabeth Hambelton, May 26, 1796.

Doss, Chas. and Sarah Harvey, dau. Thos., Jan. 27, 1793. Sur. James Martin. 52.

Doss, James L. and Katherine Ferguson, Dec. 14, 1831. Sur. Archibald Ferguson. 3.

Doss, James L. and Eliza N. R. Ferguson, Feb. 15, 1850. Sur. Geo. D. Odineal.

Doss, Josiah and Lucinda Davis, Nov. 1853. 132.

Doss, Stephen and Judah Hodges, Feb. 14, 1809. 8.

Doss, Wiley and Joycey Bowles, Apr. 19, 1847. Sur. Armistead Hodges. 132.

Doss, Wm. and Catherine Harrison, Aug. 27, 1858.

Doughton, James and Ann J. Lavinder, Nov. 26, 1849. Sur. Samuel Lavinder. 19.

Doughten, John and Sarah Willis, May 30, 1837. Sur. Moses G. Carper. 18.

Doughten, John and Sarah Hunter, Dec. 19, 1816. Sur. John Woods.

Douglass, Wm. and Rachael Davis, Feb. 1, 1796. Sur. Samuel Davis. 37.

Douglass, Wm. and Priscilla Greer, May 10, 1786. Sur. Greenberry Greer.

Dow, Fulleurd and Sally Pedoit, Dec. 29, 1804. Sur. John Coulter.

Dowdy, Elexton and Elizabeth Hutts, dau. Leonard and Elizabeth, Dec. 18, 1810. Sur. Ezekiel Dowdy.

Dowdy, Henry and Harwood Meador, dau. John, Jan. 9, 1838. Sur. Samuel W. Smith. 140.

Dowdy, Hundley and Isabella Austin, Nov. 20, 1844. Sur. Alburtis B. Hill. 18.

Dowdy, Jebez and Hannah Fagg, Sept. 6, 1819. Sur. Henry Bowles. 98.

Dowdy, Jabez and Massalah Hopkins, dau. Mary and Chas., Nov. 9, 1810. Sur. Isaac Hopkins.

Dowdy, James and Elizabeth Wysong, dau. Joseph, Feb. 10, 1819. Sur. Abraham Childress. 98.

Dowdy, John and Nancy Hopkins, Dec. 1, 1834. Sur. Ezekiel Dowdy. 140.

Drake, Allin and Anny Wood, Dec. 29, 1793. 41.

Drake, Andrew and Betsy Ann Bradley, dau. Wm. and Cherbel, Oct. 4, 1819.

Drake, Braxton and Patsy Greer, dau. Elizabeth, Apr. 27, 1795. Sur. Asel Greer. 41.

Drake, Clayton and Sarah Meador, dau. Levine, July 26, 1791. Sur. John Drake.

Drake, Turner and Polly Graham, dau. Joseph, May 5, 1797. Sur. John Jones.

Draper, Asa and Sally Mitchell, Feb. 11, 1811. Sur. Wm. Mitchell.

Draper, John H. and Letitia A. Scott, Jan. 22, 1848. Sur. Michael W. Scott. 67.

Draper, Martin and Polly G. Williams, g. Gregory Hagood, Feb. 12, 1818. Sur. John H. Stewart.

Draper, Martin and Lucy Holcomb, Mar. 30, 1827. Sur. Jeremiah Holcomb.

Duckwiler, Joseph and Miriam Wright, Jan. 1, 1827. Sur. Wm. Wright. 48.

Dudley, Gwen and Mary Pasley, dau. Robt., Aug. 17, 1797. Sur. James Callaway. 141.

Dudley, Gwen Jr. and Eliza N. Smith, dau. John W., Jan. 21, 1833. Sur. Chas. H. English. 48

Dudley, James and Nancy Kemp, Sept. 19, 1804. Sur. Robt. Camp

Dudley, James A. and Mary F. Dudley, Oct. 6, 1845. Sur. Thos. W. Dudley.

Dudley, James H. and Julia A. Dudley, dau. Thos., Oct. 31, 1848. Sur. Henry F. English.

Dudley, Jesse P. and Dolly Tinsley, Jan. 24, 1816. Sur. Reubin Tinsley. 130.

Dudley, John and Lane Perdue, July 6, 1840. Sur. Isaiah Perdue.

Dudley Levi and Elizabeth Gilbert, June 2, 1817. Sur. Michael Gilbert.

Dudley, Levi and Polly Camp, dau. Thos., Mar. 27, 1802. Sur. Thos. Camp.

Dudley, Lewis and Shelley Divers, dau. Christo and Lucy, Jan. 16, 1829. Sur. Lewis Dudley. 140.

Dudley, Robt. L. and Frances Dudley, Mar. 6, 1838. Sur. Levi Dudley.

Dudley, Samuel and Lucinda Holland, John M. Holland, bro. & g., Jan. 19, 1846. Sur. Andrew Holland.

Dudley, Stephen and Charlotte Heptinstall, dau. Lizzy, Feb. 3, 1834. Sur. Thos. Dudley, Jr.

Dudley, Stephen and Patsy Kemp, Mar. 2, 1812. Sur. Thos. Camp.

Dudley, Thos. and Nancy Pasley, dau. Robt., Jan. 16, 1800. Sur. Robt. Pasley. 141.

Dudley, Thos. and Temperance Heptinstall, Aug. 7, 1826. Sur. Wm. G. Heptinstall.

Dudley, Thos., s. Levi, and Mary Frances Dudley, dau. Stephen, Dec. 7, 1840.

Dudley, Tilgham P. L. and Mary Elizabeth Holland, Nov. 17, 1849. Sur. Thos. J. Holland.

Dudley, Wm. and Frances English, dau. John, Mar. 6, 1843.

Dudding, (Duding) Jacob and Elizabeth Akers, Feb. 27, 1851. 12.

Duees, Lorenzo and Rosanna Shilling, Sept. 3, 1858.
Duease, (Duese) Wm. and Sarah Hubble, dau. Jonathan, Nov. 29, 1789. Sur. Nathan Sellers. 52.
Dulany, Wm. and Polly Davis (Divers), dau. Polly, Jan. 23, 1804. Sur. Edward Abshire.
Duncan, Allen and Celia Saynders, dau. Pleasant, Mar. 24, 1821. Sur. Geo. D. Saunders.
Dunham, Wm. D. and Martha Campbell, dau. Lucy, Oct. 9, 1834. Sur. Wm. Campbell.
Dunman, Joseph and Elizabeth M. Fralin, Oct. 14, 1844. Sur. Henry Frailin. 14.
Dunn, Alexander and Nancy Finney, Feb. 10, 1824. Sur. John Finney.
Dunn, Samuel and Sally Clarkson, Dec. 6, 1802. Sur. James L. Hail.
Dunn, Samuel and Sally Clarkson, dau. David, Dec. 22, 1801. Sur. Caleb Arthur.
Duninning, (Dunning) Stephen and Elizabeth Fry, May 6, 1852. 75.
Dunnings, Geo. and Ruthy Jenkins, Oct. 2, 1839. Sur. John Shavers.
Dyer, Benj. F. and Martha A. B. Walker, dau, Arnold, Dec. 22, 1848. Sur. Geo. D. Gravely. 80.
Dyer, Joseph and Rachael Prillaman, Sept. 2, 1826. Sur. John Prillaman. 61.
Dyer, Raleigh W. and Mary Ann Helms, Nov. 30, 1852. 68.
Eakles (Echols), James and Susannah Flora, Sept. 24, 1846. Sur. John Flora. 96.
Eames, Edward S. and Mary Farmer, dau. Mathew, Jan. 29, 1827. Sur. Freelen Farmer.
Eames, James and Sarah Finch, Dec. 31, 1845. Sur. Robt. A. Scott. 14.
Eanes, Herbert and Nancy Bernard, Nov. 3, 1828. Sur. Benj. Bernard.
Eanes, Herbert and Mary M. Bernard, dau. Priscilla S., Oct. 10, 1842. Sur. Thos. V. Bernard.

Early, Henry and Jane Early, Oct. 4, 1815. Sur. Jacob Anderson.

Early, Joab, Capt. and Ruth Hairston, dau. Samuel, Mar. 9, 1812. Sur. Wm. Cook.

Early, John and Elizabeth Cheatham, Feb. 20, 1792. Sur. Jubal Early. 131.

Early, Jubal and Jane P. Helm, Apr. 10, 1824. Sur. Robt. T. Woods. 20.

Early, Lamech and Elizabeth Gray, Nov. 26, 1818. Sur. James C. Early.

Early, Melchizadek and Louisa M. Ferguson, dau. Thos., Aug. 28, 1827. Sur. Wiley P. Woods. 48.

Early, Robert H. and Harriet A. Woods, June 9, 1842. Sur. Jubal A. Early.

Early, Samuel and Catherine A. Smithers, dau. Doshia, Jan. 17, 1838. Sur. Henry Kennon.

Easter, Geo. W. and Mary Ann Kemplin, Apr. 13, 1852. 68.

Easter, John and Catherine T. Earley, Oct. 23, 1848. Sur. Henry Kennon.

Eaton, Richard and Juliet P. Brooks, dau. Wm., Feb. 4, 1833. Sur. Ewell M. Brooks.

Eddings, Henry and Abagail Richardson, dau. Martha, Dec. 11, 1789. Sur. Richard Richardson. 52.

Edds, Joseph and Frances C. Ramsey, dau. Thos., Sept. 19, 1827. Sur. Theoderick A. Ramsey.

Edge, Jesse and Elizabeth Childress, Mar. 8, 1788. Sur. Philip Raley.

Edmonds, Esom and Sophia Green (Greer), Nov. 23, 1805. Sur. Isham Hodges.

Edmonds, Wm. and Peggy Lane, Mar. 2, 1807. Sur. James L. Hail. 8

Edwards, Abdon and Margaret Storme, dau. Peter, Nov. 29, 1789. Sur. Cornelius Storme. 52.

Edwards, Daniel C. and Martha C. Edwards, June 5, 1848. Sur. William H. Edwards.

Edwards, Hickman and Elizabeth Ozley, Apr. 18, 1811. 122.

Edwards, James and Caley Storme, Apr. 26, 1791. Sur. William Edwards.

Edwards, (Edmonds) James and Elizabeth Brizendine, dau. Wm., Dec. 19, 1820. 48.

Edwards, Jesse and Betsy Peters, June 17, 1826. Sur. Zachariah Peters. 129.

Edwards, Lewis and Frances Standley, dau. Samuel., Jan. 3, 1837. Sur. Samuel Standley. 132.

Edwards, Nathaniel and Turner F. Layman, Nov. 4, 1850. Sur. John Laymon. 18.

Edwards, Wm. and Sally Wiley, Aug. 28, 1820. Sur. Henry Gearhart. 130.

Edwards, Wm. R. and Louisa M. Tailor, Dec. 18, 1851. .19.

Edwards, Wm. and Elizabeth Peregoy, dau. Edward, Mar. 18, 1793.

Elam, Miles B. and Elizabeth Sharrocks, Nov. 9, 1814. Sur. Fleming Saunders. 130.

Eller, Abraham and Salma Flora, Nov. 20, 1851. 96.

Eller, David and Anna Prupecker (Brubaker), Dec. 21, 1802. Sur. John Prupecker. 72.

Eller, Jacob and Magdaline Peters, Aug. 5, 1850. Sur. Daniel Peters. 40.

Eller, Jacob and Susan Fisher, Nov. 28, 1846. Sur. Jacob Fisher. 18.

Eller, John B. and Marly Flora, Jan. 1, 1851. 40.

Elliott, Joseph and Mary Latteral, July 12, 1787. Sur. Samuel Litteral. 66.

Elliott, Philip and Mary Ann English, dau. Thos., Apr. 21, 1845. Sur. Henry T. English.

Ellis, John and Mildred Lee, Apr. 6, 1795 or Jan. 3, 1791. Sur. Stephen Lee. 52.

Ellis, (Eller) Jospeh and Fanny Woodson, dau. Shadrack, July 1, 1790. Sur. David Woodson. 52.

Ellis, Pleasant and Reesa Angel, June 1, 1820. Sur. Wm. Angel.

Ellis, Stephen and Rebecca Lewis, Apr. 9, 1795. Sur. Joseph Lewis. 52.

Ellis, Thos. M. and Susannah Meador, dau. Joel, Jan. 13, 1820. Sur. James Meador.
Ellis, Warren and Julia A. Kemp, dau. James, Dec. 11, 1841. Sur. Robt. Cunningham.
Ellis, Zachariah and Linda Dehaven, Aug. 12, 1809. Sur. Wesley Mattox. 15.
Ellison, Amos and Sarah Price, dau. John, Dec. 19, 1797. Sur. David Price. 21.
Ellison, Davis M. and Ruth Spencer, Feb. 10, 1836. Sur. Jubal Willis. 60.
Ellison, Ezekiel and Christina Vanover, Dec. 6, 1796. Sur. John Abshire.
Ellison, John and Lucy Sharp, Feb. 3, 1788. Sur. John Chitwood. 66.
Ellison, Joseph and Aleshey Vanover, Feb. 21, 1791. Sur. Matthew Vanover.
Ellison, Levi and Betsy Lewis, dau. Thos. and Betsy, Sept. 23, 1790. Sur. James Burns.
Ellison, Robt. and Nancy Keys, dau. James, Sept. 23, 1836. Sur. Wm. Brammer.
Ellison, Thos. and Mary Brammer, Mar. 4, 1833. Sur. Noah Brammer. 60.
Ellison, Wm. and Patsy Perdue, widow of David, Aug. 6, 1813. Sur. Jesse Perdue. 8.
Elkins, John and Elizabeth Stephens, Sept. 20, 1794. 52.
England, Titus, and Elizabeth Sewart, Dec. 26, 1795. Sur. James Sewart.
English, Chas. H. and Lucy English, Feb. 23, 1833. Sur. James Robertson. 3.
English, Coalman and Martha Robertson, dau. Richard, July 26, 1843. Sur. James Robertson.
English, Geo. W. and Nancy Poindexter, dau. Elizabeth, Sept. 9, 1848. Sur. Thos. L. Poindexter. 18.
English, Given and Mary F. Lynch, Dec. 4, 18——.
English, Henry and Ann Kemp, dau. Thos., Jan. 3, 1831. Sur. James Kemp. 3.
English, Henry and Charlotte Dudley, Jan. 5, 1835. Sur. James Dudley. 3.

English, James and Lucy Craghead, dau. Elizabeth, Jan. 24, 1820. Sur. Isaiah Craghead.
English, John and Catherine Beasley, dau. Susannah, Dec. 5, 1814. Sur. Floyd Payne. 8.
English, John K. and Mary Jane Smith, dau. Lucy, May 23, 1842. Sur. Samuel W. Smith.
English, Lewis and Sarah W. Divers, dau. Ananias, Oct. 15, 1828. Sur. Samuel Arrington. 26.
English, Parmenas and Sally Johnson, dau. Thos., Apr. 8, 1822. Sur. Isaiah Craghead.
English, Stephen and Elizabeth Dudley, dau. Gwyn, Jan. 3, 1791. Sur. John Hail.
English, Stephen H. and Charlotte T. Housman, Aug. 27, 1849. Sur. Adam Houseman. 18.
English, Thos. T. B. and Ann E. Powell, July 22, 1848. Sur. Silas J. Dudley.
English, Thos. and Nancy Kemp, June 16, 1817. Sur. Wm. Kemp.
English, Wm. and Millie Robertson, dau. Richard, Feb. 15, 1826. 48.
Epperson, Anthony and Ellender Divers, dau. John, Jan. 17, 1800. Sur. John Divers.
Epperson, Benj. and Polly Starkey, dau. Joshua, Jan. 30, 1797.
Erbb, Daniel and Nancy Clowers, July 4, 1797.
Estes, Elisha and Nancy Harris, dau. Henry, Aug. 29, 1791. Sur. Leonard Turley.
Estes, (Easter) Ephraim and Mary Snider, Aug. 14, 1809. Sur. James Martin.
Estes, Jesse and Elizabeth Napier, dau. Robt. and Elizabeth, Mar. 14, 1789. Sur. James Napier. 37.
Estes, Joel and Elizabeth Bradley, June 12, 1801. Sur. William Bradley. 106.
Estes, Joel and Lucy Saunders, Oct. 12, 1807. Sur. Philemon Saunders.
Evans, John and Nancy Eubank, July 24, 1793. 52.
Evans, Mark and Frances Lambert, Dec. 4, 1820. Sur. Miles Lambert. 130.

Evans, Peter and Jane Likens, dau. Marcus, July 9, 1791. Sur. Wm. Lykins. 52.
Evans, Wm. and Nancy Cunningham, dau. Thos., Aug. 5, 1816. Sur. Isaac Prillaman.
Fagg, Daniel and Hannah Bowles, Dec. 11, 1818. Sur. Wm. Bowles.
Fallas, (Folass) Hugh and Barbary Henley, Dec. 5, 1791. Sur. Lewis Davis.
Faris, (Pharis) Amariah and Elizabeth Beheler, dau. David, Jan. 10, 1791. Sur. Edward Shoat. 52.
Faris, Valentine and Hannah Underwood, July 15, 1842. Sur. Wm. Bagley. 60.
Farley, Archibald and Jane Farley, dau. Sarah, Dec. 3, 1787. Sur. Jonathan Richardson.
Farmer, Dudley and Sally Law, dau. Nathaniel, Oct. 31, 1814. Sur. Adam Law.
Farmer, Pleasant and Mary Lindsey, Sept. 14, 1819. Sur. Wm. Lindsey. 130.
Farmer, John and Sarah Wyatt, dau. Alice, May 10, 1803. Sur. Matthew Farmer. 106.
Farmer, John and Polly Showalter, Apr. 20, 1820. Sur. Abraham Showalter. 130.
Farmer, John G. and Susannah H. Richards, Aug. 12, 1828. Sur. Joel Richards.
Farmer, Wm. and Jean Wyatt, dau. John, Oct. 21, 1799. Sur. Matthew Farmer. 130.
Farner, Allen and Elizabeth Prillaman. ...., 1852. 132.
Feazel, Jacob and Jane Key, Sept. 5, 1835. Sur. Robt. McKendree. 68.
Feazel, Wm. E. and Cynthia Steagall, dau. William, Sept. 6, 1838. Sur. Drinkard Steagall. 132.
Feller, John and Nancy Jones, dau. Ann, Jan. 31. 1804. Sur. James Jones.
Ferguson, Alexander and Ann Wood, Apr. 20, 1790. Sur. Stephen Wood. 37.
Ferguson, Alexander and Nancy Wood, Dec. 1, 1788. Sur. Stephen Wood. 37.
Ferguson, Bainbridge and Sophia E. Powell, dau. Mary, Aug. 22, 1842. Sur. Courtland Cabaniss.

Ferguson, Chas. and Elizabeth Ferguson, Aug. 8, 1825. Sur. Joseph Hiett. 48.
Ferguson, Chas. D. and Lydia Ann Becker, Aug. 11, 1848. Sur. Washington Brooks Hill. 132.
Ferguson, Chas. D. and Laura Ann Belcher, ..., 1849.
Ferguson, Daniel, s. John, and Ann Heptinstall, dau. Caleb, Jan. 27. 1816. Sur. John Ferguson.
Ferguson, Daniel and Sallie Moore, Mar. 10, 1834. Sur. Wm. Robertson. 140.
Ferguson, Daniel and Jemima Saunders, Nov. 28, 1805. Sur. Pleasant Saunders.
Ferguson, David and Susannah Brum, May 3, 1799.
Ferguson, Davis and Rhoda H. Rogers, Jan. 23, 1828. Sur. James C. Tate. 26.
Ferguson, Dectator and Louisa Custer, dau. Henry, Nov. 3, 1846. Sur. James Willis. 18.
Ferguson, Eli and Mahala Ellyson, Dec. 7, 1835. Sur. Littleberry Robertson. 140.
Ferguson, Eli and Nancy Childress, Mar. 12, 1805. Sur. Robt. Childress.
Ferguson, Geo. and Polly Crump, Oct. 25, 1797. Sur. James Calloway. 21.
Ferguson, Isham M. and Sarah D. Childress, dau. Wm., Nov. 22, 1841. Sur. Abraham Childress, Jr. 18.
Ferguson, Jacob and Jane Webster, Mar. 1, 1837. Sur. Wm. Webster. 134.
Ferguson, Jeremiah and Frances Kennett, dau. Zechariah, Aug. 17, 1830. Sur. Hullen Scott.
Ferguson, Jeremiah and Polly Thornton, Jan. 26, 1837. Sur. Sandford Scott. 134.
Ferguson, John and Susannah (Suky) Abshire, Jan. 1, 1810. Sur. Geo. Wright.
Ferguson, John U. L. and Mary David, Dec. 3, 1837. Sur. Isaac David. 3.
Ferguson, John and Sally Willis, Jan. 28, 1818. Sur. Henry Akers. 130.
Ferguson, John and Ann Dowdy, dau. Ezekiel, Sept. 21, 1825. Sur. Abraham Childress. 48.

Ferguson, John and Sophia Heptinstall, July 27, 1825. Sur. Wm. G. Heptinstall.
Ferguson, John C. and Sallie M. J. Hatcher, July 2, 1851. 19.
Ferguson, John and Mary Hill, Jan. 21, 1790. Sur. Geo. Ferguson. 52.
Ferguson, Joseph and Elizabeth Griffith, Aug. 18, 1851. 11.
Ferguson, Joseph, s. John, and Sarah Hughes, May .2, 1801. Sur. Ephraim Agee. 141.
Ferguson, Joshua and Jane Johnson, Dec. 3, 1804. Sur. John Johnson.
Ferguson, Joshua and Rebecca Toney, dau. Wm., Aug. 18, 1792. Sur. Edmund Toney. 23.
Ferguson, Josiah and Sally Booth, dau. Benj., Nov. 30, 1819. Sur. John D. Booth.
Ferguson, Lafayette and Frances Dodd, dau. John, Dec. 27, 1850.
Ferguson, Lafayette and Frances Atkins, Jan. 1, 1851. 18.
Ferguson, Moses and Sophia Phelps, Dec. 4, 1815. Sur. John Ferguson. 98.
Ferguson, Noah and Fanny Short, dau. Winnefred, Mar. 11, 1799. Sur. Thos. R. Short. 21.
Ferguson, Obediah and Elizabeth Martin, dau. Sarah, Sept. 9, 1786. Sur. Randolph Martin.
Ferguson, Oliver P. and Nancy Brown, Jan. 26, 1837. Sur. Elijah Brown.
Ferguson, Otey and Ruth A. Bernard, Nov. 10, 1858.
Ferguson, Otey and Polly Arrington, Mar. 3, 1823. Sur. Daniel Arrington. 49.
Ferguson, Patrick H. and Anne E. Wood, dau. G. H., Oct. 13, 1843. Sur. Robt. A. Scott. 58.
Ferguson, Robt. and Nancy Edmunds, Feb. 16, 1807. Sur. Wm. Edmunds. 8.
Ferguson, Samuel H. and Polly King, dau. Stephen, May 10, 1822. Sur. Solomon King. 130.
Ferguson, Samuel H. and Harriet Cooper, Aug. 16, 1848. Sur. Iles Cooper. 134.
Ferguson, Standifer and Lucinda T. Lewellen, dau. Greer B., Nov. 17, 1829. Sur. Chas. Ferguson. 26.

Ferguson, Stephen and Eleanor Grotty, Apr. 10. 1843. 18.
Ferguson, Stephen D. and Margaret A. Turner, dau. Micajah, Aug. 17, 1846. 19.
Ferguson, Stephen and Rhoda Greer, Jan. 21, 1809. Sur. Ezekiel Greer.
Ferguson, Thaddeus and Alean Turnbull, Dec. 28, 1840. Sur. John D. Taylor.
Ferguson, Thos. B. and Sarah Hambrick, Jan. 29, 1811. Sur. Joseph Hambrick. 130.
Ferguson, Thos. and Mary Solsbury, Apr. 28, 1802. Sur. Lewis Davis. 72.
Ferguson, Thos. and Agnes Chambers, dau. John, Dec. 5, 1796. Sur. Alexander Ferguson.
Ferguson, Wiley and Lurelia Young, Oct. 25, 1837. Sur. John Young. 132.
Ferguson, Wm. and Susannah Simmons, May 20, 1818. Sur. Skelton Simmons.
Ferguson, Wm. and Sarah Wood, Feb. 11, 1839. Sur. Charles H. Ashworth. 3.
Field, John and Elizabeth Thurman, dau. David, May 6, 1834. Sur. Sutherland Ross.
Fielder, Isaac and Elizabeth Chambers, Nov. 6, 1851. 127.
Finch, Anthony and Elizabeth F. Jenkins, Aug. 1, 1842. Sur. Henry Jenkins.
Finney, Amos and Elizabeth Wingfield, Jan. 6, 1834. Sur. Thos. Prunty.
Finney, John and Cynthia Mitchell, dau. Floriann, Oct. 17. 1832. Sur. Peter Finney, Jr.
Finney, John and Susannah Mitchell, Nov. 17, 1824. Sur. Wm. Mitchell.
Finney, John and Polly Prunty, Jan. 18, 1802. Sur. Robt. Prunty.
Finney, John and Ruth Smith, dau. Mary, Sept. 2, 1805. Sur. Elisha Rakes. 122.
Finney, Lewis and Elizabeth Stuart, Feb. 5, 1808. Sur. David Stewart.
Finney, Riley and Ellender Slone, or (Sloan), Mar. 27, 1793. Sur. Benj. Buster. 52.

Finney, (Fleming) Squire and Mary Prunty, dau. Nancy, Sr., Jan. 22, 1828.
Finney, Wesley L. and Martha C. Finney, dau. Zachariah, Oct. 30, 1846. Sur. Wm. A. J. Finney. 80.
Finney, Zachariah and Sarah P. Brown, Dec. 7, 1821. Sur. P. Dickinson.
Fishburn, Frederick and Nancy Beheler, Feb. 2, 1807. 117.
Fishburn, Jacob and Anne Waggoner, May 6, 1809. Sur. Melcher Waggoner. 117.
Fishburn, Peter and Celia (or Callah) Harger, Apr. 1, 1805. Sur. Aaron B. Wilson.
Fishburn, Peter I. and Martha Ann Hamilton, Oct. 9, 1848. Sur. James M. Hamilton. 62.
Fishburn, Samuel and Frances Tinsley, Mar. 27, 1832. Sur. Willis Tinsley. 62.
Fisher, Abraham and Nancy Nafe, Aug. 18, 1831. 18.
Fisher, Daniel and Nancy Boone, dau. Catherine, Dec. 25, 1814. Sur. Jacob Kesler. 130.
Fisher, Daniel and Martha Jane Sence, May 6, 1850. Sur. Joel Fisher. 96.
Fisher, Daniel and Sarah Teel, Jan. 1, 1844. Sur. Abraham Teel. 18.
Fisher, Elias and Lidia Howry, Jan. 22, 1828. 18
Fisher, Jacob and Mary Moss, Sept .23, 1816. Sur. Edmund Moss. 130.
Fisher, Joel and Nancy Flora, Apr. 5, 1819. Sur. Joseph Flora. 130.
Fisher, Joel and Letitia Hall, Oct. 21, 1851. 18.
Fisher, John and Aley Teal, dau. Jamima, Sept. 23, 1829. Sur. Wm. Teel. 48.
Fisher, John and Nelly Arthur, Feb. 20, 1818. Sur. John Arthur, Jr. 130.
Fisher, John B. and Parmelia Barns, June 22, 1851. 19.
Fisher, John and Delilah Sink, dau. Mary, Feb. 21, 1843. Sur. Isaac H. Boon. 18.
Fisher, John and Tabitha Martin, May 13, 1853. 68.
Fisher, Jonathan and Charlotte Teal, Oct. 6, 1843. Sur. Abram Teel. 18.

Fisher, Jonathan and Susannah Naff, Nov. 10, 1824. Sur. David Naff. 130.
Fisher, Manuel and Sally Angle, Nov. 14, 1828. 18.
Fisher, Nathaniel and Fanny Altiz, Apr. 17, 1832. 18.
Fisher, Peter and Polly Abshire, dau. Abraham, Feb. 4, 1839. Sur. Wm. B. Martin.
Fisher, Peter and Elizabeth Brower, June 27, 1818. Sur. Daniel Brower. 130.
Fisher, Peter and Elizabeth Altic (Alleck), Mar. 12, 1792. Sur. John Allick. 23.
Fisher, Solomon and Elizabeth Kesler, Oct. 19, 1812. 130.
Fitzgerald, Theodoric and Sarah Huff, (Hoff), dau. Philip and Rachael, June 10, 1793. Sur. Joshua Rentfro. 52.
Fitzpatrick, Thos. J. and Mary Cundiff, Nov. 19, 1841. Sur. James Cundiff. 18.
Fleaman, Elias and Martha Gothard, June 9, 1823. Sur. Howard G. Hix.
Flennan, John, s. Elias, and Cynthia Lookado, July 19, 1842. Sur. John Pinckard. 38.
Fleeman, Joseph and Delilah Hodges, May 7, 1825. Sur. John Hodges. 48.
Fleet, Wm. and Elizabeth Sink, Oct. 29, 1818. Sur. Powell Sink.
Flora, Abraham and Elizabeth Naff, Dec. 7, 1840. Sur. Geo. Nafe. 18.
Flora, Abraham and Nancy Overholt, dau. Abraham and Versy, Sept. 11, 1797. Sur. John Prupecker.
Flora, Daniel and Hannah Barnhart, Dec. 22, 1842. Sur. Abraham Barnhart. 18.
Flora, Daniel and Judith Fisher, Aug. 14, 1832. 18.
Flora, Henry, s. Jacob, and Sarah Brubaker, Feb. 20, 1843. Sur. Christopher Brubaker. 18.
Flora, Isaac and Elizabeth Florah, Aug. 2, 1836. 18.
Flora, Isaac and Emaline Boone, Dec. 2, 1852. 96.
Flora, Jacob and Eve Peters, Nov. 28, 1842. Sur. Jacob Peters.
Flora, Jacob and Elizabeth Barnhart, Mar. 31, 1853. 11.
Flora, Jacob Jr. and Mary Flora, Dec. 22, 1848. Sur. Joseph Flora. 18.

Flora, Jacob, Jr, and Sally Peters, May 1, 1811. Sur. Stephen Peters. 130.

Flora, Jacob, Jr. and Hannah Brower. 1811.

Flora, Joel and Elizabeth Peters, Oct. 30, 1826. Sur. Jacob Peters. 48.

Flora, John and Hannah Tilman, Jan. 29, 1821. Sur. Michael Peters. 130.

Flora, John and Sarah Fisher, May 1, 1820. Sur. Peter Fisher. 130.

Flora, John and Susannah Ikenberry, June 24, 1808. Sur. John Ikenberry 130.

Flora, Jonathan and Mary Bowman, Nov. 28, 1814. Sur. Joseph Flora. 130.

Flora, Jonathan, s. Jacob and Hannah, and Barbary Naff, dau. Isaac and Elizabeth July 14, 1853. 96.

Flora, Joseph and Elizabeth Naff, Jan. 2, 1826. Sur. Isaac Nafe.

Flora, Peter and Jane Stover, Mar. 27, 1851. 96.

Flora, Reuben and Otway Ann C. Wray, July 16, 1849. Sur. Burd Wray. 18.

Flora, Samuel and Elzery Anne Boitnott, June 4, 1849. Sur. Geo. Boitnott. 18.

Flora, Samuel and Elizabeth Delman (Dilmon), dau. Jacob and Christina, Apr. 7, 1788. Sur. Michael Peters. 52.

Flowers, James and Jane Moore, dau. Jane, Dec. 13, 1790. Sur. Thos. Staton. 52.

Flowers, James and Elizabeth Amos, dau. Wilson, July 22, 1841. Sur. Wilson Amos. 86.

Flowers, Samuel and Sally Compton, Sept. 21, 1838. Sur. Edward Beard.

Flowers, (Fowler) Thos. and Mary Spangler, dau. Mary, Dec. 20, 1790. Sur. Chattin Pollard. 52.

Flowers, Wm. P. and Mary H. Slaughter, dau. Nancy, June 24, 1835. Sur. Elijah Basham. 140.

Flowers, Wm. T and Easter Hartman, Aug. 4, 1845. Sur. Henry C. Smith.

Forbes, Calvin E. and Sarah H. Brown, Dec. 7, 1858.

Forbes, Fleming and Clary Swanson, dau. Gabriel, Jan. 15, 1831. Sur. Jacob Bowles. 48.

Forbes, John R. and Lydia Wright, dau. John and Mary, Nov. 2, 1818. Sur. Joseph Wright.
Forbes, Otey T. and Lucy Brown, dau. Daniel, July 9, 1844. Sur. Wm. Bradley.
Forbes, Peter and Sallie R. Dillion, Mar. 20, 1823. Sur. John Pasley.
Forbes, Philip L. and Emeline Hieth, Oct. 1, 1842. Sur. Harvey Hieth.
Forbes, Robt. P. and Harriet L. Wray, dau. Jecoras Wray, Aug. 30, 1849. Sur. Giles W. B. Abshire. 86.
Forbes, Sparrel and Mary Wright, Apr. 18, 1851. 18.
Forbes, Thos. J. and Elizabeth Dillion, June 29, 1825. Sur. Henry Dillion.
Forbes, Thos. and Elizabeth Hodges, Nov. 15, 1852. 11.
Fortune, Alexander and Susannah Kitterman, dau. Annah, Jan. 14, 1817. Sur. John Kitterman.
Fortune, Benj. and Milly Carter, dau. Barnard, Oct. 13, 1804. Sur. Walker Carter.
Foster, Chas. and Leona (or Exiona) Turner, Jan. 2, 1804. Sur. Josiah Turner.
Foster, Gabriel and Polly Hudson, Oct. 6, 1828. Sur. Joel Hudson.
Foster, Geo. P. and Sylvia Gusler, dau. Jane Foster, Nov. 7, 1831. Sur. Jacob Gusler. 61.
Foster, Hugh and Susan Gusler, dau. Jacob, Oct. 17, 1835. Sur. Thos. Smith. 132.
Foster, Isaac, s. Janet, and Caninhopic Powers, Mar. 26, 1830. Sur. John Powers, Jr.
Foster, John and Ruth Smith, dau. David, Jan. 13, 1825. Sur. Samuel Smith.
Foster, Larkin and Sarah W. Janney, Dec. 9, 1839. Sur. Sparrel Janney. 68.
Foster, Richard A. and Mary Board, Jan. 3, 1853. 18.
Foster, Wm. and Polly Cuff, July 1, 1816. Sur. Henry Kennon. 130.
Fowler, Jacob and Martha Dillion, Dec. 7, 1812. Sur. Jesse Dillion. 8.

Fowler, Richard and Sarah Wade, Jan. 1, 1838. Sur. John H. Wade.
Fralin, Daniel and Margaret A. Fralin, July 1, 1814. Sur. Henry Frailin.
Frailin, David and Sarah Prunty, Nov. 1, 1824. Sur. Henry Frailin. 130.
Frailin, John and Elizabeth Showalter, June 26, 1816. Sur. Joseph Showalter.
Fralin, John Q. and Ludiney H. Oaks, Dec. 23, 1852. 18.
Fralin, Josiah and Cynthia E. Fralin, Nov. 10, 1846. Sur. David Fralin. 18.
Frailin, Riley and Tabitha Showalter, Dec. 17, 1830. Sur. John Showalter. 96.
Fralin, Robt. and Mary J. Fralin, Jan. 25, 1851. 18.
Fralin, Robt. and Sarah Ferguson, Jan. 11, 1853. 18.
Frailin, Thos. T. and Sarah E. Metts, dau. John, Oct. 19, 1850. Sur. John C. Hutcherson.
Frame, Jesse and Nancy Asbhire, dau. Abraham, Jan. 10, 1803. Sur. Abraham Abshire. 106.
Frame, Paul and Susannah Hickman, Nov. 20, 1798. Sur. Peter Hickman. 89.
Frame, Wm. and Nancy Crowe, Sept. 2, 1805. Sur. Devault Crowl. 130.
France, Mical (from Boteotourt Co.) and Hannah Good, Dec. 25, 1826. 18.
Frantz, David and Elizabeth Flora, Apr. 5, 1841. Sur. John Flora. 18.
Frantz, Mical and Elizabeth Barnhart, Dec. 24, 1833. 18.
Frantz, Peter and Hannah Barnhart, Dec. 23, 1845. Sur. Jonathan Barnhart. 18.
Frans, Michael, s. John, and Rebecca Henry, dau. John, and gfr. Abraham Picard Simmons, Feb. 5, 1798. Sur. Jacob Kingery. 89.
Franklin, Aaron and Milly Richeson, dau. Jonathan, Sept. 23, 1799. Sur. Booker Richeson. 21.
Franklin, Jesse H. and Lockey Metts, Oct. 20, 1853. 80.
Franklin, John and Mary Waid, Dec. 21, 1816. Sur. Capelton Waid. 44.

Franklin, John and Sarah Ann Pugh, Aug. 31, 1826. Sur. Richard Pugh. 48.
Frasier, Creed, s. Alexander Frasher, and Charlotte Mullins, Apr. 16, 1831. Sur. Meshack Turner. 129.
Frayl, (Trail) Elijah and Jinny Moore, Nov. 4, 1816. Sur. Jacob Moore.
Freeman, John and Permelia Smothers, July 13, 1816. Sur. Sur. Henry Kennon. 130.
Freeman, Thos. and Sally Hale, dau. James F., Nov. 15, 1814. Sur. Walter Kemp.
French, Richard and Diney Greer, dau. Mary, Feb. 22, 1800. Sur. Benj. Greer. 21.
Frith, Jacob and Mary J. Beheler, Jan. 28, 1845. Sur. John Beheler. 132.
Frith, John and Elizabeth Payne, dau. Frances, Nov. 16, 1840. Sur. Thos. A. Payne.
Frith, Joseph and Letitia Fowler, dau. Susannah Blankenship, July 23, 1792. Sur. Isham Blankenship. 23.
Frith, Robert R. and Mary E. Waggoner, dau. Jane, Mar. 12, 1850. Sur. Chilton Lavinder. 97.
Frith, Thos. and Elizabeth Scarborough, July 4, 1817. Sur. Robt. Scarborough. 130.
Frith, Thomas D. and Caroline E. Wingfield, Nov. ....., 1853. 132.
Fuller, Jesse and Mary Estes, dau. Frances and Lishe, Jan. 10, 1789. Sur. Jesse Estes.
Fuller, Moses and Elizabeth Prillaman, Nov. ___, 1805, Sur. John Wineter.
Fuller, Wm. B. and Elizabeth Jane Eanes, dau. Herbert, Nov. 25, 1850. Sur. Joseph Dickinson.
Furrow, Adam and Mary Cox, July 24, 1788. Sur. John Ferrow. 52.
Furrow, Chas. and Deborah Graham, Apr. 4, 1796. Sur. Sarah Ferrow.
Furrow, John and Sarah Cox, dau. Sarah Farley, Nov. 27, 1787. Sur. James Slone.
Gaby, Isaac P. and Harriet Hardberger, July 11, 1829. Sur. Henry Hardbarger. 62.
Gadd, James W. and Rhoda W. Thornton, Aug. 17, 1827. Sur. Wm. W. Gadd.

Gadd, Wm. and Dicey Young, dau. James, May 21, 1802. Sur. Thos. Gadd. 72.

Gallaspy, Jeremiah and Patsy Troup, Mar. 18, 1833. Sur. John Troup. 48.

Gallaspy, Wm. and Mary Jane Dowdy, Dec. 22, 1853. 127.

Gallamore, Wm. and Sarah Grimmett, dau. John, Apr. 8, 1787. Sur. Absom Gallamore.

Gardner, Obediah and Lucy Thacker, —, 1795. 37.

Garner, James and Tabitha Martin, May 17, 1798. Sur. Wm. Griffith.

Garrett, Silas and Judith Booth, Oct. 31, 1808. Sur. Peter Booth. 8.

Garst, David and Mary Overfelt, Dec. 28, 1835. Sur. John Overfelt. 68.

Gearhart, Henry and Elizabeth Quigley, Aug. 6, 1822. Sur. Edward T. Akers.

Gearhart, Henry and Polly Willis, May 1, 1823. Sur. Wm. Slone. 49.

Gearhart, Henry and Elizabeth Edwards, Sept. 12, 1817. Sur. John Gearhart. 130.

Gearhart, Henry and Hannah Rentfro, dau. Moses, Dec. 5, 1791. Sur. Bartlett Wade. 52.

Gearhart, Herman and Susannah Edwards, Feb. 5, 1817. Sur. Benj. Edwards.

Gearhart, John and Frances Dewese, dau. Mary, Oct. 26, 1819. Sur. Edward T. Akers. 130.

Gearhart, John and Elizabeth Teel, dau. Jamima, Dec. 31, 1833. Sur. Terry Teel. 48.

Gearhart, Lewis and Amelia Quigley, dau. Sarah, July 22, 1813. Sur. Leonard Gearhart. 130.

Gearhart, Wm. and Elizabeth Wright, dau. John, Apr. 16, 1804. Sur. Joseph Willis.

Gee, John and Nancy Amos, July 8, 1809. 8.

George, John and Catherine Bryans, Jan. 10, 1797. 89.

Gibson, Absalom and Elizabeth Highley, Dec. 11, 1817. Sur. Jacob Bowles. 130.

Gibson, Abner and Jane Howven (Howser), Mar. 3, 1853.

Gibson, Absalom and Nancy Hambrick, Mar. 6, 1853. 134.

Gibson, John and Elizabeth Harvey, Apr. 7, 1834. Sur. John Nafe.
Gibson, Jonathan and Madalene Powers, Jan. 11, 1817. Sur. John Powers.
Gibson, Miles, s. John, and Minerva Bocock, Sept. 3, 1833. Sur. Castello Mills. 110.
Gibson, Miles, s. Absolem, and Catherine Wimmer, dau. James, Jan. 10, 1846. Sur. Tazewell Gibson. 18.
Gibson, Wm. F. and Ann Guilliams, dau. Nancy, Feb. 20, 1837. Sur. David Moore. 38.
Gibson, (Gipson) Wm. and Sarah McVey, dau. James, Nov. 10, 1806. Sur. Thos. McVey.
Gilbert, ... and Elenor Charter, May 15, 1798.
Gilbert, Henry M. and Martha H. Pasley, Aug. 17, 1840. Sur. Robt. Pasley.
Gilbert, James and Christina Keen, Dec. 3, 1803. Sur. Elisha Keen.
Gilbert, Kenniel and Polly Smith, Nov. 4, 1805. Sur. Wm. Smith. 8.
Gilbert, Kemuel C. and Dicey Mason, June 4, 1827. Sur. Samuel Smith. 48.
Gilbert, Michale, Jr. and Elizabeth Ashworth, Dec. 1, 1817. Sur. Mathew Wyatt.
Gilbert, Preston and Fanny Law, dau. Henry, Jan. 11, 1803. 106.
Gilbert, Samuel and Susannah Kemp, Mar. 7, 1814. Sur. Thos. Kemp.
Gilbert, Samuel and Nancy Weatherford, (1st h. Chas. A. Weatherford), Oct. 4, 1847. Sur. Moses G. Carper. 137.
Gilbert, Thos K. and Frances McCall, Feb. 5, 1838.
Gilbert, Wm. W. and Mary S. Bell, dau. James, Oct. 5, 1835. Sur. Peter H. Bell.
Gill, Hezekiah and Dorothy Graves, dau. John, Jan. 24, 1809. Sur. Pleasant Dickinson. 8.
Gillinwater, Absalom and Hany Underwood, dau. Mary, Dec. 19, 1821. Sur. Spencer Cockran.
Gillingwater, Elijah, s. Joshua, and Nancy Underwood, dau. Mary, Aug. 3, 1820. Sur. Spencer Cockran. 61.
Gillinwater, James, s. Joshua, and Catherine Underwood, dau. Mary, June 22, 1829. Sur. David Underwood.

Gillingwater, Joshua and Susanna Jones, Aug. 17, 1815. 122.

Gillingwater, Nathan and Nancy Turner, May 5, 1841. Sur. Pleasant Nowlin.

Gallaspy, Evan and Nancy Lee, dau. Elizabeth and John Frashier, Mar. 17, 1789. Sur. Owen Griffith. 52.

Gillispie, Evan, Jr. and Dicey Atkins, dau. John, Nov. 3, 1834. Sur. Joseph Adkins. 60.

Gillispie, Henry L. and Letitia Menefee, Aug. 6, 1849. Sur. Robt. A. Scott. 64.

Gillispie, Isaac and Eleanor Howell, Dec. 16, 1848. Sur. Moses Howell. 134.

Gillispie, Wm. and Polly Faris, Nov. 16, 1811. Sur. Samuel Taylor. 122.

Gillispie, Wm. and Allie Wade, Oct. 20, 1820. Sur. Castleton Wade.

Gilpin, James and Rebecca Meedlin, dau. Frederick, Oct. 16, 1812. Sur. Wm. McCormack.

Gish, Abraham and Susannah Smith, Oct. 7, 1822. Sur. John Smith. 130.

Gish, Geo. and Nancy Gearhart, Dec. 4, 1845. 18.

Gish, Jacob and Elizabeth Smith, Nov. 3, 1827. Sur. Luke Smith. 48.

Givins, John and Patty Talley, Aug. 3, 1800. Sur. Moses Poor. 72.

Glancy, Hugh and Rhoda Ellison, dau. John, Aug. 8, 1807. Sur. Patrick Hix.

Goggin, Wm. L. and Elizabeth L. Cook, Nov. 11, 1840.

Goings, Thos. and Elizabeth Marrs, Jan. 11, 1829. Sur. Hercules Marrs. 48.

Goode, Abraham and Catherine Fisher, Aug. 7, 1824. Sur. Jonathan Fisher. 130.

Goode, David, Sr. and Lucy Arthur, Dec. 1, 1848. Sur. Abraham Williams. 19.

Goode, David, Jr. and Nancy Thomas, Dec. 20, 1841. Sur. Nathaniel Thomas. 132.

Goode, David, Jr. and Mary Turner, Mar. ...., 1852. 132.

Goode, David, Jr. and Charity Ramsey, May 15, 1822. Sur. Woodson Ramsey.

Goode, David, Jr. and Ruth Feazel, Apr. 9, 1829. Sur. Aaron Feazel. 132.

Goode, David and Malinda W. Miles, Mar. 27, 1825. Sur. Joseph Miles.

Good, Geo. and Sarah Williams, Dec. 24, 1839. Sur. John Williams. 132.

Goode, Geo. and Eleanor Davis, Feb. 6, 1832. Sur. Thos. Davis. 90.

Goode, Geo. W. and Partheny Mason, Oct. ___, 1853. 132.

Goode, Jacob and Alice Mullen, Jan. 6, 1817. Sur. Bowker Mullins. 44.

Goode, James and Julia Ann Goode, ..., 1851. 132.

Goode, John and Jane Standley, Mar. 31, 1813. Sur. Wm. Standley. 44.

Goode, John and Euseby Barnes, dau. Pamela, Dec. 25, 1832. Sur. Meshack Turner. 46.

Goode, Samuel and Nancy Craig, Dec. 23, 1822. Sur. David Craig.

Good, Stephen and Rachael Smith, dau. John, Mar. 5, 1792. Sur. John Smith.

Goode, Wm. and Anne E. Oxley, Dec. 20, 1845. 20.

Goodson, Wm. W. and Lydia Moore, dau. John, Dec. 21, 1846. Sur. David Moore. 60.

Gore, Amos and Mary Jane Webb, Oct. 21, 1852. 18.

Gore, Wm. and Betsy Prater, Mar. 28, 1829. Sur. Joseph D. Meador. 140.

Gorman, Armistead and Nancy W. Brown, Feb. 27, 1826. Sur. Wm. L. Pearson.

Gossard, Daniel and Nancy Noftsinger, Mar. 4, 1805. Sur. John Nofsinger.

Gossett, Abraham and Elizabeth Ikenberry, Nov. 24, 1819. 130.

Gossler, Jacob and Sally Janney, dau. Hannah, Dec. 22, 1810. Sur. John Janney. 117.

Gossnell, Dawson and Rebecca Frith, Sept. 1804. Sur. Richard Goggins.

Gossnell, Dawson and Nancy Cooley, Jan. 16, 1815.

Gossnell, Dawson and Mima Saul, July 30, 1814. Sur. Jacob Anderson. 8.

Gragg, (Crigg) John and Elizabeth Booth, gdau. John, Jan. 6, 1800. Sur. James Reese. 21.
Graham, Jacob and Elizabeth Radford, Jan. 23, 1823. Sur. Lewis Radford. 61.
Graham, Robt. and Rachael Delany. dau. Samuel, Mar. 2, 1790. 52.
Graham, Silas and Elizabeth Askue, Mar. 28, 1816. Sur. Philip Askue. 130.
Graham, Wm. and Sarah Slone, Sept. 6, 1839. Sur. Abraham Griffith.
Granbel, Francis and Nancy Castle, Dec. 14, 1798. 89.
Grant, Gardner and Mary Holland, Oct. 3, 1836. Sur. Thos. Holland.
Grant, Geo. W. and Sarah A. Swepston, dau. Geo., Nov. 17, 1848. Sur. Joseph Edds.
Graves, David and Nancy Pinkard, Jan. 27, 1793. Sur. Chas. Pinckard.
Graves, John and Nancy Ryan, dau. Wm., Dec. 13, 1790. Sur. Wm. Ryan.
Graves, Peyton and Charlotte Pinkard, dau. John, Nov. 11, 1788. Sur. Nathan Ryan.
Graves, Simon and Elizabeth Rinehart, May 10, 1809. 130.
Gravly, James and Sally Traile, Apr. 2, 1812. 122.
Gray, Cary and Rebecca Sowder, Dec. 29, 1828. Sur. Benj. Lambeth. 48.
Gray, Edley and Polly Akers, Sept. 11, 1832. Sur. Daniel Akers. 48.
Gray, Edward and Elizabeth Key, May 1, 1834. Sur. Wesley Key.
Gray, James and Polly Moore, dau. Benj., Jan. 29, 1824. Sur. James Mavity. 130.
Gray, Joseph and Margaret Wiatt, Mar. 12, 1839. Sur. Henry Wiatt. 68.
Gray, Rouzee P. and Martha Ann Glass, July 21, 1847. Sur. Jacob G. Machenheimer.
Gray, Wm. and Polly Hale, Nov. 12, 1812. Sur. Jacob Moore. 130.
Gray, Wm. R. and Elizabeth Prillaman, Oct. 28, 1851. 68.

Green, Barny and Polly Clarkson, dau. David, Dec. 2, 1792. Sur. Robt. Powell.
Green, Jesse and Mary Smithers, Feb. 2, 1847. Sur. Samuel Early.
Green, John and Leney Murphy, Oct. 23, 1810. Sur. Butler Murphy. 130.
Green, Samuel and Elizabeth Early, Apr. 4, 1836. Sur. Thos. Smithers. 140.
Greenwood, Abraham and Sophia Cooper, Dec. 21, 1818. Sur. Lewis Cooper. 98.
Greenwood, Demarquis L. and Emeline Mays, Mar. 9, 1841. Sur. Silas Mays. 86.
Greer, Andrew and Polly Guthrey, Nov. 20, 1813. Sur. Benj. Guthry.
Greer, Aquilla and Elizabeth Smith, dau. John, Aug. 8, 1796. Sur. Asa Dillion. 141.
Greer, Asa and Rebecca Neighbors, dau. Francis, July 22, 1791. Sur. Thos. Wilson.
Greer, Benj. and Sally Compton, dau. Richard, Jan. 9, 1799. Sur. Joel Estes.
Greer, Benj. Jr. and Sally Early, dau. Elizabeth Carraway, Mar. 19, 1812.
Greer, Chas. and Agnes Sumpter, Aug. 8, 1793. 52.
Greer, Chas. and Rebecca Henson, June 10, 1806. Sur. Wm. Curtain. 122.
Greer, Ezekial and Jemima Saunders, dau. Philemon, Oct. 7, 1813. Sur. Stephen Ferguson.
Greer, Geo. and Sarah Elizabeth Taylor, dau. Sarah, Aug. 4, 1795. Sur. Skelton Taylor. 41.
Greer, Geo. and Wilmeth Kirby, dau. Francis and Elizabeth, June 30, 1789. Sur. Daniel Brown. 37.
Greer, Henry T. and Julia Ann Divers, dau. Francis, Sept. 10, 1833. 140.
Greer, Isaac and Ann Saunders, Apr. 1, 1811. Sur. Pleasant Saunders.
Greer, Isaiah and Joannah Saunders, dau. Philemon, Apr. 24, 1819. Sur. Stephen Ferguson.
Greer, James and Elizabeth Fraser, Sept. 22, 1800. Sur. John Frazer.

Greer, John and Elizabeth Fowler, Jan. 14, 1813. 130.
Greer, John H. and Nancy Overfelt, Sept. 4, 1839. Sur. David Overfelt.
Greer, John and Louisa Robertson, dau. John, Dec. 29, 1828. Sur. Littleberry Robertson. 140.
Greer, (Green) Joseph Jr. and Catherine Webster, dau. James, Oct. 3, 1825. Sur. Wm. Kemplin. 48.
Greer, Joseph and Fannie Lyon, May 1, 1786. Sur. Elisha Lyons, 66.
Greer, Matthew and Rhoda Chambers, dau. Joel, Feb. 3, 1812. Sur. Thos. Ferguson.
Greer, Moses and Susannah Wood, Nov. 4, 1794. 52.
Greer, Moses and Elizabeth Powell, June 29, 1840. Sur. Edward Powell. 86.
Greer, Moses and Charity Salmon, Sept. 8, 1795. 52.
Greer, Moses C. and Nancy R. Childress, dau. Wm., Jan. 7, 1845. Sur. John O. Taylor. 68.
Greer, Nathan and Elizabeth Wysong, dau. Jacob, Nov. 10, 1834. Sur. Albert G. Ferguson. 140.
Greer, Peter and Mary Ann Noell, dau. Stephen, Dec. 2, 1829. Sur. Chas. R. Noell. 140.
Greer, Samuel and Nancy Divers, Nov. 4, 1850. Sur. Moses C. Greer. 134.
Greer, Samuel W. and Frances D. Pollard, May 15, 1823. Sur. Henry Carper. 49.
Greer, Thos. S. and Ann I. Tate, Jan. 15, 1840. Sur. Wm. Turnbull.
Greer, Thos. B. and Ursula Webb, Mar. 6, 1816. Sur. Joseph H. Turner.
Greer, Thos. B. and Celestia A. Taliaferro, July 10, 1852. 134.
Greer, Wm. and Elizabeth Harkrider, dau. Conrad, Apr. 30, 1791. Sur. Daniel Brown. 52.
Greer, Witherston S. and Mary Kyle, Nov. 26, 1821. 130.
Gregory, Wm. H. and Mary Amos, Aug. 22, 1850. Sur. Geo. K. Williams.
Greso, Haulkin (of Botetourt) and Hannah Barnhart, Feb. 19, 1835. 18.
Gresso, John and Fanny Barnhart, Feb. 8, 1838. 18.

Greybill, Daniel and Elizabeth Kinzer, —, 1894. 89.
Grice, Eli and Phoebe Trout, Jan. 31, 1825. Sur. David Trout. 48.
Griffith, Abner and Sally Turk, Sept. 23, 1802. 72.
Griffith, Abraham and Margaret Livesay, dau. Thos., July 8, 1789. Sur. Robt. Carter. 77.
Griffith, Abraham and Selah Webb, Mar. 18, 1812. Sur. Joseph Webb. 8.
Griffith, Alexander and Rachael Griffith, Dec. 16, 1806. Sur. Geo. Griffith. 130.
Griffith (Griffin), Chisholm Holland and Elizabeth Bowman, June 29, 1811. Sur. John Bowman. 130.
Griffith, Daniel and Alley Shierden, Dec. 29, 1808. 122.
Griffith, Elijah and Susan Young, g. John, Jan. 1, 1842. Sur. Jubal Young. 60.
Griffith Greenberry and Fanny Smith, Apr. 20, 1848. Sur. John O. Smith.
Griffith, Isaac and Ruth Hale, dau. Thos., Dec. 28, 1819. Sur. Daniel Griffith. 61.
Griffith, Isaac and Peggy Gallaspy, Jan. 12, 1795. Sur. Daniel Gillaspy. 52.
Griffith, Jackson and Catherine Sigmon, ..., 1799. 66.
Griffith, James H. and Mary Jane Cannaday, Feb. 10, 1853. 60.
Griffith, John and Martha Griffith, Dec. 28, 1830. Sur. Daniel Griffith. 60.
Griffith, John and Martha Griffith, Jan. 13, 1832. 60.
Griffith, John and Nelly Bowles, Jan. 21, 1812. Sur. Jacob Clower.
Griffith, John and Martha Campbell, Oct. 8, 1833. Sur. Peter Cannaday. 60.
Griffith, Meshack and Lucy Chitwood, Jan. 18, 1830. Sur. Wm. Cabaniss. 26.
Griffith (Griffin), Samuel and Charlotte Hook, dau. John, Jan. 11, 1800.
Griffith, Sparrell H. and Mary E. Campbell, Oct. 9, 1843. Sur. John Griffith.
Griffith, Wm. and Nancy Edwards, dau. Edward Brill, Aug. 24, 1820. Sur. Isaac Griffith. 61.

Griggs, Jeremiah and Elzira E. Carper, Nov. 25, 1847. Sur. Robt. A. Scott.
Grigg, (Gregg) John and Christina Lemon, dau. Mary, June 30, 1791. Sur. Isaac Lemon. 52.
Grimmett, Solomon and Sarah Hale, Sept. 18, 1795. 52.
Grimmett, Wm. and Delila Polston, Mar. 7, 1791. Sur. Andrew Polston. 52.
Grist, Geo. and Polly Reynolds, Feb. 1, 1827. Sur. Wm. Reynolds.
Ground, Geo. and Elizabeth Landers, Mar. 28, 1808. Sur. John Landers. 117.
Grove, Simon and Elizabeth Rinehart, May 10, 1809. Sur. Jacob Rinehart.
Grubb, Alfred and Jemima Greer, dau. Joseph, Mar. 1, 1820. Sur. David Grubb.
Grymes, Jesse and Margaret Ray, dau. Moses, June 28, 1790. Sur. Moses Wray. 52.
Guerrant, Peter Jr., s. Peter Sr., and Sarah Akers, Feb. 2, 1842. Sur. Wm. Blochess.
Guilliams, John and Jean McClary, dau., Richard and Jean, Feb. 1, 1796. Sur. David Lykins.
Guilliams, John and Lydia Hill, Jan. 23, 1851. 68.
Guilliams, Luke and Elizabeth Kingery, Dec. 20, 1833. Sur. Geo. Abshire. 48.
Guilliams, Richard and Rosannah Scott, Aug. 3, 1814. Sur. Wm. Hunter Jr.
Guilliams, Robt. and Miriam Jones, dau. Wm., Jan. 2, 1843. Sur. Isaac M. Jones. 68.
Guilliams, Robt. and Elizabeth Luke, Dec. 26, 1805. 122.
Guilliams, Wm. and Sarah Ferguson, Dec. 24, 1797. Sur. Thos. Gadd.
Guilliams, Wm. and Sophronia Hill, Feb. 3, 1851. 68.
Gusler, Jacob, s. Jacob Sr., and Martha Powers, dau. Nancy, Nov. 3, 1845.
Gusler, John and Elizabeth Roberts, stdau. Moseley Vest Jr., Jan. 2, 1815. Sur. John Roberts.
Gusler, John and Sarah Boulds, Nov. 22, 1836. 18.
Gustler, John and Elizabeth Janney, Aug. 24, 1818. Sur. Jacob Gossler.

Guthry, Bluford and Fanny Snidor, Jan. 7, 1830. Sur. John Snider, Jr. 26.
Guthrey, Benj. and Sarah Bradley, Feb. 23, 1799. Sur. Wm. Bradley.
Guthry, David and Mary Booth, dau. John, Sept. 13, 1786. Sur. Stephen Booth.
Hagood (Haywood), Wm. and Ruth Helms, Nov. 11, 1850. Sur. Daniel Helms. 20.
Hail (Hale), James Lewis and Anne Craghead, dau. John, July 20, 1789. Sur. Thos. Camp. 37.
Hail, Nicholas and Jinsey Jackson, Aug. 3, 1807. Sur. Thos. Jackson.
Haines, Geo. and Sally Walden, Oct. 7, 1802. 122.
Hairston, Marshall and Anne Hairston, Mar. 9, 1829. Sur. Samuel Hairston, Jr.
Hairston, Robt. and Elizabeth Saunders, Nov 17, 1852. 47.
Hairston, Samuel and Judith Saunders, Feb. 9, 1790. 52.
Hairston, Wm. and Rachael Hufman, Jan. 17, 1804.
Haislip, Arthur J. and Elizabeth Peters, dau. Johathan, Oct. 30, 1848. Sur. Geo. Peters. 18.
Haslip, Henry and Betsey Taylor, Sept. 4, 1809. Sur. Willis Luttrell. 8.
Haizlip, Joel John and Drucilla Haizlip, Apr. 2, 1804. Sur. Robt. Hazlip.
Haizlip, Wm. and Polly Roach, dau. Gideon, Apr. 13, 1801. Sur. Benj. Potter. 141.
Hale, Alfred and Emaline Hodges, Apr. 8, 1843. Sur. Elisha Hodges.
Hale, Armstrong and Elizabeth Ruble, dau. Owen, Jan. 16, 1789. Sur. David Willis. 52.
Hale, Benj. and Dicie Franklin, Nov. 13, 1788. Sur. Benj. Hale Sr. 66.
Hale, (Hall) David and Elizabeth Webb, dau. Hannah, Dec. 25, 1818. Sur. Isaiah Welch.
Hale, David and America Easter, June 7, 1847. Sur. Wiley Easter. 68.
Hale, Frances and Nancy Leffew, June 11, 1844. Sur. Thos. Leffew. 68.

Hale, Geo. T. and Temperance Winfrey, dau. Mary, May 10, 1822. Sur. John Jones. 61.
Hale, Hiram and Sarah Franklin, dau. Francis Hale, Aug. 15, 1835. Sur. Jeremiah Hale.
Hale, Isaac, s. Francis, and Cerena Shiveley, dau. David and Celia, Sept. 30, 1814. Sur. Wm. Hixson. 28.
Hale, James and Jenny Craghead, dau. John, Oct. 2, 1786. Sur. Richard Edmundson.
Hale, Jeremiah, s. Francis, and Nancy Wade, dau. Lewis, Jan. 3, 1827. Sur. Castleton Wade.
Hale, Jehu John and Elizabeth Woods, Oct. 10, 1807. Sur. Robt. Woods, Jr.
Hale, (Hail) John and Joan Hatcher, Oct. 5, 1812. Sur. Caleb Heptinstall. 15.
Hale, John and Susannah Wade, dau. John, Mar. 17, 1789. Sur. David Willis. 66.
Hale, John S. and Margaret I. Saunders, Jan. 30, 1850. Sur. Jubal A. Early. 47.
Hale, John and Phoebe Akers, Dec. 15, 1834. Sur. Daniel Akers.
Hale, John S. and Judith Early, May 12, 1834. Sur. Wm. B. Williams.
Hale, John and Doshia Saunders, dau. Peter, Sept. 12, 1792. Sur. Wm. Crump. 52.
Hale, Jonathan, s. Thos., and Mary Cockran, dau. Isham, Feb. 7, 1825. Sur. Joseph Edwards.
Hale, Joseph and Elizabeth Truman (Turman), dau. Francis, Feb. 13, 1789. Sur. Elijah Jones. 66.
Hale, (Hall) Joseph and Sally Turnbull, July 21, 1797. Sur. Geo. Turnbull. 21.
Hale, Lewis and Sarah Sigmon, dau. Catherine, Nov. 20, 1840. Sur. Peter Sigmon. 68.
Hale, Maxey and Dicey Craghead, dau. John, Oct. 25, 1789.
Hale, Peter and Sarah Gibson, Nov. 25, 1850. Sur. Nicholas Cassell. 68.
Hale (Hall) Peter and Sarah Morris, dau. Ezekiel, Mar. 14, 1791. Sur. John Hale.
Hale, (Heil) Philip and Judith Meador, dau. Jonas, Sept. 7, 1841. Sur. Francis W. Robertson.

Hale, Richard and Tabitha Jones, dau. Robt., Oct. 24, 1788. Sur. Elijah Jones.
Hale, Samuel and Frances Sigmon, dau. Joseph, Aug. 18, 1842. Sur. Lewis Hale. 60.
Hale, Simons and Evelyn R. Johnson, Mar. 3, 1845. Sur. Francis Hale.
Hale, Thos. Jr. and Susannah Menefee, Nov. 24, 1810. Sur. Geo. Menefee.
Hale, Thos. and Harriett Woods, Nov. 20, 1819. Sur. Samuel H. Woods.
Hale, Thos. and Ann Troup, Apr. 8, 1824. Sur. Henry Troup. 48.
Hale, Vincent and Jane Morgan, Aug. 6, 1818. Sur. Wm. Martin. 61.
Hale, (Hall) Washington and Polly Clowers, Nov. 10, 1823. Sur. John Clowers. 49.
Hale, Wm. and Sarah Wade, Jan. 20, 1817. Sur. Casselton Wade. 44.
Hall, Andrew J. and Ann E. Mountcastle, Aug. 18, 1858.
Hall, Armistead and America Townley, Jan. 22, 1844. 132.
Hall, Bailey and Frances Chitwood, Aug. 16, 1836. Sur. Moses Carper. 134.
Hall, Bailey and Ann M. Creasey, Nov. 4, 1850. Sur. Obediah Creasey. 18.
Hall, Curry and Milly Hodges, Dec. 20, 1792. Sur. John Hodges.
Hall, Elisha and Polly Leffue, Aug. 20, 1834. Sur. John Leffue.
Hall, Fleming, s. Rebecca and Edward, and Mary Pugh, dau. Wm. and Susan, Oct. 22, 1853. 18.
Hall, Hiram and Catherine V. Bird, dau. Luke. Mar. 6, 1837. Sur. Wm. Bird.
Hall, James and Miriam Pugh, Feb. 26, 1822. Sur. Richard Pugh.
Hall, John and Emily Leffew, May 6, 1852. 127.
Hall, John, s. Ned, and Jane Hall, dau. Jim, Dec. 2. 1853. 134.
Hall, Jonathan and Joanna Barton, Nov. 9, 1792. Sur. David Barton. 52.
Hall, Joseph and Frances Clark, dau. Jesse, Mar. 3, 1821. Sur. Daniel Pedigo.

Hall, Joshua and Jane Griffith, dau. John, Apr. 2, 1836. Sur. James Ingram, Jr.
Hall, Lunsford and Julia Ann Belcher, Aug. 5, 1847. Sur. Shadrack Barnes.
Hall, Merida and Jane C. Woodward, July 25, 1848. Sur. Wm. Whitlow.
Hall, Middleton and Mary Wray, May 21, 1828. Sur. Henry Thurman. 26.
Hall, Peter and Mary Jane Mullins, Aug. 18, 1852. 18.
Hall, Randolph and Mary M. Bird, dau. Luke, Sept. 28, 1833. Sur. Benj. Bird. 48.
Hall, Robt. and Lucy Hodges, ―――――, 1797.
Hall, Samuel and Mary Lloyd, dau. Thos., Aug. 5, 1840. Sur. Lankford Brizendine.
Hall, Vandiver and Martha Wray, Nov. 4, 1850. Sur. Jonas Wray. 18.
Hall, Wiley and Winney Hodges, Feb. 22, 1830. Sur. Wm. Hodges. 48.
Hall, Wm. and Judy Woodall, ―――――, 1795. 37.
Hall, Wm. and Amy Hodges, Dec. 19, 1826. Sur. John Hodges. 48.
Halpain, Joseph and Nancy Smith, dau. S. C., Feb. 11, 1808. Sur. Booker Smith. 130.
Halstead, Preston and Malinda L. Phillips, stdau. Caleb and Agnes Newman, Mar. 16, 1843. Sur. Wm. P. Flowers.
Hambrick, Eli and Miriam Willis, May 18, 1847. Sur. Moses G. Carper. 18.
Hambrick, Joseph Jr. and Susan Dodd, Mar. ―, 1808. Sur. John Dodd. 130.
Hambrick, Otey and Frances Chitwood, Feb. 6, 1832. Sur. Joel Chitwood. 48.
Hambrick, Thos. and Elizabeth Ferguson, Aug. 13, 1814. Sur. Jonathan Klingenpeel. 98.
Hambrick, Henry and Lockey Martin, Mar. 31, 1825. Sur. Littrell Martin. 61.
Hammock, Peter and Nancy Prunty, Jan. 26, 1788. Sur. Macajah Beck. 37.
Hampton, Geo. and Sallie Hodges, Aug. 2, 1806. Sur. John Hodges. 8.

Hancock, Abraham B. and Martha E. Walker, dau. Moses and Frances, (later Keen), Nov. 16, 1847. Sur. John H. Smith. 137.

Hancock, Allen and Susannah Smith, Mar. 4, 1816. Sur. Wm. Smith.

Hancock, Benj. and Sally Fanny Holland, Jan. 6, 1806. Sur. Peter Holland. 8.

Hancock, Benj. and Elizabeth Booth, Oct. 6, 1817. Sur. Peter Booth.

Hancock, Peter L. and Mary Ann English, dau. Parmenas, Nov. 13, 1843. Sur. John K. English.

Hancock, (Hamock) John A. and Sally Ryan, Nov. 2, 1801. Sur. Pleasant Saunders. 141.

Hancock, Wm. T. and Agnes Booth, Jan. 23, 1838. Sur. John Booth. 3.

Handy, James and Hannah Rentfro, dau. Jesse, Feb. 11, 1786. Sur. John Handy.

Handy, John, s. Wm., and Grace Grimmett, dau. John, Nov. 5, 1792. Sur. John Grimmet. 52.

Handy, Peter and Sarah Dixon, Apr. 1, 1799. Sur. Nathaniel Dixon.

Handy, Thos. L. and Polly Gillespie, May 9, 1842. Sur. Wm. Gallaspie.

Handy, Wm. and Mary Butler, Aug. 6, 1792. (of age, ps. dcd.) 52.

Hanes, Drury and Crecy Lovel (Savel), Jan. 29, 1812. Sur. Richard Newton. 122.

Hankins, Hezekiah and Elizabeth Starkey, Mar. 26, 1813. Sur. John Coleman. 8.

Harbour, Richard and Judith Nowlin, dau. John, Aug. 9, 1824. Sur. Chas. Nowlin. 65.

Hardwick, Carey and Catherine Edwards Saunders, Oct. 17, 1794. Sur. Isham Edwards. 52.

Hardy, Joseph and Leannah Payne, dau. Joseph, May 2, 1831. 48.

Hardy, Robt. and Fanny Payne, Sept. 19, 1831. Sur. Reed Payne. 140.

Harkrider, David and Anna Mikesell, Feb. 18, 1799. Sur. John Fishburn. 89.

Harkrider, Jacob and Judith Young, July 26, 1811. Sur. Geo. Payne.

Harkrider, (Hearkrider) John and Becky Houston, dau. Wm., Mar. 23, 1800. Sur. John Huston.

Harkrider, John and Aley Angel, Feb. 5, 1821. Sur. Pleasant Beard. 49.

Harkrider, Solomon and Rachael Houston, Nov. 3, 1800. Sur. Thos. Huston. 21.

Harman, Robt. and Mary Drake, May 20, 1794. Sur. John Drake. 41.

Harman, Thos. and Lucy Blankenship, dau. Smith, Jan. 5, 1820. Sur. John Oyler.

Harper, Absalom and Elizabeth Birchfield, dau. John, July 20, 1790. 52.

Harper, James C. and Mary Showalter, dau. Joseph, Nov. 17, 1842. Sur. Stephen Showalter.

Harper, Joel and Mary Ann Noble, June 3, 1844.

Harper, Josiah and Sarah Parrott, dau. Winea, Dec. 27, 1787. Sur. Joseph Parrot. 37.

Harper, Robt. M. and Mary A. Betz, Jan. 6, 1852. 19.

Harper, Robt. M. and Lydia Hill, Sept. 3, 1838. Sur. Lot Hill.

Harral, James and Elizabeth Ellis, Apr. 3, 1793. Sur. Joseph Ellis. 52.

Harris, Benj. and Jaminia Greer, Dec. 13, 1830. Sur. Demarquis D. Ferguson. 140.

Harris, James and Elizabeth Ross, Jan. 22, 1819. Sur. David Ross.

Harris, John and Polly Saunders, Jan. 18, 1810. Sur. Clayton Saunders.

Harris, Jubal and Sally Ross, Apr. 1, 1816. Sur. James Williamson.

Harris, Micajah and Dilsey Cousins, Jan. 20, 1836. Sur. John Shavers.

Harris, Rolen and Elizabeth Bates, Nov. 4, 1800. 72.

Harris, Samuel and Nancy Saunders, Sept. 9, 1811. Sur. Daniel Ferguson.

Harris, Samuel and Drucilla Huff, Sept. 4, 1793. 52.

Harrison, Amos and Rachael Dodd, Apr. 25, 1816. Sur. Solomon Harrison.
Harrison, Greenville and Mildred Harrison, Oct. 9, 1840. Sur. Joseph Harrison.
Harrison, Ignatius and Glicy Jarrol, Sept. 5,. 1803. Sur. Wm. Harrison. 72.
Harrison, John and Mary Hopkins, Oct. 17, 1835. Sur. Ezekiel Dowdy. 140.
Harrison, Joseph and Lucy Kennett, Feb. 29, 1812. Sur. Peter Kenett. 8.
Harrison, Perry and Julia S. Beheler, Nov. 19, 1852. 80.
Harrison, Peter and Pamelia J. Hudson, Apr. 2, 1834. Sur. Edmund Hudson.
Harrison, Samuel and Lucy Bratcher, dau. Allen, Jan. 14, 1813. Sur. Seth Bratcher.
Harrison, Solomon, s. Wm, Sr., and Polly Dodd, dau. Sarah, Mar. 30, 1811. 130.
Harrison, Thos. and Nancy Crawley, Jan. 24, 1807. Sur. Lewis Hammick.
Harrison, Wm. and Elizabeth Thurman, ... 1811. 130.
Harrison, Wm. and Cynthia Dillon, Oct. 23, 1826. Sur. John Dillion. 48.
Harrison, Wm. and Avis S. Frith, Apr. 15, 1845. Sur. Thos. Frith. 132.
Harter, David and Polly Beckner, Aug. 6, 1804. Sur. Geo. Harter.
Harter, Geo. and Mary Miller, Feb. 13, 1798. Sur. Tobias Miller. 89.
Harter, Henry and Elizabeth Young, dau. Joseph, June 4, 1799. Sur. Peter Young.
Harter, Jacob and Elizabeth Houts, (Hautz) dau. Christian, (of Roanoke), Mar. 17, 1798. 89.
Harter, John and Sarah Webb, dau. Mary, Aug. 14, 1797. Sur. James Webb.
Hartman, Geo. and Nancy Broaker, ..., 1811. 130.
Hartman, Henry, s. Jacob and Elizabeth, and Claressa Smith, dau. Henry and Margaret, Dec. 27, 1853. 11.
Hartman, John Lewis and Susannah Dishong, Mar. 13, 1838. Sur. Samuel Wart. 18.

Hartman, John, s. John Sr., and Lockie Wood, Feb. 9, 1841. Sur. Anthony Simmons.
Hartman, Michael and Polly Philips, July 30, 1816. Sur. Wm. Lindsay. 130.
Hartwell, Lorenzo D. and Cecily Hodges, dau. Lewis, Nov. 4, 1829. Sur. Absalom Hodges. 48.
Hartwell, Silas E. G. and Miriam Webb, Feb. 28, 1842. Sur. Wm. Webb. 86.
Hartwell, Silas and Sally Beckner, Feb. 18, 1837. Sur. Jonathan Beckner. 140.
Hartzell, Abraham and Eve Houtz, dau. Christian, May 23, 1796. Sur. Sur. Christian Houtz. 89.
Hartzell, Geo. and Nancy Goode, June 2, 1823. Sur. Cornelius Kinsey. 130.
Hartzell, Geo. and Sally Clark, July 11, 1838. Sur. Otey Hambrick. 18.
Hartzell, Geo. and Susannah Toney, Mar. 28, 1809. Sur. James Toney.
Hartzell, Jacob and Hannah Capper, Nov. 19, 1816. Sur. Jacob Wimmer. 130.
Harvey, James and Nancy C. Chandler, July 29, 1839. Sur. Gerutin Chandler.
Harvey, Lewis P. and Lavenia Jane Helm, Aug. 13, 1851. 68.
Harvey, Robt. and Julianna H. Holland, dau. Asa, Nov. 13, 1839. Sur. Richard M. Taliaferro. 99.
Harvey, Robt. and Elizabeth Helm, July 9, 1850. Sur. Skelton T. Helm. 97.
Hatcher, Edmund and Polly Maxey, dau. Pheby, Nov. 9, 1803. Sur. Elijah Hatcher.
Hatcher, Edward C. and Miriam Hambrick, ..., 1851. 132.
Hatcher, Henry and Sally Greer, dau. Mary and Henry, Feb. 4, 1801. Sur. Henry Greer.
Hatcher, Henry and Mary Napier, dau. Robt., Jan. 7, 1805. Sur. Champion Napier.
Hatcher, James and Agnes Booth, Apr. 4, 1808. Sur. Richard Booth.
Hatcher, Jeremiah and Jane Johnson, dau. Thos., Oct. 26, 1832. Sur. Chas. English. 3.

Hatcher, John and Charlotte Thurmond, dau. David, June 7, 1822. Sur. Wm. Baker.
Hatcher, Lewis and Polly Lyon, dau. Elisha, Apr. 22, 1826. Sur. Elijah Lyon. 48.
Hatcher, Richard and Elizabeth Hatcher, Aug. 4, 1817. Sur. Jonathan Waid.
Hatcher, Samuel and Nancy Greer, dau. Nathan, Dec. 8, 1819. Sur. James Smith.
Hatcher, Ward and Mary Smith, July 29, 1823. Sur. James Hutz.
Hatcher, Wm. and Catherine Payne, Mar. 3, 1819. Sur. Thos. Payne.
Hatcher, Wm. and Patsy Hale, Aug. 8, 1796. Sur. James Edmundson Hale. 93.
Haven, (Hoven) Geo. and Elizabeth Saul, Jan. 8, 1846. Sur. James D. Saul. 18.
Hawkins, Thos. M. and Elizabeth M. Bernard, dau. Judith, Mar. 27, 1846. Sur. Wm. L. Bernard, 138.
Haynes, Drury and Barsheba Adams, Feb. 28, 1821. Sur. Jacob Sigmon. 122.
Haynes, Henry W. and Mary Wheat, July 4, 1797. Sur. Stephen Haynes.
Haynes, Henry and Susannah Walker, Jan. 16, 1789. Sur. Robt. Boulton. 37.
Haynes, James and Rhoda Gipson, Oct. 31, 1809. Sur. Richard Platt.
Haynes, (Haines) James, s. Drewry and Basheeba, and Sarah Campbell, Jan. 3, 1848. Sur. Thos. Campbell. 68.
Haynes, John O. M. and Elizabeth Anne Keen, dau. Ashford, Mar. 2, 1840. Sur. Thos. S. Keen.
Haynes, John and Elizabeth Martin, May 3, 1821. Sur. Luttrel Martin. 130.
Haynes, John and Jane Campbell, Aug. 21, 1837. Sur. Thos. Campbell. 134.
Haynes (Hayes) Levi and Anna Adney, dau. Thos., June 7, 1802. Sur. Wm. Richeson.
Haynes, Lewis and Frances Powell, dau. Robt., Feb. 27, 1821. Sur. James Worley.
Haynes, Thos. and Mary Campbell, Feb. 3, 1843. Sur. Thos. Campbell. 68.

Hays, Joseph and Jemima Alley, dau. Joseph Hale, Mar. 31, 1788. Sur. Richard Hale.
Hazelwood, Chas. W. and Susan A. DeWitt, Oct. 19, 1848. Sur. Geo. G. Richardson. 19.
Hazelwood, John W. and Frances J. Merryman, Jan. 10, 1849. Sur. John Brown.
Hazelwood, Wm. and Jane Cooper, dau. John, Jr., Jan. 18, 1823. Sur. Abram Greenwood.
Heard, Chas. and Sarah Carter, Oct. 18, 1795. Sur. Wm. Stinnett. 66.
Heard, Geo. and Rhoda Hill, Feb. 22, 1806. Sur. Joshua Rogers.
Heard, John and Hannah Underwood, dau. Samuel, Jan. 24, 1788. Sur. Joseph Underwood.
Heard, Stephen and Sarah Marcum, dau. Ogge and Janey, Mar. 11, 1790. Sur. Wm. Austin. 37.
Heath, Timothy and Mary Ferguson, Dec. 25, 1793. 52.
Heckman, Jacob and Mary Overfelt, May 13, 1793. Sur. David Overholt.
Heckman, Nicodemus, s. John, and Charlotte Edwards, dau. Thos., Mar. 25, 1792. Sur. Thos. Edwards.
Helm, Adam and Conny Webb, dau. Molly, Apr. 25, 1789. Sur. John Kelley. 52.
Helm, Daniel P. and Jane Turner, Apr. 21, 1830. Sur. Geo. Turner.
Helm, Fleming and Elizabeth Prillaman, Mar. 12, 1828. Sur. David Prillaman. 129.
Helm, Jacob, s. Jacob Sr., and Nancy Webb, Mar. 8, 1806. Sur. Thos. Helms.
Helms, James and Mary Webb, dau. Hannah and Jacob, Feb. 2, 1818. Sur. Thos. Helms. 130.
Helm, John and Sally M. Livesay, Feb. 3, 1823. Sur. Peter Livesay. 130.
Helm, Samuel and Alian Taylor, July 12, 1806. Sur. Abraham Taylor. 130.
Helm, Samuel S. and Sarah Hoy, Mar. 21, 1838. Sur. Madison S. Helm. 134.
Helm, Sebert and Ann Radford, dau. James, Mar. 3, 1823. Sur. John B. Williams.

Helms, Thos. and Betsy Prillaman, Mar. 7, 1808. Sur. Thos. Helms. 117.
Helm, Thos. and Olivia Smith, Aug. 15, 1812. 130.
Helm, Thos. and Sally Lemon, Apr. 23, 1832. Sur. Isaac Lemon.
Helm, Thos. and Molly Webb, dau. Mary and Theodorick, Aug. 10, 1795. Sur. Theo. Webb. 52.
Helm, Wm. and Barbara Helm, dau. Thos., Nov. 9, 1818. Sur. James Helm
Henderson, Henry Andrew and Asenah Harris, dau. Evan, Nov. 3, 1791. Sur. Daniel Brown. 52.
Henderson, Wm., s. Samuel, and Mary McClure, dau. Mary, Mar. 3, 1786. Sur. Wm. Camp. 66.
Henley, James B. and Elizabeth Dodd, dau. Sarah, June 4, 1804. Sur. Elijah Poteet.
Hennes (Harris) John and Rhoda Candy, dau. Wm. Sept. 9, 1787. Sur. Wm. Candy. 66.
Henry, John R. and Frances E. Edwards, June 5, 1848. Sur. Wm. H. Edwards.
Henry, Samuel W. and Matilda J. Fralin, June 2, 1842. Sur. Henry Frailin.
Henry, Thos. T. and Elizabeth Anderson, Dec. 9, 1844. Sur. Jesse Anderson. 133.
Henry, Thos. H. and Nancy Martin, Mar. 25, 1800.
Henry, Wm. and Rachael McIlhaney, May 26, 1806. Sur. Samuel McAlhancy. 130.
Hensley, Solomon and Evah Hickman, Mar. 9, 1800. 72.
Hensley, Solomon G. and Catherine Kinsey, dau. Jacob Kinsey, Dec. 2, 1833. Sur. Cornelius Kinsey. 48.
Heptinstall, Caleb and Lize (Tege) Greer, g. Thos. Demoss, Nov. 7, 1796. Sur. Thomas Demoss.
Heptinstall, Caleb and Gilley S. Dudley, dau. Martha, Oct. 10, 1839. Sur. Thos. Dudley.
Heptinstall, Wm. and Permelia Phelps, dau. Polly, Dec. 7, 1819. Sur. John Ferguson.
Hepner, Henry and Mary Hysor, dau. Mary, Dec. 30, 1794. Sur. Conrade Overloe. 89.
Herndon, Dr. A. and Mary A. Keen, Mar. 4, 1850. Sur. Ashford Keen.

Herndon, Dr. A. and Elizabeth C. Perkins, dau. Temple, Apr. 4, 1831. Sur. Wm. T. Perkins.

Herndon, D. A. and Elizabeth Brumley, Oct. 14, 1831.

Harold, Benj. and Mary M. Boon, dau. Peter, June 26, 1840. Sur. Isaac Boon.

Hewitt, Daniel and Bridget Rowland, Feb. 7, 1803. Sur. Philmer Whitworth. 106.

Hickman, (Heckman) David and Polly Snauffer, Feb. 11, 1804. Sur. Jacob Snawffer.

Hickman, Henry and Barbara Prillaman, dau. John, Oct. 6, 1823. Sur. Isaac Prillaman.

Heckman, Jacob A. and Elizabeth Dodd, Apr. 5, 1819. Sur. Wm. Dodd. 48.

Heckman, Joseph Jr. and Jane Akers, June 7, 1824. Sur. Luke Akers. 130.

Hickman, Peter and Catherine Kesler, Feb. 5, 1821. Sur. Geo. Kesler. 130.

Hickman, Peter Henry and Mary Kinsey, Sept. 5, 1803. Sur. Henry Kinsey.

Hickerson, (Hickman) Daniel and Sally Lane, May 4, 1790. Sur. Hugh Pratt. 51.

Hiatt, Joseph and Elizabeth Ann Waid, dau. John E. McCrery, Aug. 16, 1828. Sur. John E. McGrery. 132.

Hiett, Harvey and Elizabeth C. Tinsley, dau. Willis, Aug. 2, 1842. Sur. Sterling M. Thornton. 104.

Highly, James Jr. and Polly Wright, dau. Mary and John, Dec. 23, 1810. Sur. Samuel Akers.

Highly, John and Susannah Brown, June 9, 1801. 72.

Highly, Thos. and Patty Brown, dau. Lucy, Aug. 22, 1795. Sur. James Highly. 52.

Highly, Thos. Jr. and Phebe McWaine, g. Franky Calley, Dec. 30, 1810. Sur. Samuel Akers. 130.

Highly, Wm. and Mary Coger, Feb. 8, 1808. Sur. James Smith. 130.

Hill, Costillo and Ruth Jones, dau. Thomas, Jan. 9, 1809. Sur. Abraham Jones.

Hill, Francis and Elizabeth Woods, Feb. 24, 1796. Sur. John Woods. 37.

Hill, Isaac and Tabitha Hill, May 23, 1816. Sur. John Hill. 44.
Hill, John and Elizabeth Hill, May 6, 1816. Sur. Isaac Hill. 44.
Hill, John and Patsey Price, Apr. 9, 1795. 52.
Hill, John and Nancy Cabaniss, Apr. 8, 1830. Sur. Lewis P. Stearnes. 26.
Hill, Lot and Sophronia Jones, July 15, 1833. Sur. Wm. Jones.
Hill, Luke and Charlotte Richeson, dau. Jonathan, Oct. 22, 1810. Sur. Skelton Richeson.
Hill, Madison and Sarah Bramer, Sept. 7, 1846. Sur. Wm. Brammer. 83.
Hill, Thos. S. and Nancy Hill, dau. Jesse, Apr. 8, 1807. Sur. Abraham Jones.
Hilton, Elijah and Hannah Bowman, Feb. 3, 1853. 18.
Hilton, Samuel and Hannah Hurd, Feb. 23, 1825. Sur. Thos. Austin.
Himer, David and Sarah More, June 17, 1802. 72.
Hinson, Joseph and Nancy Aaron, May 10, 1801. 141.
Hinson, Wm. and Nancy Perkins, July 6, 1800. 141.
Hisor, (or Hisaw) John and Elizabeth Rudy, Oct. 10, 1795. Sur. Daniel Rudy.
Hix, Patrick and Dolly Early, Jan. 7, 1811. Sur. Joseph Wright.
Hix, Tyree and Susannah Sink, Oct. 1, 1832. Sur. Henry Sink.
Hix, Tyree G. and Doshia M. Simmons, July 26, 1849. Sur. Thos. Simmons. 18.
Hix, Wm. and Sally Board, Feb. 11, 1826. Sur. Elijah Beard. 48.
Hix, Wm. and Rebecca Boles, dau. Jesse and Hannah, Nov. 18, 1797. Sur. Jesse Hix.
Hixon, Daniel and Sally Graham, Oct. 6, 1810. Sur. Wm. Graham. 117.
Hixon, John and Polly Phillips, dau. Sallie, Oct. 7, 1805. Sur. Salter Phillips. 122.
Hixon, Wm. and Conny Janney, July 6, 1833. Sur. Thos. Smith.
Hobson, John W. and Mary E. Bennett, Dec. 23, 1850. Sur. Geo. A. Bennett. 132.

Hockaday, (Hochaba) Geo. and Catherine Whiteneck, Dec. 30, 1827. Sur. Jacob Abshire. 26.
Hodges, Aaron and Elizabeth Markham, Aug. 13, 1792. Sur. James Markham.
Hodges, Abednego, Jr. and Sarah Webb, dau. Sarah, Feb. 6, 1833. 145.
Hodges, Achilles and Mary E. Weaver, Dec. 13, 1858.
Hodges, Alexander and Clarissa Steagall, dau. Wm., Feb. 1, 1849. Sur. Wm. Steagall. 132.
Hodges, Anderson and Nancy Hodges, Nov. 25, 1831. Sur. Joel Hodges. 48.
Hodges, Andrew and Avarilla Hodges, dau. John, Dec. 26, 1825. Sur. Jonathan Hodges. 48.
Hodges, Andrew and Cynthia Clowers, dau. John, Sept. 22, 1829. Sur. Jacob Clowers, Jr.
Hodges, Armistead and Nancy Leffew, Jan. 25, 1842. Sur. Joseph Hodges. 18.
Hodges, Asa and Jemima Cockran, Feb. 2, 1807. Sur. Samuel Cockran. 8.
Hodges, Bowker and Sophia Martin, Apr. 2, 1827. Sur. John Martin.
Hodges, Caleb and Lucy Bird, dau. Elijah, June 13, 1848. Sur. Seth Burton. 18.
Hodges, Camell, s. Wm., and Polly Walker, Mar. 11, 1850. Sur. Sur. Wm. Hodges.
Hodges, Coleman and Chloe Hodges, Dec. 1, 1829. Sur. Wm. Hodges. 48.
Hodges, Curl and Elizabeth Hall, Sept. 30, 1839. Sur. Hebron Hodges.
Hodges, Currell and Elizabeth Hall, Nov. 21, 1844. Sur. Caleb Hodges.
Hodges, Denin and Frances Dearin, dau. Martha, Oct. 13, 1835. Sur. Abednego Hodges, Jr.
Hodges, Drury and Dinah Griffith, Jan. 21, 1800. Sur. Geo. Griffith. 21.
Hodges, Elbert and Adaline M. Jones, dau. Wm., Jan. 2, 1847. Sur. Randolph M. Jones. 68.
Hodges, Elisha and Anna Parsell, Feb. 4, 1833. Sur. Wm. Lavender.

WINGFIELD'S WORKS 117

Hodges, Elisha and Polly Hodges, June 6, 1825. Sur. Joel Hodges. 48.

Hodges, Elijah and Judy Hodges, dau. Robt., Nov. 26, 1821. Sur. Robt. Hodges.

Hodges, Elkanah and Lucinda E. Woody, Dec. 20, 1858.

Hodges, Gabriel and Elizabeth Hunt, dau. Stephen and Caty, Nov. 29, 1825. Sur. Peter H. McCall. 48.

Hodges, Gresham, s. Wm., and Jane Laprade, Dec. 8, 1845. Sur. Joel Fisher. 18.

Hodges, Hebron and Anna Fisher, dau. Jacob, Nov. 5, 1840. Sur. Anderson Hodges.

Hodges, Henry and Nancy Chandler, Jan. 12, 1822. Sur. Moses Chandler.

Hodges, Isham Jr. and Sally Cockran, Mar. 6, 1812. Sur. Samuel Cockran. 8.

Hodges, Jeter and Avey Ann R. Hall, Jan. 15, 1849. Sur. Wm. Hall. 18.

Hodges, Jacob and Nancy Richards, Jan. 5, 1819. Sur. Shadrach Richards.

Hodges, Joel and Susannah Hodges, Nov. 5, 1792. Sur. Wm. Hodges.

Hodges, John and Lucea Dalton, Aug. 8, 1786. Sur. David Dalton.

Hodges, John and Catherine Sigmon, dau. Wm., Nov. 27, 1845. Sur. Wiley P. Ferguson. 68.

Hodges, John and Elizabeth Leffew, Dec. 1, 1834. Sur. Josiah Webb.

Hodges, John and Polly Warren, dau. Zachariah, Aug. 17, 1811. Sur. Edmund Richards.

Hodges, Joseph and Sally A. H. Wingfield, dau. John, Oct. 10, 1848. Sur. Isaac Semones. 11.

Hodges, Josiah and Vicey Hodges, Dec. 16, 1826. Sur. Joel Hodges. 48.

Hodges, Lewis and Elizabeth Doss, Aug. 8, 1803. Sur. Abednego Hodges. 72.

Hodges, Lewis and Caroline McNeil, July 24, 1836. 18.

Hodges, Paton and Elizabeth Hall, June 8, 1808. 8.

Hodges, Rivers and Nancy Dunn, dau. Thos., Dec. 23, 1814. Sur. Thos. Dunn, Jr. 8.

Hodges, Rivers and Jane Woodall, Oct. 12, 1812. Sur. Wm. Steagall. 8.
Hodges, Rivers and Elizabeth Hodges, Apr. 21, 1812. Sur. John Hodges.
Hodges, Rivers and Jane Burtchet, Feb. 20, 1837. Sur. Josiah Webb.
Hodges, Rivers and Martha C. Steagall, Dec. 10, 1840. Sur. Drinkard Steagall. 132.
Hodges, Robt. and Susannah Hall, dau. Isham, May 18, 1791. Sur. John Keen.
Hodges, Robt. and Amy Woody, Oct. 17, 1825. Sur. Edward Jones.
Hodges, Rowland and Catherine Nunnery, Dec. 17, 1810. Sur. Benj. Brizendine. 8.
Hodges, Rowland and Mary A. Davis, Nov. 24, 1845. Sur. Wm. Davis. 132.
Hodges, Samuel and Harriet Hodges, Sept. 19, 1851. Sur. John Bowman.
Hodges, Samuel P. and Lucinda Frith, Dec. 6, 1858.
Hodges, Thos. and Tabitha Hall, Jan. 23, 1835. Sur. Curril Hall. 53.
Hodges, Thos. and Lucinda Burton, Nov. 9, 1850. Sur. Seth Burton. 18.
Hodges, Welcome and Polly Pines, Feb. 3, 1807. Sur. Brice Stewart. 8.
Hodges, Wm. and Amey Hall, Mar. 16, 1796. Sur. Wm. Hall. 87.
Hodges, Wm. and Elizabeth Marcum, dau. Sally, May 3, 1838. Sur. Robt. Haynes. 3.
Hodges, Wm. R. and Jane Robertson, Sept. 9, 1852. 18.
Hodges, Wm. and Lavinia Hodges, Dec. 23, 1825. Sur. Peyton Hodges. 48.
Hodges, Wm. and Nancy Lavinder, Aug. 18, 1853. 47.
Hodges, Wm. and Anne Howser, Oct. 19, 1843. Sur. Wm. H. Dent. 132.
Hofawger, Samuel and Elizabeth Hays, Mar. 9, 1829. Sur. Levi Hats. 48.
Hoffman, Wm. H. and Mary F. Millirons, dau. Sarah, Aug. 2, 1847. Sur. Alexander B. Millirons. 68.

Hogan, John and Anney Campbell, dau. Jeremiah, Jan. 18, 1843. Sur. John Barton. 18.
Hoggs, Asey and Cloa Marcum, ..., 1796. 21.
Holcomb, John and Nancy Jamison, ..., 1795. 37.
Holcomb, Joseph W. and Mary Jane Howser, dau. John, Jan. 2, 1847. Sur. Jeremiah Holcomb. 67.
Holcomb, Lewis and Martha Akers, Aug. 27, 1839. Sur. Jeremiah Holcomb. 132.
Holdeman, John and Mary Kinsey, Jan. 26, 1797. 89.
Holland, Andrew and Sarah J. Holland, Oct. 16, 1845. Sur. Andy S. Holland.
Holland, Andrew S. and Mary Susan English, dau. John, Jan. 20, 1846. Sur. Geo. W. English.
Holland, Andrew and Nancy Smith, dau. Wm., Oct. 1, 1821. Sur. Stephen Smith, Jr. 48.
Holland, Asa and Catherine Sample, dau. John, Feb. 12, 1833. Sur. Richard M. Taliaferro. 53.
Holland, Chas. and Dotia Craghead, dau. John, Feb. 26, 1827. Sur. John Craghead, Jr.
Holland, Chas. and Mary Payne, Apr. 7, 1809. Sur. James Payne.
Holland, Ebenezer H. and Mary J. F. Smith, Sept. 4, 1848. Sur. Stephen Smith.
Holland, (Hollins) Floyd and Elizabeth Justice, Jan. 4, 1847. Sur. Sparrel Griffith.
Holland, Jeremiah B. and Mary E. Holland, dau. Andy S., Dec. 16, 1844. Sur. John M. Holland, Jr. 18.
Holland, John and Sarah W. Holland, Nov. 15, 1827. Sur. Asa Holland.
Holland, John M., Jr. and Frances A. Holland, dau. Andy. S., Dec. 16, 1844. Sur. Jeremiah Holland. 18.
Holland, Mastin and Polly Bradley, dau Wm., July 20, 1801. Sur. Wm. Bradley. 106.
Holland, Meador and Mary Smith, Jan. 2, 1797. Sur. Peter Holland.
Holland, Peter D. and Franky Hancock, Jan. 26, 1807. Sur. Lewis Hancock. 8.

Holland, Peter H. and Sarah Kemp, Feb. 18, 1834. Sur. James Kemp. 3.
Holland, Peter L. and Elizabeth Ferguson, Dec. 5, 1836. Sur. James Ferguson. 134.
Holland, Sandy and Nancy Smith, Oct. 1, 1821.
Holland, Thos. and Sally Candler, Sept. 25, 1806. Sur. Zedekiah Candler.
Holland, Thos. and Patsy Smith, Dec. 6, 1819. Sur. Wm. Smith.
Holland, Thos. J. and Elizabeth Smith, Mar. 26, 1838. Sur. Thos. J. Holland.
Holland, Thos. J. and Miriam Smith, Nov. 5, 1827. Sur. Andrew H. Turner. 26.
Holland, Thos. and Sarah Gilbert, dau. Michel and Willmuth, Dec. 27, 1790. Sur. John Smith.
Holland, Wm. R. and Mary Moore, Dec. 27, 1843. Sur. John Moore.
Holland, Wm. W. and Nancy Gray, Dec. 19, 1817. Sur. Alexander Gray.
Holliday, Jeremiah and Margaret Martin, dau. James, Aug. 15, 1788. Sur. John Martin.
Holliday, Levi and Amy Pugh, Feb. 17, 1826. Sur. Richard Pugh. 48.
Hollinsworth, Chesley and Nancy J. Stone, Oct. 7, 1850. Sur. John Stone. 1.
Holloway, Hugh and Frances Bowles, Aug. 25, 1824. Sur. Hezekiah Brammer. 130.
Holloway, John and Elizabeth Crum, dau. Abraham and Martha, Jan. 12, 1841. Sur. Martin Perdue. 18.
Holley, Smithson G. and Katherine Oyler, dau. John, Dec. 16, 1831. Sur. Wm. Allbright. 70.
Holly, David and Nancy Pew, dau. Mary, Dec. 16, 1836. Sur. James Foster. 129.
Holley, Joseph and Frances Hancock, dau. Sabrah, Aug. 25, 1840. Sur. Wm. Hinson.
Holly, Wm. M. H. and Catherine Meador, dau. Prudence, Aug. 4, 1834. Sur. Lewis Wysong.
Holt, Ambrose and Lucy Richardson, Sept. 9, 1788. Sur. John Burgiss.

Holt, Newt, s. Sprattley, and Martha Cannaday, July 28, 1834. Sur. John Huff. 134.
Hood, Lawson and Irena Ferguson, Feb. 5, 1844. Sur. Thos. B. Ferguson. 18.
Hoover, Matthew and Fanny Altick, July 21, 1829. Sur. Jacob Altick. 48.
Horn, Jefferson and Jane Trail, dau. Marvel, Dec. 31, 1845. Sur. Joel Leftwich. 68.
Horn, John D. and Malinda Lemon, May 6, 1851. 127.
Hopkins, Geo. W. and Elizabeth Dowdy, Dec. 22, 1828. Sur. Ezekiel Dowdy. 140.
Hopkins, Henry C. and Elizabeth Sence, Jan. 5, 1828. Sur. Moses Simmons. 140.
Hopkins, Isaac and Rhoda Nimmo, Feb. 7, 1825. 48.
Hopkins, John and Polly Dowdy, Jan. 1, 1816. Sur. James Dowdy. 98.
Hopkins, Jonathan, s. Chas., and Mary Simmons, dau. Moses, Apr. 14, 1821. Sur. Skelton Simmons. 130.
Hopkins, Otey and Ann Simmons, Jan. 6, 1825. Sur. Moses Simmons.
Hopkins, Tilgham P. and Mary A. Roach, July 22, 1852. 18.
Hopkins, Wm. L. T. and Julia A. Muse, Dec. 22, 1850. 47.
Horsley, Joseph and Mary Board, dau. Henry, June 10, 1840. Sur. Eli Board. 86.
Horsley, Wm. and Elizabeth Potter, dau. Lewis, Aug. 27, 1802.
Hough (Huff), Daniel and Hannah Hale, dau. John, Aug. 30, 1790. Sur. Wm. Hoff. 52.
Howser, Josiah and Matilda Grubb, Aug. 20, 1823. Sur. Edward Miles.
Housman, Adam and Martha Pelter, Feb. 25, 1831. Sur. Pleasant M. Pelter. 48.
Housman David and Lucy Kemp, dau. Thos., Nov. 1, 1819. Sur. John Kemp.
Housman, David and Milley Law, dau. John Sr., Oct. 1, 1810. Sur. John Law, Jr. 8.
Housman, Geo. and Elizabeth M. Kemp, Feb. 6, 1832. Sur. Wm. Kemp, Jr. 3.
Housman, Madison and Elivira W. Walker, Aug. 16, 1858.

Housman, Wm. R. and Martha R. Mattox, Nov. 28, 1846. Sur. Gabrial Mattox. 104.

Howery, Preston and Elizabeth Cannaday, Dec. 2, 1844. Sur. James P. Cannaday. 68.

Howell, David and Susan Hilton, Oct. 6, 1789. Sur. Elijah Hilton.

Howell, Lewis and Frances Ann Carter, dau. Lawson H., May 26, 1845. Sur. James B. Anderson.

Howell, Riar Alfred and Ann Gallaspy, Aug. 21, 1847. Sur. Thos. Handy. 134.

Howell, Thos. and Mary Kennett, Nov. 20, 1853.

Howry, Michael and Eleanor Sheriden, Sept. 26, 1816. 122.

Howser, James and Polly Martin, Mar. 24, 1818. Sur. Jeremiah Bowles.

Howser, (Houser) and Frances Young, Feb. 12, 1817. Sur. John Young. 44.

Hoy, Samuel J. and Ruth Turner, Aug. 21, 1833. Sur. Geo. Turner.

Hoy, Thos. and Priscilla Gallaspy, Sept. 25, 1810. Sur. Evan Gallaspy. 130.

Hoy, (Hay), Thos. and Jane Taylor, Mar. 31, 1813. Sur. Samuel Taylor. 130.

Hubbles, (Hubbler) Isham and Cally (Catey) Hughes, g. Goettnick Johnson, May 3, 1789. Sur. Abraham Abshire. 52.

Hubble, Isham and Demorass Lewis, dau. Thos., Mar. 12, 1787. Sur. Thos. Arthur. 66.

Huddleston, Abraham and Elizabeth W. Bagley, June 8, 1824. Sur. Woodson Bagley. 48.

Huddleston, Henry Abraham and Martha Pate, dau. Anthony, Jan. 8, 1790. Sur. Stephen Pate.

Huddleston, Henry and Abagail Oyler, June 28, 1851. 18.

Huddleston, Richard and Elizabeth Oyler, dau. John, Dec. 1, 1845. Sur. Valentine W. Oyler.

Hudson, Abel and Susannah Pratt, Mar. 20, 1809. Sur. John Ashworth. 8.

Hudson, Alexander and Nancy Smith, Sept. 30, 1858.

Hudson, Peyton and Elizabeth J. Bird, dau. Hannah and Wm., Jan. 30, 1843. Sur. Benj. K. Bird.

Huff, Jacob and Elizabeth Cannaday, Feb. 1, 1847. Sur. Peter Cannaday. 60.

Huff, (Hoff) John and Mary (Polly) Gearhart, July 14, 1786. Sur. Wm. Kelly.

Huff, John and Polly Wade, Mar. 16, 1830. Sur. John Huff, Jr.

Huff, John, Jr. and Orrina M. Livesay, Nov. 5, 1821. Sur. Peter Livesay.

Huff, (Hoff) Wm. and Lydda Miller, dau. Thos., Feb. 2, 1791. Sur. Samuel Wilson. 102.

Hughes, Burwell and Nancy Coon, Jan. 7, 1828. Sur. Adam Weaver. 48.

Hughes, David and Susannah Hammond, Apr. 7, 1786. Sur. James Vest.

Hughes, Elijah and Susannah English, dau. Geo. L., Oct. 15, 1828. Sur. Lewis English. 26.

Hughes, Geo. H. and Jane Hale, dau. James L., Feb. 17, 1810. Sur. Henry Law. 8.

Hughes, Reese and Polly Lyon, Aug. 5, 1801. Sur. Joseph Greer. 141.

Hundley, John and Diannah Basham, dau. Lucinda, Dec. 9, 1850. Sur. Will Wilson. 86.

Hunt, James, s. John, and Elizabeth Bird, Jan. 4, 1834. Sur. John Hunt. 3.

Hunt, John and Catherine Kessler, Jan. 3, 1842. Sur. Henry Kesler.

Hunt, Richard and Patty Chavers, Aug. 31, 1808. Sur. Jesse Chavers.

Hunt, Stephen A. and Mary Metts, dau. Lucy, Dec. 4, 1848. Sur. James B. Anderson. 18.

Hunter, John and Sarah Price, Aug. 7, 1786. Sur. Joseph L. Price.

Hunter, Robt. and Sally Martin, dau. John, Feb. 23, 1798. Sur. Dabney Garland.

Hunter, Samuel and Martha Feazel, Dec. 18, 1827. Sur. Joseph Feazel. 48.

Hurd, (Heard) Garner C. and Rhoda Jamison, Nov. 12, 1834. Sur. Lewis Jamison.

Hurd, Stephen and Sarah Marcum, Apr. ...., 1790.
Hurd, Wm. and Asenath Sink, Sept. 25, 1828.
Hurt, Colby and Polly Ballard, Mar. 5, 1788. Sur. Stephen Stone.
Hurt, Ira M. and Lavinia J. Harvey, Oct. 21, 1858.
Hurt, John and Susannah Barnhart, Feb. 16, 1837. 18.
Hurt, Milton R. and Elizabeth Wray, dau. Wm., Dec. 7, 1846. Sur. Matthew R. Allen. 132.
Hurt, Wm. and Elizabeth A. Martin, dau. Elizabeth, Dec. 22, 1840. Sur. Lorenzo Bousman. 86.
Huston, Hugh M. and Susan Woody, Dec. 17, 1833. Sur. Geo. L. Johnson. 48.
Huston, (Hutson) Samuel and Jinny Abshire, Apr. 16, 1802. Sur. Philemon Saunders.
Huston, Samuel and Elizabeth Brown, dau. Richard, Dec. 31, 1790. Sur. Wm. Brown. 52.
Huston, Thos. and Tabitha Wright, dau. John, June 8, 1799. Sur. Wm. Wright.
Huston, Thos. Jr. and Ellender Wright, Aug. 23, 1816. Sur. Thos. Turner. 130.
Huston, Wm. and Rachael Huff, (Hook) Jan. 2, 1804. Sur. John Huston.
Hutcheson, David and Synthaetta Anderson, Nov. 9, 1837. Sur. Jesse Anderson. 3.
Hutcheson, Wm. and Lucinda Woody, Oct. 18, 1823. Sur. Henry Woody. 49.
Hutcheson, Wm. and Catherine Cook, Sept. 30, 1796. Sur. Jesse Prunty.
Hutson, Chas. and Betsy Doran, Feb. 8, 1831. Sur. Geo. Doran. 48.
Hutson, Joel and Polly Bell, Jan. 8, 1801. 141.
Hutson, Joel and Fanny Vest, dau. John, Jan. 9, 1808. Sur. James Worley. 117.
Hutson, Joseph and Elizabeth Brumley, Oct. 14, 1831. Sur. Thos. Sigmon. 60.
Hutson, Wm. and Ailey Packet, Oct. 15, 1800. 141.
Hutts, Bluford and Rebecca Heptinstall, July 20, 1835. Sur. Wm. G. Heptinstall. 34.

WINGFIELD'S WORKS 125

Hutts (Hiett), Edward H. and Martha A. James, (Jones), Oct. 5, 1840. Sur. Abraham Betz.

Hutts, Francis and Mary Divers, dau. Wm. R., Jan. 7, 1835. Sur. Baley Divers. 140.

Hutts, James P. and Ellender Law, dau. Elizabeth, June 26, 1839. Sur. Jesse Brooks.

Hutts, John and Sophia E. Boothe, Dec. 3, 1851. 19.

Hutts, Joseph and Nancy Forbes, Oct. 17, 1817. Sur. John R. Forbes.

Hutts, Joseph and Susan Ferguson, Dec. 27, 1821. Sur. Caleb Tate.

Hutts, Leonard and Sally Sparks, Oct. 2, 1851. 19.

Hutts, Michael Jr. and Judith McCormack, Aug. 25, 1817. Sur. Wm. McCormack. 98.

Hutts, Shelton and Nancy Trant, Sept. 7, 1849. Sur. Ransom Dudley.

Hutts, Thos. G. and Virginia Bond, Nov. 11, 1841. Sur. Bluford Burnett. 86.

Hutts, Wiley and Celina Bond, dau. Malinda, May 9, 1843. Sur. James McDowell.

Hymlick, John and Elizabeth Clingenpeale, Dec. 28, 1811. Sur. Joseph Klingenpeale. 130.

Ikenberry, Henry and Mary Landis, ..., 1794. 89.

Ikenberry, (Eichenberry) Peter and Elizabeth Landis (or Landers), dau. Henry, Oct. 22, 1791. Sur. Henry Landis. 52.

Ikenberry, Samuel and Lidia Flora, Feb. 26, 1833. 18.

Ingles, John and Elizabeth Saunders, Jan. 27, 1814. Sur. Samuel Hairston.

Ingram, Elkanah T. and Matilda Ann Willis, Apr. 17, 1843. Sur. Jubal Willis. 68.

Ingram, James, Jr. and Adaline Cannaday, dau. Jane, Mar. 24, 1841. Sur. James Ingram, Sr. 60.

Ingram, Pleasant and Nancy Welch, dau. James, Dec. 1, 1826. 61.

Jackson, Andrew and Hannah Flora, Dec. 22, 1846. Sur. Jacob Flora. 18.

Jackson, Moses and Elizabeth James, Jan. 15, 1825. Sur. David Young. 130.
Jackson, Wm. and Patsy Amos, Aug. 2, 1815. Sur. James Amos. 98.
Jacoby, John and Anney Dalton ——, 1790.
James, Daniel and Polly Harmon, dau. Levicy and John Drake, Aug. 5, 1801. Sur. Archibald Drake. 106.
James, David and Catherine McClannahan, July 3, 1811. Sur. John Kelly.
James, Ezekiel and Fanny James, dau. Spencer, Mar. 7, 1808. Sur. Waddy Thompson. 44.
James, Hardin and Jane Graham, Nov. 8, 1837. Sur. Patrick Graham. 132.
James, Isaac L. and Harriet E. Carter, dau. E. S., Oct. 21, 1850. Sur. John H. Carter. 134
James, Jamey and Elizabeth Huston, dau. Thos., Feb. 21, 1789. Sur. Samuel Huston. 52.
James, John and Polly Abshire, Aug. 3, 1812. Sur. Nathaniel Mitchell. 130.
James, John and Elizabeth Adney, Dec. 15, 1818.
James, John and Dotherine Craghead, dau. John, Jan. 17, 1815. Sur. Chas. Powell.
James, John and Fanny Estes, dau. Franny, June 22, 1798. Sur. Elisha Estes.
James, John P. and Malinda Williams, dau. Wm., Oct. 12, 1842. Sur. John Bower.
James, Nicholas and Elizabeth Philips, dau. Sally, Dec. 2, 1805. Sur. Benj. Hancock. 122.
James, Pyrant T. and Emily R. Woods, Dec. 2, 1850. Sur. Thos. D. Childress.
James, Reuben, s Faney Hancock, and Jane Smith, dau. David (Daniel), Nov. 10, 1828. Sur. John Foster. 129.
James, Samuel and Patsey Sneed, dau. John, Apr. 6, 1791. Sur. Ralph Thomas. 52.
James, Smith and Martha Radford, Nov. 11, 1851. 68.
James, Waddie T. and Mary Jane Warren, Oct. 26, 1858.
James, Wm. and Hannah Janney, Jan. 2, 1823. Sur. Moses Jinney.

James, Wm. and Elizabeth James, Sept. 20, 1821. Sur. Catlett James.
Jamison, Henry and Sarah Showalter, Nov. 7, 1842. Sur. John Showalter.
Jamison, Jacob and Lavinia F. Fralin, dau. John and Elizabeth, Apr. 26, 1849. Sur. Riley Fralin. 18.
Jamison, John and Mary F. Smith, Dec. 2, 1844. Sur. Smith Wyatt. 132.
Jamison, John and Caty Boon, Jan. 6, 1806. 130.
Jamison, John Jr. and Elizabeth Akers, Aug. 5, 1844. 18.
Jamison, Lewis and Barbara Prillaman, Jan. 1, 1844. Sur. Jacob Prillaman. 132.
Jamison, Samuel and Catherine Brubaker, Oct. 21, 1852. 11.
Jamison, Samuel and Winnie Bird, Dec. 9, 1806. Sur. John Bird.
Jamison, Samuel and Sarah Webster, dau. Jesse, Feb. 18, 1832. Sur. Wm. Webster. 48.
Jamison, Thos. and Mary R. Anglin, dau. Robt, Dec. 15, 1849. Sur. Marshall Waid. 132.
Jamison, Wm. and Sarah McGhee, dau. Martin, Feb. 3, 1840. Sur. Correll McGhee. 132.
Janney, (Jennings) Burwell and Mary Radford, dau. Elender, Dec. 17, 1840. 60.
Janney (Jinney), Fleming and Rachael Hale, Sept. 23, 1824. Sur. John Hale. 48.
Jinny, Aaron and Lelah Webb, Dec. 9, 1807. Sur. Adam Helm. 122.
Jenney (Jinney), Isaac and Polly Underwood, Oct. 17, 1818.
Janney, Isaac and Martha Radford, Feb. 9, 1830. Sur. James Radford. 61.
Janney, Moses and Peggy Dixon, Apr. 28, 1802. Sur. Nathaniel Dixon. 72.
Janney, Nathaniel and Lucy Younger, Apr. 14, 1831. Sur. Anthony Young. 48.
Janney, Wm. and Sarah Radford, dau. James, Mar. 1, 1834. Sur. Isaac Janney, Jr. 61.
Jacques, James and Nancy Harger, dau. John, May 29, 1806. Sur. Geo. Harger.

Jarrett, Allen and Polly Spangler, Oct. 17, 1805. Sur. Wm. Hawkins.
Jarrett, Adda and Winnie Bobbitt, Nov. 7, 1815. Sur. Willis Lutrell.
Jarrett, Young and Nancy Hill, dau. Thos. and Margaret, Oct. 24, 1816. Sur. John Hill. 130.
Jarrett, (Janel) Isham and Lucy Webb, Jan. 19, 1790. Sur. Mark Rentfro. 52.
Jarrold, John and Fanny Vandover, Nov. 14, 1808. Sur. Robt. Bond. 117.
Jarrell, Joseph and Lucy Peters, Oct. 4, 1827. Sur. Zachariah Peters.
Jefferson, Archibald and Lavinia Ramsey, Jan. 8, 1798.
Jefferson, Field and Elizabeth Beasley, dau. Elizabeth, Sept. 7, 1789. Sur. Ashford Napier.
Jefferson, Field and Lucy Golman Johnson, Sept. 5, 1806. Sur. Daniel Law.
Jefferson, Greenville P. and Sarah H. Brown, dau. L. H., Jan. 6, 1840. Sur. Andrew S. Brooks.
Jefferson, John and Anna Ramsey, Jan. 8, 1798.
Jefferson, Oglesby and Lucy Ann Pearson, Dec. 29, 1853. 63.
Jenkins, Anderson, s. Gentry, and Polly Blankenship, June 7, 1841. Sur. Asa Ward. 18.
Jenkins, Chas. H. and Sarah A. Dillion, Dec. 31, 1851. 18.
Jenkins, David C., s. Gentry Jenkins, and Mary Fielder, dau. Cobley, Feb. 5, 1844. Sur. Benjamin Trent. 18.
Jenkins, Edward F., s. J. and Mary, and Loueasy Morris, dau. Ambrose and Polly, Dec. 21, 1853. 96.
Jenkins, Johnson and Miriam Hendley, Jan. 20, 1829. Sur. Amos Harrison. 48.
Jenkins, Thos. G. and Betsey M. Barton, Sept. 30, 1851. 18.
Jenkins, Vincent A. and Arlena C. Divers, Aug. 10, 1858.
Jesse, Chas. W. and Sarah J. Gallaspy, Aug. 30, 1847. Sur. Wm. Galaspy. 134.
Jesse, John and Rachael Minnix, Nov. 27, 1821. Sur. Daniel Minnix.
Jesse, John and Lucy Akers, dau. Daniel, Feb. 11, 1833. Sur. James Shepherd. 48.

Jett, Edgar M. and Nancy Lancaster, June 7, 1853. 68.
Johnson, Alexander and Nancy D. Brooks, Oct. 19, 1841. Sur. Isaac D. Brooks.
Johnson, Creek T., s. Henry B., and Harriet Shiveley, dau. David, Feb. 15, 1843. Sur. Burwell Shiveley. 68.
Johnson, Geo. S. and Margaret Hunt, Sept. 3, 1832. Sur. Owen Hunt.
Johnson, Henry and Jane Wray, Sept. 24, 1837. Sur. Benj. Wray. 18.
Johnson, James M. and Harriet H. Cloughton, Sept. 22, 1852. Sur. J. W. Lewis.
Johnson, James M. and America Stone, Oct. 2, 1858.
Johnson, Jacob and Nancy Hall, dau. Martha, Jan. 30, 1790. Sur. Wm. Johnson. 52.
Johnson, John and Milly Green, Feb. 12, 1801. 21.
Johnson, John W. and Mary E. Haynes, dau. Frances, Sept. 10, 1844. Sur. Peter F. Jefferson.
Johnson, John and Elizabeth Reeson, 1795. 37.
Johnson, John and Nancy Cooper, Feb. 2, 1824. Sur. Gideon Cooper.
Johnson, John and Elizabeth Watson, Sept. 4, 1786. Sur. Isaac Rentfro.
Johnson, Joseph and Sarah Hundley, dau. Nehemiah, Oct. 3, 1825. Sur. Robt. Hundley.
Johnson, Marten and Doshie Griffith, July 29, 1812. 130.
Johnson, Nathan and Elizabeth Osborne, Oct. 16, 1809. Sur. John Osborne.
Johnson, Nathaniel, s. Elizabeth and Nathaniel, and Sarah E. Chitwood, dau. Jefferson and Lucy, Oct. 27, 1853. 18.
Johnson, Presley and Sally Bowles, Feb. 16, 1819. Sur. Samuel Jamison.
Johnson, Samuel and Matilda Brockman, dau. Elizabeth, Dec. 20, 1811. Sur. John Dodd. 130.
Johnson, Silas and Elizabeth Craig, Dec. 28, 1812.
Johnson, Silas and Polly Woody, Dec. 23, 1806. Sur. Martin Woody.
Johnson, Wm. and Mary Maynor, dau. John, May 19, 1790. Sur. John Maynor.

Johnson, Wm. H. and Mary Jane Hale, Dec. 2, 1852. 68.
Johnson, Wm. and Edith Wattson, dau. Alexander and Elizabeth, Sept. 13, 1786. Sur. Wm. Roberts.
Jones, Abraham and Sally Hall, July 26, 1813. Sur. P. Saunders.
Jones, Anselm and Lener Noles, dau. Joshua, Dec. 21, 1799. Sur. Joshua Noles. 66.
Jones, Barnet and Sisley Blankenship, Oct. 23, 1795. 41.
Jones, Beverly G. and Delilah Hodges, Sept. 29, 1846. Sur. Habron Hodges.
Jones, Creed and Sally Jones, Sept. 23, 1835. Sur. Lewis Jones.
Jones, Creed F., s. Abraham, and Dorothy Prillaman, dau. Abraham, Nov. 3, 1853. 68.
Jones David and Polly Trent, dau. Wm., Mar. 15, 1827. Sur. Bluford Guttery. 140.
Jones, Edward and Elizabeth Harger, Dec. 1, 1823. Sur. Josiah W. Dickinson. 49.
Jones, Edward and Betsey Hodges, dau. Robt., July 25, 1805. Sur. Wilson Mattox. 8.
Jones, Elijah and Rebecca McCuthon, dau. James, Feb. 13, 1789. Sur. Joseph Hale. 66.
Jones, Ezekiel and Elizabeth Prindle, Mar. 3, 1824. Sur. Wm. Prindle. 130.
Jones, Henry and Cassandra James, May 23, 1817. Sur. Castillo Hill. 61.
Jones, Henry and Sophia Sink, dau. Henry, Dec. 5, 1831. Sur. Otey Sink. 48.
Jones, Isaac M. and Emma Hill, dau. John, Nov. 25, 1833. Sur. Owen Price.
Jones, Isaac, Jr. and Rhoda H. Jones, dau. Wm., Mar. 15, 1833. Sur. Isaac M. Jones. 60.
Jones, James and Susan A. Hodges, June 5, 1848. Sur. Wm. Hodges. 18.
Jones, James M. and Elizabeth Blankenship, dau. Mary, Nov. 15, 1792. Sur. John Smith. 23.
Jones, Jeremiah and Susannah Agee, dau. Mathew, Oct. 2, 1800. Sur. Obadiah Jones. 141.
Jones, Jesse and Hannah Hale, dau. John, Sept. 2, 1788. Sur. Richard Hale.

Jones, Jesse and Sarah E. Helm, Nov. 18, 1858.
Jones, John and Lily King, Apr. 6, 1813. Sur. David Via.
Jones, John and Abagail Hale, dau. Abraham Jones, Jan. 17, 1826. Sur. Isaac Jones.
Jones, John and Peggy Hartzel, Apr. 3, 1843. Sur. Joel Fisher. 18.
Jones, John and Sarah Sumpter, dau. Geo., July 5, 1790. Sur. Solomon Jones.
Jones, Jonathan and Sarah Barton, Nov. 7, 1803. Sur. David Barton.
Jones, Martin and Mary Jones, dau. John L., June 26, 1839. Sur. Jesse Scott. 68.
Jones, Reuben and Judy Moore, Oct. 19, 1829. Sur. Wm. Moore. 61.
Jones, Reuben, s. Robert Cole, Sr., and Agnes Stewart dau. James, Mar. 11, 1811. Sur. Wm. Stewart and Edward Jones.
Jones, Sampson and Sarah Miles, June 20, 1793. 52.
Jones, Samuel and Martha Jane Arrington, Oct. 1, 1851. 18.
Jones, Robt. and Violet Barton, Feb. 1, 1796, Sur. David Barton. 66.
Jones, Thos. E. and Elizabeth F. Cannaday, Dec. 2, 1844. 68.
Jones, Thos. E., s. Wm. and Elizabeth, and Sarah E. Jones, dau. John and Abagail, Sept. 7, 1853. 47.
Jones, Wm. and Abagail Willis, g. Wm. Turnbull, May 10, 1844. Sur. Wm. Turnbull.
Jones, Wiley and Jane Heard, dau. John, Oct. 16, 1826. Sur. Stephen Heard. 61.
Jones, Wm. and Betty Hill, July 26, 1806. Sur. John Hill.
Joplin, James W. and Emily Booth, Nov. 25, 1835. Sur. Moses G. Booth.
Jopling, Thos. B. and Sarah E. Webb, dau. Creed T., Aug. 23, 1845. 13.
Jurnell, John and Sally Idle, Oct. 10, 1821. Sur. Joe Sweeny.
Justice, James and Elizabeth Underwood, Nov. 15, 1809. Sur. James and Samuel Underwood. 112.
Justice, Simeon and Polly Abshire, Jan. 2, 1809. Sur. Peter Abshire. 130.

Kailer, John and Selmy Kinsey, June 14, 1792. Sur. Henry Kinsey. 52.
Kaler, John and Susanna Haltaman, Apr. 27, 1797. 89.
Kasey, John N., s. Wm., and Elizabeth Saunders, dau. Phillemon, Oct. 14, 1820.
Keen, Anderson and Elizabeth Robins (or Rollins), Aug. 20, 1804. Sur. John Smith.
Keen, Ashford and Frances Walker, Sept. 3, 1836. Sur. Moses G. Carper. 3.
Keen, David S. and Julia H. Holland, dau. John M., Aug. 17, 1830. Sur. Wm. A. Street. 3.
Keen, Gideon E. and Sarah A. Taylor, dau. Christoper C., Feb. 4, 1846. Sur. Hay Turnbull. 19.
Keen, (Kerr) John and Elizabeth Rodman (Redmand), July 8, 1786. Sur. Hugh Innes.
Keen, John and Nancy Shockley, dau. Levi and Rebecker, Mar. 22, 1802. Sur. Benj. Potter.
Keen, Thos. and Elizabeth Brown, dau. Tier, Jan. 6, 1818. Sur. Tarlton Brown.
Keeney, Thos. B. and Lucy A. Dowdy, Sept. 20, 1858.
Kelley, Geo. W. and Sarah Webster, Dec. 17, 1819. Sur Benj. Woodson.
Kelly, John and Frances McKlewain, Nov. 5, 1798. Sur. Wm. Kelly. 89.
Kelley, Richard and Rebecca Underwood, dau. Mary, Dec. 28, 1829. Sur. Absalom Gillinwater. 61.
Kelly, Richard and Keziah Hutson, July 9, 1843. Sur. Creed T. Jones. 68.
Kelly, Wm. and Hannah Martha Richeson, Nov. 26, 1792. Sur. Ambrose Rains. 52.
Kembleton, John Henry and Margaret Robbins, Jan. 17, 1848. Sur. Robt. James. 86.
Kemmonds (or Kimmons), Robt. and Lydia Kimmons Reese, Jan. 2, 1798. Sur. James Reese, Jr. 21.
Kemp, Dudley and Martha Dudley, Apr. 2, 1827. Sur. Levi Dudley.
Kemp, James, s. Adam, and Nancy English, June 5, 1820. Sur. Ezekiel Kemp.
Kemp, John and Fanny Dudley, Aug. 13, 1799. 141.

Kemp, Jordan and Peggy Mattox, Dec. 1, 1795. Sur. Richard Robinson.
Kemp, Michael and Nancy Kemp, Jan. 31, 1823. Sur. Ezekiel Kemp.
Kemp, Nathan and Judith C. Dickerson, Jan. 3, 1831. Sur. Andrew E. Brooks. 48.
Kemp, Robt. and Mary Holland, Nov. 17, 1823. Sur. John Holland, Jr. 49.
Kemp, Thos. and Regina M. Rachel Newbill, dau. G., Nov. 25, 1826. Sur. Wm. R. Kemp. 119.
Kemp, Walter and Jerusha Key, dau. Geo., Feb. 6, 1815. Sur. Stephen Standifer.
Kemp, Wm. and Catherine Housman, Apr. 25, 1817. Sur. Peter Housman.
Kemp, Wm. W. and Susannah Meador, Jan. 12, 1833. Sur. John Meador.
Kemp, Wm. R. and Millie Dudley, dau. James, Dec. 21, 1825. Sur. John Law, Jr.
Kemp, Wm. and Ardra English, Aug. 2, 1819. Sur. Stephen English.
Kemp, Wm. R. and Sarah Glenn Newbill, Mar. 5, 1827. Sur. John G. Newbill. 48
Kemp, Wm. and Delila Kemp, Feb. 24, 1827. Sur. Wm. R. Kemp. 48.
Kemplin, Nicholas and Stella Austin, Sept. 3, 1846. Sur. Henry Huffman. 68.
Kemplin, Nicholas and Ann Mullins, Jan. 23, 1832. Sur. Wiley Easter. 48.
Kemplin, Thos. and Eliza Pugh, Feb. 6, 1827. 48.
Kemplin, Wm. and Lucy Greer, Oct. 4, 1819. Sur. Joseph Greer. 130
Kendrick, Samuel and Mary M. Calhoun, Aug. 25, 1847. Sur. Edward J. Calhoun.
Kennett, Barnabas and Phebe Scott, Nov. 6, 1826. Sur. Daniel McNeil. 48.
Kennett (or Kinnett), Caleb and Susannah Handy, dau. Gray, Dec. 14, 1829. Sur. Nicholas Handy. 61.
Kennett, John F. and Martha A. Simmons, dau. Sarah, Sept. 4, 1843. Sur. Fletcher Simmons.

Kennett, Joseph and Polly Bowles, Dec. 18, 1826. Sur. Joseph Bowles. 129.

Kennett, Nehemiah D. and Catherine Robertson, dau. John, Apr. 5, 1834. Sur. Richard R. Shoar.

Kennett, Solomon and Rebecca W. Hudson, Mar. 30, 1836. Sur. Edmond Hudson.

Kennett, Zachariah and Frances Ferguson, Mar. 2, 1830. Sur. Jeremiah Ferguson. 132.

Kennon, Henry and Nancy Echols, Dec. 31, 1845. Sur. Robt. A. Scott. 14.

Kesler, Andrew and Margaret Housman, Mar. 6, 1824. Sur. Peter Housman.

Kesler, Anthony, s. Stephen and Susannah, and Elizabeth H. Forbes, dau. Thomas and Elizabeth, Nov. 17, 1853. 18.

Kesler, David and Martha F. Cabaniss, dau. Clarissa, Jan. 6, 1843. Sur. Courtland Cabaniss.

Kesler, Elias and Elizabeth Sink, Feb. 3, 1845. Sur. Henry Sink. 18.

Kesler, Henry and Elizabeth Howsman, Jan. 14, 1818. Sur. Peter Howsman.

Kessler, Jacob and Hannah Flora, Mar. 3, 1812. 130.

Kesler, Jacob and Elizabeth T. Robertson, dau. Richard, Aug. 12, 1839. Sur. Wm. English.

Kesler, Jonathan and Elizabeth Wray, dau. Adam, Jan. 8, 1844. Sur. Jabez Wray. 18.

Kesler, Lodwick and Mary Boon, dau. Jacob, Aug. 1, 1789. Sur. Jacob Mullendon. 52.

Kesler, Peter and Lydia Montgomery, May 8, 1849. Sur. Joel Montgomery. 11.

Kesler, Peter and Eve Barnhart, dau. Francis, Oct. 23, 1843. Sur. John Barnhart. 18.

Kesler, Samuel and Sarah Goode, Sept. 6, 1825. Sur. Abraham Goode.

Kesler, Stephen and Susannah Barnhart, Oct. 14, 1816. 130.

Kesler, Stephen and Sophia Sink, Nov. 19, 1851. 11.

Keys, Bolling and Theresa T. Wysong, dau. Benj. and Catherine, Apr. 16, 1834. Sur. Hullum Scott.

Keys, Floyd B. and Carolina McMelon, Nov. 2, 1858.

Keys, James and Anney Bowles, dau. Geo., Sept. 19, 1810. Sur.
Reuben Bowles. 122.
Keys, James and Polly Smith, Apr. 24, 1829. Sur. John Kemp.
132.
Keys, John and Phebe Akers, Sept. 12, 1806. Sur. Nathaniel
Akers. 130.
Keys, (or Keep) Mathew, Jr. and Lucy Bowles, Jan. 19, 1806.
Sur. Geo. Bowles, Jr. 130.
Keys, Maxcy and Polly Agee, June 4, 1810. Sur. Jesse Agee.
Keys, Thos. and Ester Brammer, dau. John, Nov. 17, 1802.
Sur. John Brammer. 122.
Keys, Worley and Susannah Akers. Sept. 3, 1804. Sur. Wm.
Akers. 122.
Kezee, Geo. and Nancy Hail, Dec. 18, 1810. Sur. James F.
Hail. 8.
Kidd, Benj., s. Jane, and America Manning, dau. Charity, July
26, 1850. Sur. Lorenzo D. Brock. 80.
Kidd, Geo. and Lidia Chiles, Apr. 17, 1805. Sur. David Hunt.
King, Alexander and Nancy Payne, dau. Mary, Aug. 7, 1811.
Sur. Wm. McCormack.
King, Anthony and Peggy Wright, Apr. 21, 1831. Sur. James
G. Wright. 48.
King, Columbus and Sally L. Stockton, dau. Peter C., Dec. 27,
1837. Sur. Jeffery Woody. 132.
King, Geo. C. and Exony Prillaman, Jan. 14, 1850. Sur. Geo.
Prillaman. 1.
King, Hiram and Elizabeth Barrett, Dec. 6, 1814. Sur. Carre
Pyrtle.
King, Jacob and Polly Mills, dau. Arthur, Mar. 5, 1838. Sur.
Cornelius Mills.
King, Moses and Mary Pugh, Nov. 5, 1810. Sur. John Shivley.
112.
King, Samuel and Mary Richardson, dau. Frances and Stanhope,
Sept. 29, 1790. Sur. Avery King. 52.
King, Samuel and Nancy McLand, dau. Daniel, Oct. 16, 1816.
130.
King, Solomon and Elizabeth Turner, Sept. 6, 1824. Sur. Geo.
Turner.

King, Stephen and Betsey E. McComach, Sept. 18, 1848. Sur. Peter McCormack. 68.

King, Thos. and Nancy Witcher, g. Vincent Witcher, Sept. 27, 1830. Sur. Sterling Cooper, Jr.

King, Thos. B. and Nancy Cook, Oct. 30, 1807. Sur. Benjamin Cook.

King, Thos. and Christina Stockton, Nov. 7, 1803. Sur. Richard Stockton.

King, Wm. and Liddia Edwards, dau. Isham, Mar. 22, 1803. Sur. Abraham Harper.

King, Wm. L. and Eliza W. Stockton, dau. Mary Meredith, Oct. 16, 1838. Sur. Herbert Cooper.

Kingery, Abraham and Catherine Stump, dau. Thos. Stump, Aug. 12, 1841. Sur. Geo. Abshire. 18.

Kingery, Albert and Usley Rite, dau. Jane and Burnice Arthur, sfr., Mar. 16, 1840.

Kingery, Anderson and Charlotte Eleanor Knight, Aug. 16, 1845. Sur. Rhoda H. Monday. 18.

Kingery, Christian and Jinney Hudson, dau. Abraham Abshire, Nov. 9, 1805. Sur. Philemon Smith. 130.

Kingery, Fleming, s. Thos. and Elizabeth, and Martha Ann Jones, dau. Abraham and Eliza, Dec. 22, 1833.

Kingery, Henry and Polly Miret, Mar. 31, 1812. 130.

Kingery, Hiram and Nancy McIlhaney, Nov. 22, 1832. Sur. John A. Smith. 48.

Kingery, Jacob and Leah Kelley, dau. Wm. and Rachael, Jan. 7, 1799. Sur. John Vincent (or Vinson). 21.

Kingery, Jacob and Barbary Lybrook, dau. Philip, Feb. 2, 1801. Sur. Abraham Miller. 21.

Kingery, James (or Joseph) and Caty Kelly, June 27, 1796. Sur. Wm. Kelly.

Kingery, Joseph and Eva Ritter, Aug. 12, 1794. Sur. Jacob Miller. 89.

Kingery, John and Anny Richardson, dau. Caty, May 15, 1800. Sur. Thos. Helm.

Kingery, Peter and Sarah Davis, dau. Joseph, Dec. 20, 1800. Sur. Absalom Pollson. 66.

Kingery, Peter and Caty Abshire, Dec. 24, 1806. Sur. Abraham Abshire. 117.

Kingery, Samuel and Sally Hickman, dau. Barbara, Apr. 4, 1803. Sur. Jacob Hickman. 122.
Kingery, Sebert and Mary A. Brammer, dau. Sarah, Mar. 1, 1841. Sur. Nicholas Cassel. 68.
Kingery, Thos. and Sarah Gearhart, dau. Leonard and Sarah, Sept. 30, 1813. Sur. Hiram Gearhart. 130.
Kingery, Thos. J. and Ann Eliza Jane Dickinson, Apr. 6, 1852. 141.
Kingery, Tobias and Charlotte Dodd, May 26, 1832. Sur. Wm. Dodd. 48.
Kinsey, Abraham and Charlotte Showalter, dau. John, Nov. 16, 1839. Sur. Randolph Showalter.
Kinsey, Cornelius and Mariah Hill, dau. John, Mar. 20, 1838. Sur. James Harper.
Kinsey, David and Elizabeth Vinson, Oct. 1, 1811. Sur. Nathaniel Mitchell. 130.
Kinsey, Edmond and Martha Wade, Feb. 8, 1806. Sur. Castleton Wade. 122.
Kinsey, Geo. W. and Frances Akers, dau. James, Sept. 30, 1840. Sur. David S. Webster.
Kinsey, John and Elizabeth Mullendore, Feb. 6, 1804. Sur. Jacob Mullendore.
Kinsey, John and Barbara Hickman, dau. Barbara, Sept. 3, 1804. Sur. Jacob Hickman.
Kinsey, John and Catherine Gossett, Dec. 2, 1845. Sur. David Kinsey. 18.
Kinsey, John and Sophia Wilkinson, dau. John and Lucy, Oct. 6, 1817. Sur. Thomas Cunningham.
Kinsey, John H. and Rebecca N. Bowman, Sept. 19, 1849. Sur. Daniel Bowman. 18.
Kinzie, (or Kingery), Daniel and Elizabeth Perry, May 9, 1795. Sur. Geo. Perry.
Kinzie, Jacob and Elizabeth Hartzell, Sept. 11, 1798. Sur. Philip Hartzell.
Kirby, (Kerby) Geo. and Eleanor Jamison, dau. Hannah and Thos., Oct. 10, 1795. Sur. Benj. Potter.
Kirby, John and Anna Dalton, dau. James and Elizabeth, Mar. 1, 1790. Sur. Thos. Townsend. 37.

Kirby, Joel and Mary Brammer, dau. John, June 4, 1804. Sur. Noah Brammer
Kirby, Samuel and Mary Spangler, dau. Mary, Mar. 12, 1788. Sur. Bartlett Wade.
Kirks, Wm. and Mary Horsley, Feb. 22, 1837. Sur. Stephen Martin. 3.
Kitchin, John W. and Nancy Feazel, dau. Joseph, Jan. 4, 1836. Sur. Aaron Feazel.
Kitterman, John and Sally Byrd, Sept. 4, 1815. Sur. James Bird.
Kitterman, Peter and Mary Kitterman, June 10, 1809. Sur. Henry Kitterman.
Knight, John and Jane Ferguson, Sept. 6, 1802. Sur. Isham Ferguson. 106.
Knowles, John and Susannah Reel, Feb. 23, 1791. Sur. Matthew Knowles. 115.
Knowles, Matthew and Jane Smith, dau. Elizabeth, Mar. 27, 1792. Sur. Joseph Smith. 52.
Knowles, Matten and Sarah Smith, Sept. 29, 1805. 122.
Krantz, David and Lucy Starkey, dau. Austin, Dec. 13, 1847. Sur. Reed Dillion. 18.
Kropff, Geo. H. and Mary E. Martin, Mar. 8, 1848. Sur. Pleasant M. Peltee.
Kropff, Henry and Nancy Glasspy, July 14, 1832. Sur. Jeremiah Glaspy.
Kymes, Abraham and Mary Hare, Nov. 9, 1804. Sur. Abraham Custard and Valentine Kymes.
Lackey, Wm. and Martha Turner, Sept. 11, 1835. Sur. Josiah Turner. 129.
Lacy, John and Jane Choice, Oct. 4, 1824. Sur. Armistead Gorman.
Lacy, John and Sally Brown, July 20, 1799. Sur. John Napier.
Lacy, Johnson W. and Sarah Belcher, Dec. 22, 1835. Sur. Francis Belcher.
Lacy, Thos. and Almira F. Booth, dau. Richard, Dec. 2, 1839. 5.
Lacy, Wm. L. and Clarkey Belcher, dau. Francis, Dec. 12, 1836. Sur. Chas. H. Lacy.
Laguer, Cornelius and Polly Bishop, Jan. 12, 1821. Sur. Chas. Bishop.

Lamb, Josiah and Susannah Blackburn, Mar. 22, 1831. Sur. Hutson Akers.
Lamb, Josiah and Elizabeth Barns, Mar. 7, 1832. Sur. Peyton Stanley.
Lamberth, Clayton and Adeline Cooper, dau. Lidia, Jan. 3, 1846. Sur. John McVey. 19.
Lamberth, Edward and Sarah Akers, Jan. 3, 1823. Sur. Daniel Akers. 130.
Lambert, Miles and Naomi Loving, Nov. 27, 1822. Sur. Christopher Loving.
Lancaster, John and Ellen Greer, Dec. 15, 1841. Sur. James Greer. 68.
Landes, Abraham and Polly Hickman (Hockman), Nov. 16, 1803. Sur. Daniel Nofsinger.
Landes, David and Betsy Pecklesimer, dau. Jacob, May 31, 1800. Sur. Henry Landis.
Landess, Thos. and Polly Martin, May 16, 1821. Sur. Suttrell Martin. 130.
Lane, Gilman and Mimi Martin, June 13, 1811. Sur. Joel Shrewsbury.
Lang, Abel and Margaret M. Woods, June 11, 1840. Sur. Reuben Tinsley. 132.
Lang, (Long), James and Priscilla Lanfield, dau. Moses, May 12, 1790. Sur. Daniel Chandler. 37.
Langhorne, Maurice, Jr. and Elizabeth S. Cabel, Aug. 28, 1847. Sur. Moses G. Carper. 36.
Lansdown, Johnson and Sally Meador, dau. Joseph, Feb. 7, 1825. Sur. Christopher Meador.
Laprade, Andrew and Sally Sink, Nov. 11, 1816. Sur. Henry Sink. 130.
Laprade, Benj. and Nancy Horseley, dau. Wm., Dec. 29, 1823. Sur. Jack Zink. 48.
Laprade, Benj. and Mary Altick, Aug. 7, 1848. Sur. Christopher Altick. 18.
Laprad, Ishmael C. and Sally Palmer, Mar. 16, 1853. 80.
Laprade, James and Rosina M. Ramsey, dau. Theoderick A., Oct. 23, 1849. Sur. Jas. Shorter.
Laprade, Wm. and Harriet W. Boatwright, Dec. 22, 1834. Sur. Benj. Hill.

Laprade, Wm. W. and Catherine Sink, dau. Polly, Jan. 7, 1850. Sur. Henry Sink. 11.
Laprade, Wm. and Nancy C. Dunman, Jan. 9, 1834.
Lark, Dennis and Sally Lovell, Oct. 21, 1802. Sur. Markham Lovel.
Lasly, David L. and Sarah Murphy, Nov. 24, 1830. Sur. Geo. McVey.
Laswell, Peters and Abagail Sherwood, dau. Robt., Apr. 3, 1789. Sur. Thos. Sherwood and Thos. Prunty.
Lavinder, Albert C. and Mary Dudley, Nov. 3, 1845. Sur. Levi Dudley. 14.
Lavinder, Geo. and Sarah Ann Stegall, Jan. 1851. 132.
Lavinder, Giles O. and Permella Bowles, July 1852. 132.
Lavinder, James and Thirza King, dau. Stephen, Dec. 31 ,1822. Sur. Solomon King. 130.
Lavinder, John, Jr. and Nancy Beheler, Dec. 19, 1821. Sur. Geo. Beheler.
Lavinder, John and Mary Dunn, dau. Nancy Hodges, Oct. 10, 1831. Sur. Jacob Fishburn. 46.
Lavinder, John, Sr. and Catherine S. Lesseuer, July 1, 1844. Sur. Richard M. Taliaferro. 132.
Lavinder, John A. and Juliana Dudley, Feb. 2, 1847. Sur. Robt. A. Scott.
Lavinder, Joseph and Nancy Edmondson, Sept. 2, 1822. Sur. Wm. Carmichael. 130.
Lavinder, Joseph and Cathren Nafe, Mar. 30, 1837. 18.
Lavinder, Robt. R. and Emily C. Noble, Dec. 31, 1858.
Lavinder, Robt. and Milly Willis, Sept. 23, 1795. Sur. John Highly. 52.
Lavinder, Robt. and Nancy Willis, Feb. 27, 1794. Sur. Randolph Hall.
Lavinder, Shelton and Elizabeth Ashinherst, Nov. 28, 1816. Sur. Chas. Waid.
Lavinder, Thornton and Jane Grimes, Mar. 10, 1816. Sur. John Saul. 130.
Lavinder, Thos. and Elizabeth Naff, May 4, 1835. Sur. David Naff. 68.
Lavinder, Thos. and Margaret Kely, May 28, 1795. 52.

Lavinder, Wm., Jr. and Lucinda Hodges, Dec. 2, 1850. Sur. David Hodges. 80.
Lavinder, Wm. and Rachael Parsel, Sept. 6, 1819. Sur. John Woody.
Law, Adam and Elizabeth Haynes, dau. Stephen, Dec. 17, 1835. Sur. Stephen P. Haynes. 3.
Law, Amos B. and Julia A. Ashworth, dau. Lucy, Sept. 4, 1847. Sur. Robt. Smith. 137.
Law, Booker and Nancy C. Dunman, Jan. 9, 1834. Sur. James W. Dunmon.
Law, Burnet and Betsey Wood, 1789. 37.
Law, Burwell, Jr. and Nancy Law, Jan. 30, 1817. Sur. Wm. W. Holland. 7.
Law, Burwell and Elizabeth Wood, Dec. 24, 1788. Sur. Stephen Wood.
Law, Burwell, Jr. and Lucy Smith, Apr. 1, 1811. Sur. Henry Smith.
Law, Coleman and Susannah Sutherland, Apr. 3, 1806. Sur. Samuel Sutherland. 8.
Law, Daniel and Brildy (or Biddy) Tyree, May 16, 1791. Sur. Wm. Law.
Law, David and Susannah Edmunds, Dec. 20, 1804. Sur. Wm. Edmunds.
Law, Henry David and Nancy Bell, dau. Frances, Mar. 1, 1802. Sur. Burwell Law.
Law, Henry and Sally Brizendine, Nov. 13, 1807. Sur. Leroy Law.
Law, Henry and Sarah W. Law, dau. Jesse, Dec. 29, 1834. Sur. Peter Law. 3.
Law, Henry and Frances Bell, dau. Fanny, May 7, 1810. Sur. Robt. Hodges. 8.
Law, James A. and Julia A. Dudley, Jan. 21, 1845. Sur. Cluffs M. Brooks.
Law, Jesse and Sally Hopkins, Oct. 8, 1805. Sur. Benj. Hopkins. 8.
Law, John and Sarah Maxey, dau. Jeremiah, Sept. 5, 1796. Sur. Stephen Maxey.
Law, John and Mary Ferguson, Apr. 2, 1827. Sur. Thos. Ferguson. 48.

Law, John and Mary Phillips, Nov. 4, 1844. Sur. Isaac D. Brooks.
Law, Marshall P. and Lucy J. Gilbert, Aug. 7, 1848. Sur. Samuel Gilbert. 80.
Law, Nathaniel and Sarah Campbell, Jan. 5, 1829. Sur. Peter Campbell.
Law, Ransom and Nancy Ashworth, Aug. 3, 1836. Sur. Robt. Arrington.
Law, Robin and Lucy Hopkins, Apr. 28, 1808. Sur. Jesse Law. 8.
Law, Robt. and Antheney L. Dunman, dau. Any, Oct. 3, 1842. Sur. James W. Dunman.
Law, Samuel and Elizabeth Smith, Jan. 12, 1808. Sur. Burwell Law. 8.
Law, Samuel T. and Nancy E. English, dau. John, Dec. 26, 1843. Sur. Wiley Chitwood.
Law, Samuel A. B. and Charlotte Pugh, July 16, 1846. Sur. Thos. H. Bernard. 18.
Law, Samuel and Lucinda Hodges Sept. 19, 1852. 11.
Law, Stephen G. and Martha A. Bennett, dau. Abner, Oct. 7, 1848. Sur. Geo. A. Bennett.
Law, Stephen and Dianah H. Crump, dau. Geo., May 1, 1826. Sur. Wm. Crump. 48.
Law, Thos. and Ann E. Gill, dau. Dorothy, Nov. 6, 1837. Sur. Chas. A. Gill. 140.
Law, Thos. and Mary Law, dau. John, Sr., Feb. 25, 1809. Sur. Henry Law.
Law, Thos. and Martha Gilbert, Apr. 3, 1815. Sur. Michael Gilbert.
Law, Wm. and Letty Cockran, dau. Susannah, Jan. 7, 1799. Sur. Wm. Smith. 141.
Law, Wm. H. and Margaret Mitchel, dau. James, July 1, 1841. Sur. Daniel Mitchell. 18.
Law, (Lane) Winston S. and Polly Ferguson, g. Jesse Chandler, July 27, 1824. Sur. Moses Chandler. 130.
Law, Wyatt and Hannah Law, dau. John, May 20, 1808. Sur. Cheadle Law. 8.
Lawrence, Samuel and Rebecca Campbell, dau. Lucy, Nov. 25, 1844. Sur. Peter Campbell.

Layman, Daniel and Rhoda Lumsden, Nov. 10, 1821. Sur. Dudley Lumsden. 49.

Layman, (or Lehman) Daniel and Lydie Barnhart, Sept. 3, 1849. Sur. Jonathan Barnhart. 18.

Layman, Peter and Magdaline Peters, Oct. 28, 1852. Sur. John Bowman.

Lazenby, Rezer and Polly Booth, May 6, 1822. Sur. Benj. Booth.

Lazenby, Robt., Jr., s. Robt., Sr., and Nancy Osborne, Apr. 14, 1807. Sur. Thos. Osborne. 130.

Leamon (or Seamon), John and Fanny Angle, Feb. 3, 1817. Sur. Daniel Angle. 98.

Lebart (or Libert), Chas. and Catherine Lemon, Mar. 2, 1789. Sur. Daniel Spangler. 52.

Lee, Braxton and Elizabeth Hatcher, dau. Archibald, Feb. 1, 1790. Sur. Joseph Price. 52.

Lee, Chas. C. and Louisa W. Finney, dau. Peter, Oct. 13, 1835. Sur. James Taylor. 35.

Lee, David and Susannah Barber, Oct. 9, 1792. Sur. Wm. Boid (Boyd).

Lee, John and Rachael Richards, Jan. 16, 1802. Sur. Benj. Richards.

Lee, Samuel E. and Nancy Glass, July 29, 1846. Sur. Samuel A. Kirks. 138.

Lee, Wm. and Sarah Coger, Dec. 4, 1797. Sur. Joseph Wier. 89.

Lee, Wm. and Sarah John, dau. Jehu, Jan. 13, 1801. Sur. Jehu John. 72.

Leffew, Anderson and Elizabeth Gusler, Jan. 28, 1850. Sur. Thos. Leffew. 22.

Leffew, Elias and Rebecca Quigley, dau. Thos. and Sarah, June 28, 1802. Sur. Joseph Quigley. 72.

Leffew (or Lefue), Elijah and Adelphia Webb, Dec. 7, 1807. Sur. Andrew Rogers. 8.

Leffew, John and Frances McGraw, Oct. 9, 1834. Sur. John McGraw.

Leffew, Thos. and Sarah Ann Prewitt, Oct. 26, 1847. Sur. Geo. Booth. 20.

Leffew, Wesley and Nancy E. Wray, dau. Nancy, Aug. 17, 1847. Sur. John W. Ray.

Leftwich, James M. and Maranda E. Callaway, dau. James, Sept. 16, 1847. Sur. Moses G. Carper.
Leftwich, Joel and Latitia Compton, Feb. 12, 1846. Sur. Micajah Cumpton. 68.
Leftwich, Joel and Frances Evans, Dec. 29, 1847.
Leftwich, Uriah and Nancy Williamson, May 14, 1806. Sur. Henry Williamson. 130.
Leftwich, Wm. and Catherine B. Greer, Feb. 27, 1839. 48.
Leftwich, Wm. B. and Catherine Newbill, May 18, 1831. Sur. Tyree G. Newbill.
Leftwich, Wm. W. and Serena C. Calloway, Apr. 18, 1848. Sur. James Callaway. 134.
Leftwich, Wm. B. and Sarah Smith, dau. Reuben, Oct. 19, 1824. Sur. John Smith.
Lehman, Daniel and Frances Rudy, Feb. 5, 1791. Sur. Daniel Rudy. 52.
Lemon, Benj. and Frances Walker, Apr. 19, 1824. Sur. Joel Young. 130.
Lemon, Creed, s. Benj. Lemon, and Marcia Menefee, Nov. 4, 1843. Sur. Geo. Menifee, Jr. 58.
Lemon, Isaac and Vina Richardson, May 1, 1786. Sur. David Jones.
Lemon, Sparrel and Elizabeth Deloss Helms, June 3, 1850. Sur. Thos. Helm. 132.
Lemon, Wm. and Margaret Williams, Nov. 14, 1807. Sur. Benj. Richards, Jr. 122.
Lesseuer, Grandison B. and Econey Ingram, Sept. 26, 1831. Sur. Alexander Ingram. 61.
Lesseuer, Moses and Susannah Brock, dau. Geo., July 14, 1792. Sur. Amos Richardson.
Lester, Wm. and Frances Steagall, dau. Allen, Nov. 20, 1833. Sur. Allan Steagall.
Lewis, Andrew and Jenny Bozwell, Dec. 7, 1812. Sur. Wm. Bozwell. 8.
Lewis, Edward and Polly Wright, dau. Tabitha and Winfield, Dec. 25, 1792. Sur. Jesse Burns.
Lewis, Francis and Polly Hudson, Nov. 26, 1788.
Lewis, Jesse and Rodey Bell, dau. John, Sept. 24, 1790. Sur. Sherod Bybee. 52.

Lewis, Joseph and Sarah Bell, dau. John and Sarah, May 7, 1787. Sur. Isaac Lemon. 66.
Lewis, Joseph and Nancy Griffith, dau. Hannah and Wm., Mar. 20, 1792. 52.
Lianberry, Henry and Mary Landes, 1794. 89.
Light, James and Hannah Hatherway (Hathaway), dau. Leonard and Susannah, Oct. 3, 1791. Sur. Edward Lewis.
Likens, David and Jemima Willis, dau. Isiah, Dec. 22, 1797. Sur. Joseph Willis.
Likens, Wm., s. Margaret, and Margaret Ritter, dau. Susannah, Jan. 13, 1790. Sur. Marcus Likens. 52.
Lindsay, Edward and Elizabeth Farmer, Mar. 5, 1821. Sur. Pleasant Farmer. 130.
Lindsay, James and Nancy Bryant, Dec. 10, 1840. 132.
Lindsey, Jeremiah and Nancy Mills, dau. Wm., Nov. 14, 1817. 130.
Lindsey, John and Polly Gwin, Sept. 2, 1822. Sur. Joel Chitwood. 130.
Lindsey, John M. and Nancy W. Law, dau. Burwell, Oct. 27, 1832. Sur. Thos Law. 3.
Lindsey, Wm. and Martha Vinson, Jan. 2, 1807. Sur. Chas. Vinson. 130.
Linton, Peyton and Jinny Ellison, Mar. 5, 1827. Sur. Payton. Ellison. 61.
Linza, Wm. and Nancy Highland, 1811. 130.
Lipscomb, Richard and Sarah F. Woods, Aug. 20, 1849. 18.
Little, David and Sarah Hale, Feb. 3, 1789. 52.
Livesay, Sparrell, Jr. and Mary Huff, dau. Isaac, Mar. 21, 1838. Sur. Lewis M. Livesay. 134.
Loaden, James and Susannah Gipson, Sept. 15, 1795. Sur. Wm. Gipson. 52.
Lockard, David and Mary H. Mays, May 26, 1853. 18.
Loe (or Law), John and Sally Adney, Feb. 22, 1810. 122.
Long, Edward and Milly Boulton, dau. Thomas and Fennyah, Sept. 26, 1803. Sur. John Boulton.
Long, Isaac and Nancy Boulton, dau. Thomas, Nov. 18, 1799. Sur. Thos. Boulton.

Lookado, Jackson and Frances Evans, Dec. 29, 1847. Sur. Lorenzo D. Brock.
Lookado, Jackson and Nancy Carter, Feb. 16, 1841. Sur. Benj. Pinckard. 39.
Lookade, J. A. and Martha Matherlin, Oct. 25, 1845. Sur. Elias Fleeman. 80.
Love, Henry and Caty Dent, Mar. 26, 1814. Sur. Walter Dent, Jr.
Love, James, s. Philip Love, and Polly May, dau. Stephen, Dec. 23, 1787. Sur. Stephen Mays.
Love, Josiah and Amiga Bowles, Mar. 2, 1840. Sur. Jeremiah Bowles. 132.
Love, Wm. and Margaret Ann Oxley, Feb. 1852. 132.
Lovell, Grover and Rainy Mighe, Jan. 1851. 132.
Lovell, Jesse and Betsy Worley, dau. Daniel, Dec. 30, 1809. Sur. Wm. Highley.
Lovell, John and Polly Ashinherst Parberry, June 15, 1816. Sur. James Parberry.
Lovell (Sowel), Pleasant A. and Caty Stone, May 15, 1798. Sur. Patrick Stone. 21.
Loven, Henry and Sallie Aday, Nov. 8, 1786. Sur. Walter Aday.
Lowe, James and Sarah Zeigler, dau. Robt. Napier, Aug. 12, 1794. Sur. Robt. Napier. 141.
Loyd, John and Ann Roberts, Nov. 6, 1805. Sur. Micajah Stone.
Loyd, John and Mary Miller, Nov. 4, 1805. Sur. Moses Greer, Jr. 130.
Lloyd, Robt. and Peggy Standley, Apr. 11, 1804. Sur. John Loyd.
Luke, John and Polly Hickerson, Oct. 26, 1808. Sur. Daniel Hickerson.
Luke, Wm. and Sophia Hill, Dec. 15, 1821. Sur. John Ashinhurst.
Luke, Wm. A. and Harriet Guilliams, Dec. 19, 1848. Sur. John Guilliams. 68.
Lumkin, Robt. W. and Nancy Cunningham, dau. Joseph, Oct. 20, 1821. Sur. Robt. Cunningham.
Lumsden, Chas. and Patty Rives (or Reaves), Mar. 16, 1787. Sur. Jeremiah Lumsden. 66.

Lumsden, Dudley and Sally Chitwood, June 7, 1802. Sur. John Chitwood 106.
Lumsden, Elijah and Rachael Greer, dau. Benj. Feb. 7, 1787. Sur. Jesse Lumsden.
Lumsden, Geo. and Nancy E. Hughes, Feb. 1, 1847. Sur. Elijah Hughes. 18.
Luney, Elisha, s. Judith, and Nancy Burchett, dau. Jane, Feb. 6, 1843. Sur. Nathaniel Oxley. 18.
Luney, Peter and Judith Robertson (Robinson), dau. Thos., Mar. 10, 1786. Sur. Wm. Crump.
Littrell (Lutrell), James and Nancy Helm, Aug. 22, 1814. Sur. Thos. Helms. 130.
Luttrell, John and Sarah Elliott, Nov. 13, 1788. Sur. Moses Crammer. 37.
Luttrell, Richard and Susannah Walker, Sept. 17 1787. 37.
Luttrell, Willis and Sally Via (or Viar), Aug. 20, 1810, Sur. James Viar. 8.
Lynch, Christopher and Elizabeth Custer, dau. Henry, May 3, 1838. Sur. James Lynch.
Lynch, Henry and Mary Ann Johnson, dau. Nathan, Mar. 12, 1849. Sur. Nathaniel Johnson.
Lynch, James and Mary Custer, Mar. 12, 1838. Sur. Henry Custer, Jr.
Lynch, John and Frances Thurmond, Nov. 24, 1851. 11.
Lyon, Daniel and Lucy Dillion, dau. Squire, Oct. 9, 1829. Sur. Asa Wood.
Lyon, Elisha and Patsey Ward, Nov. 17, 1814. Sur. John Ashworth.
Lyon, John B. and Polly M. Forbes, dau. John, Jan. 1, 1826. Sur. John R. Forbes.
Lyon, John and Lydia Arrington, dau. Samuel, Nov. 25, 1800. Sur. Chas. Arrington. 21.
Lyon, Peter and Elizabeth Bernard, Apr. 16, 1808. Sur. Peter Bernard. 8.
Lyon, Wm. and Celia Brown, dau. Jinnion, Aug 11, 1795. Sur. Joseph Wright. 106.
Lyon, Wm. and Sarah Hatcher, Oct. 31, 1829. Sur. Roddy McConnell. 48.

Mackenhimer, Jacob and Patience Glass, dau. John, Mar. 2, 1829. Sur. Dudley Glass. 3.
Maddox, Andrew and Ester Martin, Mar. 2, 1812. Sur. John Martin.
Maddox, Wilson and Elizabeth Richards, dau. Edwards, Apr. 11, 1796. Sur. Wateman Richards. 93.
Magers, Roland and Elizabeth Stanley, Oct. 29, 1795. 41.
Mannin, Franklin and Charity Carter, Mar. 5, 1832. Sur. Dabney Carter.
Manning, Henry and Seny Arrington, Oct. 18, 1815. 122.
Manning, John and Sally More, July 2, 1809. 122.
Manning, Meredith and Catherine Burnett, dau. Chas., Mar. 7, 1796, Sur. Moses Brock. 120.
Manning, Samuel and Patsy Brock, dau. Lucy and Joshua, Mar. 19, 1804. Sur. John Mannin and Tarlton Brock.
Manning, Samuel and Nancy Edmunds, Mar. 13, 1823. Sur. Wm. Hood.
Manning, Samuel and Elizabeth Hale, dau. Thos., Mar. 7, 1835. Sur. John Manning. 60
Manor, Wm. and Elizabeth Clardy, dau. Archibald, Dec. 7, 1824. Sur. John Clay. 48.
Maple, John Van and Susannah Pergram, Jan. 18, 1814.
Marcum, Barnett and Lucy Belcher, dau. Isham, June 6, 1791. Sur. John Tyree.
Marcum, Beverly and Elizabeth Ward, dau. Betsey and Daniel, Oct. 8, 1792. Sur. Daniel Perdue.
Marcum, James and Elender Terry, Dec. 1, 1814. 8.
Marcum, John and Dicey Greer, Dec. 19, 1789. Sur. Thos. Demoss. 37.
Marcum, Licley and Sally Keen, 1796. 21.
Marrs, Benj. and Margaret Saunders, dau. Samuel and Catherine, Feb. 24, 1804. Sur. Abraham Marrs.
Marrs, Geo. and Elizabeth Beverly, Feb. 23, 1808. Sur. Beverly Herod. 117.
Marrs, Geo. and Charity Hickman, Mar. 3, 1828. Sur. Aaron Marrs. 48.
Marrs, Hercules and Lydia Cuff, dau. Wm. and Rachael, Mar. 1, 1828. 48.

Marrs, Hercules and Betty Chavers, Feb. 11, 1806. Sur. Jesse Chavers.
Marrs, Samuel and Anna Marrs, dau. George, Sr. and Elizabeth, Apr. 18, 1827. Sur. Abraham Marrs.
Marshall, Lewis and Martha Jamison, Jan. 1, 1798. Sur. Wm. Jameson.
Marshall, Lewis R. and Mary Ann Nance, gdau. Hughey O'Neil, Sept. 2, 1828. Sur. Nathaniel Clart. 26.
Marshall, Robt. and Susannah Dodd, dau. Sally, Dec. 26, 1800. Sur. Elijah Poteet. 21.
Martin, Abraham and Ann Beckner, Feb. 22, 1823. Sur. Lewis Oyler. 49.
Martin, Abraham and Ann Beckner, Oct. 7, 1822. Sur. Mathias Croak.
Martin, Abraham and Sally Real, Aug. 10, 1809. 44.
Martin, Absalom and Senah Henderson, May 14, 1794. Sur. Daniel Barnhart. 52.
Martin, Andrew and Tempe Meador, dau. Tempey, Dec. 24, 1821. Sur. Burwell Meador.
Martin, Benj. and Judith Walker, Mar. 17, 1792. Sur. Edward Beard. 131.
Martin, Drury and Sally Ramsey, Nov. 6, 1813.
Martin, Geo. and Judith Willis, dau. Davis, Oct. 8, 1804. Sur. John Napier.
Martin, Hezekiah and Sally (or Sarah) Allen, dau. Wm., June 16, 1846. Sur. David Allen. 68.
Martin, Hugh and Jane Craig, Mar. 6, 1815. Sur. David Craig. 71.
Martin, James Sr. and Mary McGhee, Aug. 22, 1805. Sur. Hugh Martin.
Martin, James and Rebecca Percy, dau. James, Oct. 18, 1811. Sur. John Percy.
Martin, James and Frances Johnson, dau. John, Mar. 6, 1829. Sur. Baley Johnson.
Martin, James L. and Sarah Lacy, dau. John, Aug. 29, 1833. Sur. Thos. Lacy.
Martin, James and Polly Starkey, Dec. 2, 1837. Sur. Austin Starkey.

Martin, James and Jane Miles, Feb. 12, 1839. Sur. Moses G. Carper. 132.
Martin, James and Margaret Bowman, Dec. 10, 1794. Sur. John Watson. 20.
Martin, James and Doria Mullins, June 6, 1803. Sur. Thos. Roberts. 72.
Martin, James and Agnes Saunders, dau. Robin, Feb. 4, 1837. Sur. Peter Via. 60.
Martin, Jesse and Betsy Ramsey, Feb. 3, 1806.
Martin, Jesse and Jean Hunter, Sept. 19, 1808. Sur. John Hunter.
Martin, John and Sally Huston, dau. Wm., May 30, 1803. Sur. John Huston.
Martin, John R. and Elizabeth Webb, Apr. 1, 1850. Sur. Wm. H. Turner.
Martin, John and Meley Meadow, Jan. 13, 1795. Sur. Jesse Fears. 41.
Martin, John and Polly Helms, dau. Thos., Sept. 27, 1829. Sur Fleming Helms. 26.
Martin, John R. and Susan L. Wingfield, Aug. 5, 1840. Sur. Christopher Wingfield.
Martin, John D. and Eliza Doran, Sept. 14, 1848. Sur. Jubal A. Doran. 134.
Martin, John R. and Elizabeth M. Wade, dau. John, July 2, 1849. Sur. Moses G. Carper. 132.
Martin, Jonathan and Eliza J. Wright, Mar. 28, 1842. Sur. Joseph Wright.
Martin, Jordan and Milley Swanson, dau. Gabriel, July 23, 1830. Sur. Fleming Forbes. 18.
Martin, Joseph and Anne Langdon, dau. John, Sept. 12, 1786. Sur. Moses Greer.
Martin, Joshua and Mary Runels, Apr. 9, 1799. 89.
Martin, Joshua W. and Martha J. Ingram, Aug. 16, 1858.
Martin, Levi and Nancy Maynor, dau. John and Ruthy Briant, Feb. 8, 1808. Sur. Daniel Prillaman. 122.
Martin, Littrell and Anne Pelter, May 11, 1822. Sur. John Pelter.
Martin, Littrell and Lucy Young, dau. James, Feb. 11, 1829. Sur. Stephen Mullins. 129.

Martin, Mathew B. and Minerva Hopkins, Oct. 7, 1858.

Martin, Robt. and Susannah Robinson, dau. Wm., Dec. 16, 1799. Sur. Wm. Bolles.

Martin, Robt. and Susannah Ray, Feb. 13, 1798. Sur. Richard Stanley.

Martin, Samuel H. and Jane Cooper, dau. Langston, Mar. 18, 1830. Sur. Wm. Cooper.

Martin, Samuel H. and Jane Given, Mar. 17, 1830.

Martin, Sebret and Mina Richardson, Oct. 7, 1808. Sur. John Martin.

Martin, Thos. and Susannah Hawkins, Feb. 7, 1825. Sur. Geo. McVey. 130.

Martin, Thos. and Mary Jane Martin, Dec. 22, 1849. Sur. Hugh Martin. 19.

Martin, Wm. and Anny Craig, Jan. 7, 1805. Sur. Thos. Craig.

Martin, Wm. and Nancy Heard, dau. John, Sept. 14, 1818. Sur. James Via. 61.

Martin, Wm. and Sarah Armstrong, dau. Mary, Oct. 1, 1823. Sur. Anderson McCormack. 49.

Martin, Wm. and Sophia Beckner, Jan. 28, 1833. Sur. Samuel Beckner.

Martin, Wm. and Elizabeth Boon, June 5, 1828. 18.

Mason, Abner and Elizabeth Smith, Aug. 2, 1858.

Mason, Charles R. and Martha Brooks, Nov. 11, 1822. Sur. Lewis Mason.

Mason, James B. and Mary F. Boswell, May 7, 1846. Sur. Andrew L. Bozwell. 132.

Mason, John and Julia Ashworth, Dec. 24, 1822. Sur. Michael Gilbert. 49.

Mason, John, s. Nathan, and Polly Bowles, dau. Frances, Dec. 14, 1811.

Mason, John and Nancy Farmer, Aug. 23, 1808. Sur. Mathew Farmer.

Mason, Lewis, Jr., s. John, and Catherine J. Pearson, Feb. 24, 1844. Sur. Peyton Pearson.

Mason, Micajah and Miria Brizendine, Dec. 25, 1832. Sur. John Brizendine. 48.

Mason, Nathan and Sarah M. Dehaven, Nov. 17, 1847. Sur. James Bottom. 104.
Mason, Nathan and Frances Bowles, Oct. 23, 1816. Sur. Jabel Bowles.
Mason, Nathan and Hannah Aden, July 6, 1789. Sur. Swinfield Hill.
Mason, Robt. and Mary Hodges, Dec. 7, 1835. Sur. Abednego Hodges.
Mason, Wm. A. and Jane Mitchell, dau. Floriania, Nov. 21, 1826. Sur. Wm. O. Mitchell.
Massey, Obediah and Lorvinia Holly, dau. James, Feb. 21, 1840. Sur. Joel Holly.
Matthews, Banister and Wilmoth Law, Dec. 23, 1833. Sur. Thos. Law. 48.
Matthews, James A. and Perlina David, dau. Abraham, Dec. 2, 1850. Sur. John W. Ferguson.
Matthews, John and Rachel Edmonds, Sept. 4, 1820. Sur. Lankford Brizendine.
Matthews, Wm. and Martha Gilbert, dau. Samuel, June 7, 1847. Sur. Wyley W. Mathews. 137.
Mathis, Banister and Susan Wiggenton, Feb. ....., 1851. 132.
Mathis, Wyatt and Polly Ann Ashworth, Mar. 3, 1817. Sur. Stephen Ashworth. 7.
Mattox, Chas. W. and Nancy C. Ashworth, dau. Lucy, Dec. 7, 1846. Sur. Spencer L. James.
Mattox, David and Sally Hail, Dec. 1, 1806. Sur. Henry Page White. 8.
Mattox, John and Polly Cockran, Aug. 5, 1816. Sur. Samuel Cockran.
Mattox, John and Fanny Parrott, Sept. 3, 1787. Sur. Joseph Parrott. 37.
Mattox, Michael and Mary Frailey, dau. Frederick, Sept. 19, 1795. Sur. Richard Robertson. 82.
Mattox, Wesley and Jane Craghead, dau. John, Mar. 14, 1814. Sur. John Mattox.
Mattox, Wm. and Catherine Tinnis, dau. Wm., Nov. 1, 1795. Sur. Richard Robertson.
Mavity, David J. and Susannah B. Davis, June 24, 1836. Sur. Thos. Davis. 132.

Mavity, Jesse and Susannah Rigg, Mar. 1, 1819. Sur. Townley Rigg.
Mavity, John and Dorotha Reel, June 25, 1795. 65.
Maxcy, Arthur and Tilitha Russell, Apr. 2, 1821. 130.
Maxcy, Caleb and Martha Williams, Apr. 12, 1853. Sur. Geo. W. Kelly. 68.
Maxey, Edward and Elizabeth Pitner, Oct. 28, 1794. 22.
Maxey, Hail and Dicey Craghead, dau. Dicey, Oct. 25, 1789. Sur. Stephen English.
Maxcy, Isaac and Elizabeth Sowels, July 7, 1832. Sur. Wm. Bowles.
Maxey, Jabez and Betsy Shrewsberry (or Soursberry), dau. Jeremiah, Feb. 4, 1799. Sur. Thos. Shrewsberry.
Maxey, James and Sally Agee (Agnew), Jan. 4, 1796. Sur. Matthew Agee. 37.
Maxey, James B. and Aly Anne Richards, Dec. 14, 1846. Sur. Christopher Richards. 18.
Maxey, Jeremiah and Polly West, dau. Jane, Jan. 10, 1811. Sur. Arthur Mills. 15.
Maxey, John and Sarah Greer, July 21, 1794. Sur. Thos. Demoss.
Maxey, Josiah and Elizabeth Ferguson, dau. Jeremiah, Oct. 10, 1810. Sur. Maxcy Key. 15.
May, Daniel and Jane Ferris, (Faris), dau. Joel, Jan. 21, 1808. Sur. Cheadle Law. 8.
May, Frederick and Susannah Perkins, June 21, 1811. Sur. John Perkins.
Mays, Robt. G. and Ann Eliza Shelton, dau. T. C., Apr. 19, 1841. Sur. Wm. Heard.
Mays, Wm. and Jane Faris, Feb. 4, 1830. Sur. Geo. W. Ferguson.
Mayo, David M. and Anne E. Rives, dau. Joseph, Oct. 22, 1839. Sur. Joseph Rives. 142.
Maynor, Joseph and Mary Standley, July 10, 1823. Sur. Moses Standley.
Maynor, Joseph and Elizabeth Stone, Nov. 9, 1835. Sur. Obediah Turner. 129.
Maynor, Richard Tucker and Nancy Davis, dau. Martha, Jan. 15, 1793. Sur. Jesse Prunty.
Mayvey, James and Martha Richeson, May 20, 1798. 89.

McCallester, Geo. and Agnes Stewart, Aug. 24, 1796. Sur. Wm. Dillenham.
McBride, Chas. and Elizabeth Finney Zeigler, Jan 5, 1818. Sur. Wm. Zeigler.
McBride, James and Martha Ann Bird, dau. Benj., Oct. 7, 1850. Sur. Wm. Oxley. 18.
McBride, Obediah and Eliza Saunders, Dec. 5, 1838. 3.
McCabe, Wm. and Elizabeth A. R. Brown, Nov. 22, 1836. Sur. Pleasant Brown.
McCall, John and Phebe Smith, Jan. 24, 1805. Sur. Wm. McCall.
McCall, John and Julia Anne Jane Holland, June 20, 1849. Sur. John Holland. 18.
McCall, Peter H. and Zilpha Hodges, dau. John and Rebecca, Apr. 10, 1826. Sur. Gabriel Hodges. 48.
McCall, Robt. H. and Elizabeth M. Gilbert, Nov. 5, 1832. Sur. Kemuel C. Gilbert, Jr. 48.
McCall, Wm. and Milly Holland, Nov. 11, 1799. Sur. Peter Holland.
McCall, Wm. S. and Martha Jane Smith, June 25, 1839. Sur. Wiatt Smith. 132.
McCan, Edward and Mary Clawson, June 19, 1793. Sur. Wm. Bernard. 52.
McCarroll, Samuel and Polly Menefee, Dec. 8, 1806. Sur. Geo. Menifee. 130.
McComack, Jabez B. L. and Lydia Green, dau. Peggy, Feb. 8, 1844. Sur. Francis M. Harrison. 18.
McComack, Jeremiah M. and Patsy Basham, Sept. 30, 1817. Sur. Martin Wright. 98.
McConnell, John and Fernley Bernard, (widow of John Barnard who was a son of Peter Bernard, Sr.), Aug. 3, 1803. Sur. John Forbes.
McConnell, Roddy and Lucy Lyon, Oct. 30, 1822. Sur. Wm. Stewart.
McConner, John and Margaret Ruble, dau. Owen, Aug. 17, 1795.
McCormack, Abraham and Judith W. Palmore, Sept. 29, 1825. Sur. John P. Palmore.
McCormack, Anderson and Elizabeth Armstrong, June 15, 1807. Sur. Wm. McCormack and Wm. Bowles.

McCormack (McComack), Andrew J. and Mary Maxcy, dau. Martha, Mar. 10, 1846. Sur. Jas. H. Williams. 134.

McCormack, John W. and Susannah Dowdy, dau. Ezekiel and Jane, Nov. 19, 1823. Sur. James Dowdy.

McCormick, Richard and Mary Roberson, dau. Wm., Dec. 1, 1798. Sur. Wm. Roberson.

McCormick, Wright and Charlotte Payne, May 18, 1819. Sur. Joseph Payne. 98.

McCraw, Alexander and Arreaney Ray, dau. Viney, July 15, 1839. Sur. Wm. Parker.

McCutchen, Samuel and Phoebe Carter, Feb. 25, 1796. Sur. Bailey Carter. 66.

McEvett, Joseph and Catherine Kingery, dau. Abraham Abshire, Feb. 3, 1835. Sur. Thos. J. Abshire. 68.

McFalls, John and Martha Beverly, Feb. 10, 1830. Sur. Geo. Marrs. 48.

McFalls, John and Nancy Shavers, Sept. 5, 1831. Sur. Jesse Shavers. 48.

McGhee, Carroll W. and Mary Virginia Neblett, dau. Wm. S., Mar. 13, 1846. Sur. James M. Neblett. 138.

McGhee, Jesse H. and Mary Pinckard, dau. Robert, Jan. 6, 1848. Sur. Thos. Pinchard. 80.

McGhee, John and Susan Ann C. Frith, Jan. 25, 1847. Sur. Thos. Frith. 132.

McGhee, Nelson and Martha Cooper, Apr. 4, 1814. Sur. Haley Andrews.

McGhee, Nelson and Aley A. Hiett, dau. Elizabeth A., Apr. 1, 1848. Sur. Wm. Menefee. 132.

McGhee, Nelson and Susannah Richards, Oct. 13, 1831. Sur. Pleasant Richards.

McGhee, Robt. and Elizabeth A. Martin, Sept. 28, 1849. Sur. Hugh Martin. 132.

McGhee, Wm. and Frances Ramsey, Feb. 3, 1845. Sur. Thos. Ramsey. 132.

McGrady, Wm. and Milly Slone, Nov. 3, 1820. Sur. Jacob Slone. 130.

McGuffen, Joseph and Mary Ann Turner, July 8, 1837. Sur. Josiah Turner. 129.

McGuffen, Joseph and Eliza Ann Walrond, dau. Conrad, Dec. 3, 1832. 48.

McGuffen, Robt. F. and Sarah Ingram, Mar. 6, 1837. Sur. Alexander Ingram. 130.

McGuire, Elijah and Lucinda Meador, Feb. 9, 1819. Sur. Jehu Meador.

McGuire, Elijah and Sary Robertson, 23 yrs. old, Mar. 7, 1791. Sur. Ephraim Thomas.

McGuire, Joel and Jemima Meador, dau. John, Dec. 14, 1835. Sur. Elijah McGuire. 140.

McGuire, John and Nancy Hambrick, dau. Joseph, Oct. 1, 1803. Sur. James Molly.

McGuire, Jonathan and Sarah Dowdy, dau. Ezekiel and Jean, Mar. 23, 1812. Sur. Jabez Dowdy.

McGuire, Joseph and Nancy Ferguson, Jan. 3, 1830.

McGuire, Robt. and Polly Rucker, Feb. 16, 1829. Sur. Robt. Martin. 140.

McGuire, Shelbert and Sarah Pasley, dau. L., Jan. 23, 1843. Sur. Wm. Pasley. 86.

McGuire, Wm. and Mahala Hambrick, Apr. 14, 1834. Sur. Patrick Slone. 68.

McHenry, Thos. and Nancy Martin, dau. Hugh, Mar. 25, 1800. Sur. John McHenry.

McIlhaney (or McKlehaney), Robt. and Miriam Abshire, dau. Abraham, June 15, 1822. Sur. Samuel McKelhaney. 130.

McIlhaney, Samuel and Margaret Abshire, Oct. 4, 1819. Sur. Hiram Wright. 130.

McIlwain (or McLewain), Thos. and Ruth Vinson, dau. Charles and Susanna, Oct. 12, 1799. Sur. Charles Vinson. 21.

McIver, John and Elizabeth Ann Mason, Mar. 16, 1846. Sur. Chas. R. Mason. 132.

McKinsey, Thos. and Martha Webster, Aug. 20, 1801. 21.

McKinsie, Wesley and Barbara Kuhn, June 16, 1810. Sur. Henry Kuhn.

McMullin, James W. C. and Decey Chitwood, Dec. 12, 1797. Sur. Wm. Chitwood. 21.

McMullen, Samuel and Elizabeth Weaver, dau. Jacob, Jan. 27, 1803. Sur. Amos Ellison, Jr.

McNanny, Archibald and Chloe Butler, Mar. 29, 1796. Sur. Micajah Stone.

McNeil, Daniel and Elizabeth Kennett, Jan. 1, 1821. Sur. Peter Kennett. 49.

McNealy, James, s. Sally, and Jane Lawhorn, dau. Mealy, Dec. 27, 1853. 10.

McNeil (or McNeal), Jacob and Peggy Cool, Mar. 2, 1812. Sur. Peter Kennett.

McNeal, John and Rebecca Griffith, Aug. 5, 1805. Sur. Jonathan Griffith. 130.

McNeil, Jonathan M. and Catherine Perdue, July 18, 1836. 18.

McVey, James and Martha Richardson, dau. Wm. and Martha Kelly, Mar. 5, 1798. 89.

McVey, John, s. James, Sr., and Barbara S. Loyd, Dec. 18, 1810. Sur. James McVey, Sr.

McVey, Thos. and Rhoda Cooper, June 3, 1816. Sur. Thos. Cooper. 130.

Mead, Morrison and Parmetter Law, Jan. 5, 1824. Sur. Cheadle Law. 130

Meador, Abel and Polly Oyler, Sept. 4, 1820. Sur. Valentine Oyler, Sr. 48.

Meador, Abel B. and Elizabeth Basham, Aug. 20, 1831. Sur. Elijah McGuire. 140.

Meador, Ananais and Sally Anderson, Mar. 3, 1823. Sur. Joseph Anderson.

Meador, Burwell and Lucy Payne, dau. Benj., Jan. 27, 1823. Sur. Mark Payne.

Meador, David and Polly Anderson, dau. James, Dec. 16, 1817. Sur. Joseph Anderson.

Meador, Geo. and Timery Payne, Oct. 20, 1823. Sur. Joseph Payne.

Meador, Hubbard and Judy Steward, Aug. 1, 1842. Sur. Josiah Ferguson. 45.

Meador, James and Mary Divers, Sept. 13, 1797. Sur. John Divers.

Meador, James and Sarah Booth, Jan. 4, 1836. Sur. John Booth.

Meador, Jehu John and Phebe J. Crews, Apr. 30, 1833. Sur. Wm. Allbright.

Meador, Jeremiah and Elizabeth Wood, Mar. 16, 1812. Surs. Wm. Drake and Wm. Boles.
Meador, Jesse and Mary Mann, Feb. 23, 1789. Sur. Joel Meador.
Meador, Jesse and Nancy Chewing, dau. Geo., Oct. 15, 1811. Sur. Nathaniel Chewing.
Meador, Job, Jr. and Minnie Simmons, dau. Chas., Sept. 29, 1806. Sur. Uriah Basham.
Meador, Joel and Edith Clyborn, Dec. 25, 1798. Sur. John Clyborn. 21.
Meador, Joel and Arena Arrington, July 6, 1853. Sur. Daniel Arrington. 140.
Meador, John and Nancy Clack, dau. Susanah Clark, Dec. 2, 1805. Sur. Joel Meador.
Meador, John and Sally B. Harwood, Oct. 15, 1816. Sur. Francis G. Harwood.
Meador, John G. and Sarepta Simmons, Oct. 7, 1833. Sur. Anthony Simmons. 140.
Meador, John J., s. Jehu, and Adeline S. Smith, dau. John W., Aug. 23, 1836. Sur. Thos. B. Robertson. 140.
Meador, Jonas and Frances Anderson, Mar. 18, 1820. Sur. Moses Meador.
Meador, Joseph and Sally Divers, Apr. 23, 1794. 41.
Meador, Joseph and Jane Arrington, Dec. 7, 1829. Sur. Daniel Arrington. 140.
Meador, Joseph J. and Frances Dudley, Aug. 6, 1827. Sur. Levi Dudley.
Meador, Josephus and Tabitha Ray, dau. Wm., Dec. 11, 1843. Sur. Wm. Ray.
Meador, Madison and Elizabeth Slone, Feb. 11, 1839. Sur. Paschal Meador. 18.
Meador, Martin and Sophia Ferguson, Dec. 11, 1831. Sur. John Ferguson. 140.
Meador, Micajah and Nancy Cooper, dau. Eiles, Dec. 30, 1837. Sur. Paschal Meador.
Meador, Moses and Sophia W. Arrington, July 10, 1823. Sur. Arthur Arrington.
Meador, Nehemiah and Peggy Payne, Dec. 10, 1821. Sur. Andrew Abshire.

Meador, Otey and Susannah Ferguson, Dec. 22, 1829. Sur. John Ferguson. 140.
Meador, Otey and Rhoda Wright, Feb. 12, 1835. Sur. Ammon Wright. 68.
Meador, Pascal and Quintina Wright, dau. Geo., Mar. 15, 1841. Sur. John A. Wright. 18.
Meador, Richard and Lucy Anderson, dau. James, Feb. 3, 1812. Sur. Jesse Anderson.
Meador, Thaddeus and Laura A. Beach, Nov. 17, 1858.
Meador, Thos. and Elizabeth Martin, Oct. 16, 1794. 41.
Meador, Turner and Judie Richardson, Feb. 8, 1814. Sur. Benj. Richardson. 98.
Medley, Geo. and Sarah Johnson, g. Wm. Johnson, Sept. 7, 1789. Sur. Geo. Asbury. 114.
Meese, Peter and Jenny Smith, dau. Mary, Aug. 6, 1804. Sur. John Kindley. 57.
Mellon (Miller), John and Amelia Garner, Feb. 7, 1803. Sur. James Welch. 122.
Melton, Andrew and Nancy Doran, Oct. 28, 1831. Sur. George Doran. 48.
Menefee, Richard and Catherine M. Hunt, 1851. 132.
Menefee, Wm. and Naomi Jane Waid, Jan. 1, 1838. Sur. John A. Waid.
Meredith, Chas. L. and Susan Hale, Jan. 11, 1825. Sur. Abraham Jones.
Meredith, James and Mary Stockton, Aug. 4, 1828. Sur. Peter Campbell.
Meredith, John W. and Sally J. Belcher, dau. Isham, Nov. 4, 1850. Sur. Wm. Belcher. 80.
Merrill, Wm. and Caroline Bunnion, Oct. 21, 1795. Sur. Wm. Binnion.
Merriman, Edward and Eleanor Sample, Nov. 10, 1828. Sur. James L. Sample.
Merryman, James B. and Amanda Catherine Wertz, Dec. 26, 1850. 18.
Merryman, John and Mary Bowsman, (or Bowman), dau. Mary, Dec. 12, 1842. Sur. Alexander Ferguson. 122.
Merryman, Wm. and Nancy Ann Anderson, dau. Joseph, Jan. 2, 1847. Sur. Henry C. Dillion.

Metts, Geo. W. and Omey Sink, dau. Henry, Feb. 14, 1842. Sur. John Sink. 16.

Metts, Henry and Julia Jenett Mitchell, dau. Samuel, Dec. 16, 1850. Sur. Creed Bernard. 18.

Metts, John and Sallie E. Fralin, Dec. 20, 1858.

Metts, Richard and Matilda Turner, Nov. 25, 1851. 18.

Metts, Thos. and Lucy Willard, Dec. 27, 1824. Sur. Thos. Metts.

Metts, Wm. and Mary N. Mathews, Oct. 19, 1847.

Miksel, David and Molly Harter, Feb. 7, 1803. Sur. Christian Harter. 122.

Miksell, Peter and Mary Troup, dau. Mary, Aug. 15, 1797. Sur. Henry Troup.

Miles, Evan and Mary Christie, dau. James, Aug. 4, 1800. Sur. James Christie.

Miles, Enos and Anna Buckanan, July 25, 1789. Sur. Moses Beck. 52.

Miles, Isaac and Mary Jones, dau. John and Mary, Jan. 24, 1787. Sur. John Chambers. 66.

Miles, James and Caty Miksel, Feb. 3, 1799. Sur. John Miksel. 89.

Miles, James E., s. Jordon, and Mary Jane Richards, dau. Simpson, Nov. 15, 1853. 68.

Miles, John and Mary Ann McGhee, Oct. 20, 1838. Sur. Nelson McGhee. 132.

Miles, Jourdan and Oney Guilliams, Nov. 22, 1830. Sur. Robt. Guilliams. 48.

Miles, Julius and Elizabeth A. Waggoner, Nov. 1, 1841. Sur. Daniel Waggoner. 132.

Miles, Perrigon G. and Martha J. Oxley, Jan. 1851. 132.

Miller, Abraham and Mary Peary, dau. Geo., July 6, 1791. Sur. Geo. Peary. 52.

Miller, Henry and Mary Hambrick, Aug. 31, 1799. Sur. Andrew Hemlick. 89.

Miller, Isaac and Hannah Webb, dau. James and Lucy, Aug. 18, 1800. Sur. Daniel Miller.

Miller, Jacob, g. Rodney Brower, and Susannah Peary, dau. Geo., Dec. 10, 1800. Sur. Geo. Peary. 66.

Miller, Jacob and Barbara Lybrook, Feb. 2, 1801.

Miller, James W. C. and Dicey Chitwood, Dec. 18, 1797. Sur. Wm. Chitwood.
Miller, John and Cynthia Willis, Oct. 10, 1811. Sur. Joseph Willis. 130.
Miller, John and Margaret Turpin, dau. Mary, Sept. 7, 1789. Sur. Samuel Baily.
Miller, John and Susannah Scott, Dec. 7, 1789. Sur. Daniel Barnhart. 52.
Miller, John and Hester Brown, Nov. 16, 1798. Sur. Christian Brown. 21.
Miller, John and Phebe McClure, July 14, 1792. Surs. Samuel and Mary Henderson. 52.
Miller, Pierson and Nancy Hook, (Hoof), dau. Philip, Dec. 4, 1797. Sur. Thos. Miller.
Miller, Tobias and Sally Henderson, dau. Mary and Samuel, Nov. 9, 1799. Sur. Thos. Miller. 89.
Millican, James H. and Sarah Welch, Oct. 29, 1829. Sur. James Welch.
Millikin, Jesse and Rebecca Overfelt, Sept. 15, 1830. Sur. John Overfelt. 48.
Millirons, Alexander B. and Catherine D. Hoffman, dau. John Jan. 3, 1848. Sur. Joel Leftwich. 68.
Millirons, Burwell and Catherine Maxey, dau. Jeremiah, Aug. 15, 1836. Sur. Geo. Ferguson. 3.
Mills, Andrew and Elizabeth Klingenpeel, Jan. 25, 1841. Sur. Jonathan Klingenpeel.
Mills, Arthur and Nancy West, dau. Jenny, Aug. 18, 1800. Sur. Peter Abshire. 21.
Mills, Cornelius and Sarah Wray, Feb. 8, 1841. Sur. Burwell Millson.
Mills, Edward and Mahaley Oxley, June 20, 1825. Sur. Samuel Oxley. 48.
Mills, Geo., s. Wm., and Milla Bond, Nov. 6, 1832. Sur. Anderson Starkey. 48.
Mills, Hiram and Tenah Wright, June 17, 1825. Sur. Geo. Wright, Jr.
Mills, James and Nancy Frame, May 3, 1799. Sur. Wm. Brown 21.
Mills, Jesse and Saphronia Hawkins, Mar. 24, 1824. Sur. Geo. McVey. 130.

Mills, Jubal and Leona Mills, Sept. 11, 1838. Sur. Jubal Mills. 18.

Mills, Samuel E. and Mary Ann Hobson, Dec. 27, 1841. Sur. James Patterson.

Mills, Wm. and Mary Abshire, dau. Ambrose, Jan. 2, 1847. Sur. Anderson Starkey. 18.

Mills, Wm. and Elizabeth Abshire, dau. Abraham, Feb. 29, 1796. Sur. Abraham Abshire.

Mills, Wm. and Polly Showalter, Nov. 19, 1828. Sur. John Frailin. 140.

Mills, Wm. and Mary M. Mathews, dau. John, Oct. 19, 1847. Sur. Wm. C. Barber.

Mills, Wm. and Drucilla Kemp, Aug. 24, 1815.

Mills, Wm. and Sarah Boitnott, Dec. 23, 1852. 11.

Milton, Jubal and Delila Patezell, Jan. 30, 1844. Sur. Abram Patezell. 18.

Mindor, Matthias and Martha Watson, Dec. 27, 1796. 89.

Minnix, Chas., Jr. and Fanny Richmond, July 17, 1798. Sur. Henry Gearhart.

Minnix, Fleming S. and Elizabeth Peters, Jan. 19, 1849. Sur. Jacob Boon. 96.

Minnix, Fleming S. and Adaline C. Angel, dau. A. H., and Lioney, Apr. 18, 1846. Sur. Sparell Minnix.

Minnix, Jesse and Polly Henry, Jan. 12, 1810. Sur. Richard Henry. 117.

Minnix, Lewis and Lucy Wright, Mar. 28, 1832. Sur. Ezekiel Wright. 48.

Minnix, Sparrel, s. Selia, and Susan Kesler, Sept. 5, 1842. Sur. Jacob Kesler.

Minter, Mathias and Fanny Kingery, July 26, 1810. Sur. David Snider. 130.

Mitchell, Abner and Catherine Abshire, Mar. 25, 1839. 18.

Mitchell, Archilaeus and Naomi Hill, July 12, 1809. Sur. Wm. Kyle. 130.

Mitchell, Daniel and Sallie A. Hodges, Dec. 20, 1858.

Mitchell, Daniel and Martha E. Brooks, June 12, 1845. Sur. Jesse Brooks. 18.

Mitchell, Decovid E. and Matilda Wilks, Dec. 29, 1837.

Mitchell, Decovid, s. Elizabeth, and Elizabeth Craighead, Mar. 12, 1821. Sur. Cabeb Maxcy.
Mitchell, Eldred and Lucinda Chambers, Jan. 6, 1827. Sur. Samuel Chambers.
Mitchell, Elisha and Eleanor Gregory, dau. Richard F., Apr. 26, 1832. Sur. Samuel Mitchell. 90.
Mitchell, Goode B. and Mary Hunt, dau. Nephin and Catharine, Apr. 19, 1841. Sur. Riley H. Hunt.
Mitchell, James and Letitia M. Burwell, Jan. 20, 1835. Sur. Beverly Sydnor. 145.
Mitchell, James and Elizabeth Niblett, May 5, 1806. Sur. Thos. Niblett.
Mitchell, James and Calpernia Franklin, dau. Jasper, May 6, 1819. Sur. Anthony Franklin. 48.
Mitchell, Nathaniel and Elender Snodon, Mar. 7, 1797. 89.
Mitchell, Robt. and Desdemona Angle, Jan. 7, 1833. Sur. Peter Angle.
Mitchell, Tarpley and Permalia Abshire, dau. Abraham, Apr. 29, 1841. Sur. Abner Mitchell. 18.
Mitchell, Thos. H. and Nancy Prillaman, Jan. 2, 1843. Sur. Thos. H. Prillaman. 132.
Mitchell, Washington C. and Elizabeth Bradley, dau. Nancy, Jan. 17, 1838. Sur. Wm. Bradley.
Mitchell, Wm. J. and Polly Bondurant, Oct. 12, 1819.
Mitchell, Wm. C. and Penelope Angel, Apr. 10, 1820 Sur. Wm. C. Angel.
Mitchell, Wm. and Mary Jackson, dau. Thos., Jan. 31, 1803. Sur. Thos. Jackson.
Mitchell, Wm. D. and Letitia S. Bird, dau. John, Sr., Aug. 25, 1840. Sur. Goode B. Mitchell.
Mixell (Miksell), George, Jr. and Catey (Haty) Harter, Feb. 4, 1805. Sur. Christian Harter.
Molloy, James and Zeanith Richeson, dau Jonathan, June 13, 1804. Sur. Skelton Richeson.
Montgomery, Andrew and Sabina Peters, Jan. 25, 1842. Sur. Michael Peters. 18.
Montgomery, James and Susannah Nafe, Aug. 27, 1835. 18.
Montgomery, John and Becky Nafe, May 26, 1831. 18.

Montgomery, Samuel and Elizabeth Bowman, Sept. 30, 1805. Sur. Peter Bowman. 130.
Montrief, Isaac and Frances Prunty, Mar. 2, 1835. Sur. Thos. Prunty.
Moody, John, s. Thos., and Polly Lilley, dau. Robt., Jan. 17, 1786. Sur. Thos. Day.
Moody, Samuel and Nancy Reiley, Sept. 11, 1794. 41.
Moomaw, Philip and Susannah Peters, Feb. 9, 1837. 18.
Moore, Abraham and Clarky Leffew, dau. Enoc, Aug. 28, 1847. Sur. John W. Ray.
Moore, Abraham and Martha Boyd, dau. Sarah, Apr. 1, 1834. Sur. Hugh Boyd. 61.
Moore, Benj. and Polly Lumpkins, Apr. 15, 1807. Sur. James L. Hail.
Moore, David and Jane H. Brewer, Feb. 23, 1818. Sur. John Dumman.
Moore, David and Sally Craig, Jan. 4, 1819. Sur. Thos. Craig.
Moore, David and Susannah Hail, Feb. 1, 1819. Sur. Geo. H. Hughes.
Moore, David and Sarah J. Griffith, Dec. 27, 1841. Sur. Daniel Griffith. 60.
Moore, Drury and Ann Parker, June 6, 1825. Sur. Sterling Parker.
Moor, Wm. and Sarah Grimmett, __, 1787. 66.
Moore, Edmund and Ursula Underwood, May 4, 1811. Sur. Robt. Radford.
Moore, Edward and Catherine Kinnett, dau. Joseph and Isabel, June 1, 1843. Sur. Joseph L. Kinnett.
Moore, Geo. W. and Eva Adeline Anderson, Apr. 13, 1853. 80.
Moore, Henry and Sarah F. Noell, dau. Judith, Jan. 4, 1843. Sur. Chas. R. Noell.
Moore, Jacob and Rebecca Williams, Apr. 12, 1853. 68.
Moore, James and Sally McGhee, dau. Nancy Adoch, Feb. 1, 1813. Sur. Martin McGhee.
Moore, James and Susannah Sigmon, Oct. 28, 1818. Sur. Wm. Brumley.
Moore, James and Jenny Leffew, dau. Enoch, Aug. 28, 1849. Sur. Moseley Young. 47.

Moore, John and Ann Austin, May 9, 1818. Sur. David Austin. 61.
Moore, John N. and Mary Potter, Nov. 5, 1851. 79.
Moore, Joseph and Tabitha Moseley, Aug. 19, 1834. Sur. Wm. Clay. 53.
Moore, Lewis and Franky Williams, July 24, 1829. Sur. John Scott.
Moore, Mathew and Martha Mavity, dau. Wm., Aug. 19, 1811. Sur. Jesse Mavity. 122.
Moore, Melon and Nancy Marrs Moore, June 3, 1816. Sur. Elijah Brockman. 130.
Moore, Peters S. and Elizabeth Cannaday, dau. Jane Radford, June 29, 1846. Sur. Thos. Stump. 121.
Moore, Rodham and Mary Young, Aug. 24, 1833. Sur. James Young.
Moore, Richard and Margaret Kropff, Nov. 1, 1832. Sur. Henry Kropff. 48.
Moore, Wesley and Lucinda Craghead, dau. John, Dec. 21, 1844. Sur. Thos. L. Craghead.
Moore, Wm. and Lucy Brown, Mar. 1, 1814. Sur. Josiah W. Dickinson. 8.
Moore, Wm. S. and Susan Hopkins, May 7, 1847. Sur. Robt. Goodson. 111.
Moore, Wm. and Sarah Grimmet, 1787. 66.
Moore, Wm. and Tebeer Sweeny, Nov. 15, 1804. 122.
Moore, Wilson and Elizabeth Shue, Oct. 26, 1834. Sur. John Griffith. 61.
Moore, Zachariah W. and Rawsa Brewer, dau. Zackfield, Nov. 26, 1827. Sur. Jas. Dunman.
More, (or Moor), John and Elizabeth Davis, dau. Joseph, May 19, 1793. Sur. Wm. More. 52.
More, Peter (of Roanoke Co.), and Mary Dishon, Aug. 25, 1841. Sur. John Bowman.
More, Samuel and Elizabeth Stewart, Mar. 26, 1793. Sur. David Thompson.
Moran, Nelson and Sally Young, Dec. 4, 1843. Sur. James Cannaday.
Moorman, Samuel and Elizabeth Hale, Mar. 5, 1835.

Moorman, Thos. and Eliza B. Price, dau. Showers, Mar. 7, 1810. Sur. Thos. Thompson.
Morgan, Jesse R. and Catherine C. Dearen, dau. Joel, Apr. 23, 1844. Sur. Joseph Bird. 104.
Morgan, Jubal and Arena Chambers, dau. Joel, Dec. 23, 1836. Sur. Thos. J. Thomason.
Morgan, Morgan and Elizabeth Blades, May 6, 1796. Sur. Francis Blades.
Morgan, Price H. and Rebecca D. Woody, Nov. 30, 1844. Sur. Henry Woody. 134.
Morgan, Samuel B. and Elizabeth Bernard, Feb. 28, 1828. Sur. Peter Bernard.
Morgan, Stephen and Jane Bird, Sept. 29, 1833. Sur. Peter H. Bell. 48.
Morgan, Thos. A. and Anne Chambers, Dec. 23, 1836.
Morris, Andrew W. and Mary H. Adams, Aug. 11, 1840. Sur. Thos. G. Adams.
Morris, Benj. S. and Mary A. Claiborne, Oct. 5, 1852. 75.
Morris, Henry and Mary H. Bird, Nov. 12, 1812. Sur. Bartlett Bird.
Moss, Frank and Polly Webster, dau. Samuel, Aug. 29, 1809. Sur. Wm. Webster.
Moss, Henry and Frances Wilkerson, dau. John and Lucy Prillaman, July 6, 1818. Sur. John Kinsey, Jr. 59.
Moss, Wm. and Betsy Lybrook, Dec. 30, 1805. Sur. Philip Lybrook.
Motley, Geo. W. and Martha McGuire, dau. Jonathan, Dec. 21, 1842. Sur. Seth E. McGuire. 86.
Moyers, John and Catherine Nafe, dau. Jacob and Elizabeth, Feb. 7, 1797. Sur. David Nafe. 89.
Mullen (or Mullenden), Jacob and Catherine Hartzell, Oct. 20, 1794. Sur. Abraham Hartzell.
Mullen (McMullin), J. W. C. and Dicey Chitwood, Dec. 12, 1797.
Mullins, Aider and Polly Scarborough, Aug. 10, 1822. Sur. Robt. Scarborough. 49.
Mullins, Bowker and Judith Stanley, May 12, 1803. Sur. Joseph Stanley. 72.
Mullins, Edmond J. and Elizabeth Hill, dau. Wm. and Nancy, Feb. 7, 1842. Sur. Samuel A. Helms. 68.

Mullins, Jacob and Dotia Brammer, Oct. 22, 1819. Sur. John Brammer.
Mullins, Jesse and Judith Doss, Nov. 6, 1807. Sur. Wm. Stone.
Mullins, John and Lucy Bohanan, Sept. 3, 1787. Sur. Wm. Bohanon.
Mullins, Joseph and Lucy Allen, dau. Winfield, Feb. 25, 1822. Sur. James Allen.
Mullins, Joseph and Frances Prillaman, dau. Dennis, Dec. 7, 1829. Sur. Geo. Standley.
Mullins, Nehemiah and Elizabeth Doss, Feb. 21, 1804. Sur. James Martin.
Mullins, Robt. and Alline (Ollive) M. Barnes, Dec. ...., 1852. 132.
Mullins, Stephen and Charity Young, Dec. 12, 1826. Sur. James Young. 129.
Mullins, Thos. and Nancy Bowles, Dec. 30, 1826. Sur. Robt. Scarborough. 129.
Mullins, Wm. and Judith Standley, Mar. 23, 1803. Sur. Richard Stanley. 72.
Mundy, Riley and Fanny Trent, Mar. 10, 1830. Sur. Archibald Trent. 140.
Munday, Wm. R. and Rhoda H. Knight, May 17, 1842. Sur. Wm. T. Clowers. 18.
Murphy, Edward C. and Sarah E. Powell, dau. Chas., Dec. 26, 1842. Sur. Robt. N. Powell.
Murphy, Wm. and Sophia Angle, Dec. 22, 1836. 18.
Murrill, Wm. and Caroline Binnion, Oct. 20, 1795. Sur. Wm. Binnion.
Muse, Alfred and Mary Ann Muse, Oct. 17, 1835. Sur. Wm. S. Muse.
Muse, Henry L., Jr. and Elizabeth F. Muse, dau. Henry L., Dec. 20, 1841. Sur. Francis W. C. Swanson.
Muse, Peter and Jenny Smith, Aug. 5, 1804. Sur. Wm. Camp.
Muse, Wm. and Judith Glass, dau. John, June 1, 1830. Sur. Dudley Glass. 3.
Musgrave (or Musgrove), Henry and Nancy Burdett, Jan. 11, 1798. Sur. Wm. Burdet.
Naff, (Knaff, Nafe, Knafe, Knave), Abraham and Hannah Peters, Apr. 6, 1830. 18.

Naff, Abraham, Jr. and Elizabeth Naff, Nov. 25, 1850. Sur. Abraham Naff, Sr. 96.
Naff, Benj. and Martha J. Teel, Feb. 3, 1849. Sur. Terry Teel. 96.
Naff, Daniel and Lidia Barnhart, Apr. 19, 1832. 18.
Naff, Daniel and Polly Logan, Sept. 28, 1795. Surs. Wm. Logan and Wm. Knafe. 52.
Naff, David and Polly Brown, Nov. 14, 1803. Sur. Jacob Brower.
Naff, Geo. and Hannah Bowman, Dec. 30, 1817. Sur. Chrisholm Griffin. 130.
Naff, Isaac and Barbara Moyer, dau. Kohor Boon, June 1, 1789. Sur. Daniel Barnhart.
Naff, Isaac and Elizabeth Peters, Jan. 31, 1833. 18.
Naff, Isaac and Mary Peters, Apr. 22, 1839. Sur. Michael Peters. 18.
Naff, Jacob and Susannah Webster, Feb. 28, 1828. 18.
Naff, Jacob and Hannah Montgomery, Dec. 2, 1858. Sur. Samuel W. Montgomery. 18.
Naff, Jacob and Polly Rentfro, dau. Moses, June 24, 1795. Sur. Isaac Rentfro.
Naff, John B. and Sarah Naff, Mar. 1, 1841. Sur. Jonathan Nafe. 18.
Naff, John and Sally Howry, Jan. 11, 1827. 18.
Naff, Jonathan and Chatherine Hoff, Aug. 31, 1795. Sur. James Flora. 52.
Naff, Joseph and Mary Magdeline Hergerdeez, dau. Conrad Barnhart, Mar. 7, 1796.
Naff, Samuel and Elizabeth Jamison, Sept. 3, 1849. Sur. Samuel Jamison. 96.
Nance, Clement and Polly Hail, May 4, 1813. Sur. John Waid.
Napier, John and Lucy Cook, dau. Mary, Mar. 15, 1804. Sur. John Cook.
Napier, John and Elizabeth Hinson, Oct. 29, 1799. Sur. Mary Henson. 141.
Napier, Robt., Jr. and Catherine Napier, Dec. 19, 1789. Sur. Ashford Napier. 37.
Napier, Skelton and Elizabeth Throsdall, Feb. 13, 1789. Sur. John Choice.

Napier, Tarlton and Susannah Smith, Oct. 6, 1806. Sur. John M. Holland. 8.

Napier, Thos. and Susannah Napier, Aug. 7, 1809. Sur. Frances Cooper.

Neighbors, Christopher and Lucy Ann Chewing, dau. Walter, Feb. 5, 1850. Sur. Chas. A. Chewing.

Neighbors, Joshua B. and Lucy Payne, ..., 1851. 86.

Neighbors, Joseph L. and Dorothy Melton, Aug. 15, 1844. 18.

Nelson, Hugh and Lucy A. Taliaferro, July 12, 1847. Sur. John R. Fontaine.

Nemore, (Nimmo), John and Sally Harrison, dau. Reuben, Nov. 30, 1807. Sur. Reuben Harrison, Jr.

New, Edward and Jane Austin, Nov. 25, 1825. Sur. David Austin. 61.

New, Wm. and Elizabeth Jones, dau. John. Oct. 23, 1801. 106.

Newberry (or Newbury), Levi and Elizabeth Boyd, dau. Wm., Jan. 5, 1808.

Newberry, Thos., s. Wm., and Sarah Vier, dau. John, Dec. 17, 1810. Sur. Wm. Boyd. 112.

Newberry, Wm. and Margaret Martin, May 22, 1813. Sur. Matthew Martin.

Newbill, Mark A. and Jane Odineal, dau. Thos., Dec. 4, 1848. Sur. Wm. P. Newbill.

Newbill, Nathaniel P. and Mary Odineal, dau. Thos., Dec. 3, 1849. Sur. Ransom T. Newbill.

Newbill, Nathaniel P. and Hope Ann Sutherland, dau. Frances, Jan. 7, 1813. Sur. Philemon Sutherland.

Newbill, Tyree G. and Keziah Sutherland, May 10, 1819. Sur. Andrew Thompson.

Newbill, Wm. P. and Susan M. Sutherland, dau. Elizabeth H., Apr. 5, 1845. Sur. Robert A. Scott. 14.

Newman, Caleb and Agnes Phillips, Aug. 8, 1820. Sur. John Meador.

Newman, Edward H. and Elizabeth Poff, Dec. 4, 1843. Sur. Cary Gray. 68.

Newton, Isaiah and Elizabeth Canaday, —, 1797.

Niblett (Nebblett), Thos. and Elizabeth Lovell, Dec. 11, 1810. Sur. John Lovell.

Nicholas, Wm. and Elizabeth Crowder, sdau. David Thomas, Feb. 16, 1844. Sur. David Thomas. 134.
Nicholls, Gilbert and Eleanor Carter, Apr. 21, 1798. Sur. Jonathan Charter. 21.
Nichols, Elisha C. and Emaline Willis, Nov. 13, 1839. Sur. Sally Doughton.
Nicholas, Jesse and Jane Hodges, July 20, 1843. Sur. John Campbell, Jr.
Nichols, John and Martha Ann Jones, Dec. 15, 1846. Sur. Ezekiel Jones. 132.
Nichols, Nehemiah and Elizabeth Blades, dau. Frances, Mar. 7, 1791. Sur. Guy Smith.
Nicholson, James L. and Mary M. Rives, dau. Joseph, Sept. 16, 1837. Sur. Wm. W. Albea. 143.
Nimmo, James and Mary Flowers, dau. Samuel, Mar. 4, 1833. Sur. Isaac Hopkins.
Nimmo (Nemo), Robt. and Lydia Holland, Jan. 18, 1800. Sur. Peter Holland.
Nimmo, Thos. J. and Frances Brown, Nov. 6, 1826. Sur. Turner Brown.
Nimo (Nunn), Thos. and Nancy Ramsey, dau. Thos., Jan. 20, 1840. 132.
Noble, Daniel and Nancy Greer, Sept. 9, 1823. Sur. Weatherston Greer.
Noble, Wiley and Nancy Ross, Feb. 21, 1827 Sur. Thos. Ross. 140.
Noe, Nathaniel D. and Rebecca A. Standley, July 17, 1834. Sur. Larkin Standley. 132.
Noftsinger, Daniel and Susannah Boone, Apr. 15, 1807. Sur. Peter Boon. 130.
Nofsinger, Joseph B. and Susan Boon, dau. Nancy and Abram, Oct. 23, 1843. Sur. James B. Price. 18.
Noftsinger, Peter and Hannah Naff, Dec. 6, 1841. Sur. Jacob Naff. 18.
Norris, Benj. and Mary Haynes, dau. Henry, Feb. 19, 1807. Sur. Josias Wheat. 8.
Norris, Wm. and Jane Craig, Apr. 1, 1805. Sur. Williamson Davis.
Nowel, Chas. R. and Rhoda Stockton, Dec. 14, 1832. 19.

WINGFIELD'S WORKS 171

Nowlin, Robt. and Fanney Taylor, dau. John and Jane, Feb. 9, 1796. Sur. James Richardson.
Nowlin, Wm. and Nancy Booth, Feb. 4, 1806. Sur. Richard Booth
Nunn, John A. and Elizabeth Bird, Oct. 14, 1840. Sur. Thos. Bird. 132.
Nunn, Joseph and Polly Stone, Oct. 19, 1798. Sur. Stephen Stone.
Nunley, Andrew and Sarah Abshire, Dec. 23, 1851. 18.
Nunley, Jefferson and Catherine Naff, dau. Isaac, Oct. 6, 1848. Sur. John Naff. 11.
Nunley, John and Omey Wright, Mar. 13, 1839. Sur. Thos. Nunley. 18.
Nunnally, John and Omey Wright, July 7, 1835. Sur. Gabriel Swanson.
Oakes, Moses R. and Nancy Potter, dau. Lewis, Sept. 7, 1850. Sur. Nathaniel R. Oaks.
Obrian, Dennis and Ruth Manier, Sept. 5, 1792. Sur. Richard Manier.
Odineal, Thos. A. and Martha H. Newbill, Dec. 28, 1836. Sur. Chas. B. Powell.
Ogles, Hercules, Jr. and Margaret Griffith, Jan. 15, 1798. Sur. Wm. Griffith.
Oilman, Jacob and Susannah Brown, Jan. 1, 1808. 130.
Oneal, Hugh and Nancy Sheridan, July 30, 1797. Sur. Wm. Campbell.
Ordin, Wm. and Sarah Mullins, ..., 1786. 103.
Osborne, Branch and Rachael Greer, Jan. 4, 1819. Sur. Ezekiel Greer. 130.
Osborne, John and Sarah Hill, dau. Thos., Aug. 16, 1804. Sur. John Ferguson.
Oteneal (Odineal), Thos. and Polly Tunning, dau. Geo., Aug. 10, 1804. Sur. Isaiah Craighead.
Otey, James C. and Bettie H. Claiborne, Apr. 13, 1851. 134.
Ovenchain (Obenchain), Samuel and Catherine Flora, April 5, 1819. Sur. Joseph Flora. 130.
Overfelt, Berry and Martha Divers, May 8, 1837. Sur. Silas Divers.

Overfelt, Burriah and Sarah T. Greer, Dec. 22, 1834. Sur. Burd S. Webb.
Overfelt, David and Evaline C. Carper, Sept. 4, 1839. Sur. Moses G. Carper.
Overfelt, Ephraim and Mahala Turner, dau. Richard, Apr. 26, 1832. Sur. John Overfelt. 48.
Overfelt, John and Catherine Walrond, dau. Benj. Jr., Aug. 13, 1830. Sur. John Tosh. 48.
Overfelt, John and Susannah Click, Aug. 3, 1815. Sur. Christian Clack. 98.
Overfelt, Joseph and Mary Altick, Jan. 9, 1851. Sur. Abraham Barnhart.
Overholt, Abraham and Catherine Gossett, Feb. 3, 1800. Sur. Daniel Gossett.
Overholt, Abraham and Barbara Prupecker, Oct. 20, 1807. Sur. John Prupecker. 130.
Overholt, David and Elizabeth Kailer, _ ., 1794. 89.
Overlies, Conrad and Peggy Hairston, Nov. 7, 1798. Sur. Anthony Pate.
Owens, Anthony and Elizabeth Young, May 17, 1791. Sur. John Young.
Ownby, James and Alice Ann Wray, Apr. 13, 1839. Sur. Edmund Wray. 18.
Oxley, Archibald and Lucy Johnson, dau. Thos., Feb. 1, 1819. Sur. Samuel Oxley.
Oxley, Armistead and Gilly Law, Dec. 4, 1843. Sur. Thos. Law.
Oxley, Elkanah and Susan Crawford, dau. Sarah Adams, Sept. 15, 1845. Sur. Wilson Oxley. 132.
Oxley (Otley), Jinkens, Sr. and Nancy Keys, Oct. 9, 1848. Sur. Jinkens M. Oxley.
Oxley, Jenkins and Elizabeth Miles, Feb. 18, 1834. Sur. Sterling M. Thornton.
Oxley, John and Mary Mason, dau. Lewis, Dec. 12, 1831. Sur. Samuel G. Mason. 48.
Oxley, Nathaniel C. and Jane E. A. Bell, Dec. 9, 1850. Sur. John M. Bell 132.
Oxley, Peter and Jane Newman, Mar. 28, 1815. Sur. Wm. Davis. 130.

Oxley, Sanford N. and Delilia A. Bird, dau. Luke, Oct. 6, 1845. Sur. Benj. T. Bird.
Oxley, Thos. and Sarah McGhee, ..., 1852. 132.
Oxley, Wm. R., s. Nathaniel and Mary, and Rebecca J. Hudson, dau. Harriet, Aug. 30, 1853. 18.
Oxley, Wm. W. and Cynthia Bird, Mar. 4, 1844. Sur. Benj. Bird.
Oxley, Wilson and Elizabeth Carter, Nov. 17, 1823. Sur. John Oxley.
Oyler, Ammon and Susan Dillion, dau. Arthur, Jan. 2, 1843. Sur. Henry Dillion, Jr. 18.
Oyler, Ammon and Delilah Altick, Dec. 15, 1852. 18.
Oyler, Clemens and Nancy A. Chewing, dau. Walter, Dec. 21, 1839. Sur. Chas. Chewing.
Oyler, Coleman and Elizabeth J. Tate, Dec. 6, 1847. Sur. Robt. A. Scott.
Oyler, Daniel and Elizabeth Crook, Feb. 1, 1819. Sur. Matthias Crook. 98.
Oyler, David and Elizabeth Hutts, dau. Wm., Sept. 20, 1824. Sur. Wm. Hutts. 48.
Oyler, Elihue B. and Charlotte Howard, dau. Robt., Apr. 11, 1831. Sur. James C. Arthur.
Oyler, Frederick and Nancy Cockran, Nov. 10, 1808. Sur. Samuel Cockran. 8.
Oyler, Harvy and Charlotte Starkey, Oct. 28, 1852. 18.
Oyler, John and Elizabeth Wysong, Jan. 4, 1808. Sur. John Wysong.
Oyler, Lewis and Polly Roupe, Nov. 3, 1823. Sur. Henry Sink. 49.
Oyler, Valentine, Jr. and Caty Wysong, May 17, 1806. Sur. Joseph Wysong.
Ozley, Joseph and Mary Bridget, Dec. 24, 1789. Sur. James Bridgett.
Packwood (Parkwood), Samuel and Judith Sneed, May 6, 1800. Sur. John Sneed. 72.
Packwood, William and Eleanor Anderson, dau. John and Mary, Mar. 1, 1802. 72.
Pagan, David and Mary Harmon, Oct. 8, 1795. 41.
Pagan, John and Polly H. Bradley, dau. Wm. and Elizabeth, Nov. 5, 1817. Sur. Archibald Bradley. 98.

Painter, David and Catherine Hickman, July 31, 1824. Sur. Joseph Hickman, Jr. 130.

Paitzel, Martin and Harriet Webb, Jan. 11, 1833. Sur. Minor S. Webb.

Palmer, Branch and Elizabeth Gregory, dau. Wm. H., May 2, 1845. Sur. John H. Bradnor.

Palmer, John and Ruth A. Meador, dau. Benj. and Oney, Nov. 25, 1840. Sur. Paschal Meador.

Palmer, John, s. Samuel T. and Mary Emeline Williams, dau. Johnson, Feb. 19, 1846. Sur. Lewis Williams. 68.

Palmer, Joseph W. and Juliana Meador, Apr. 6, 1846. Sur. Benj. Meador.

Palmer, Samuel and Rachael Willis, Jan. 24, 1825. Sur. John Willis.

Palmer, Wm. and Minerva Noell, Dec. 20, 1834. Sur. Chas. Noell. 140.

Parberry, James and Susannah Newbill, dau. Nathale, Dec. 6, 1819. Sur. Jas. M. Newbill.

Parberry, Wm. and Dellana Clay, Mar. 17, 1819. Sur. John Clay.

Parcell, James and Delilah Hodges, Jan. 10, 1822. Sur. Joab Hodges.

Parcell, John and Jane Ashworth, Jan. 16, 1819. Sur. Wyatt Mathews.

Parcell, Joel and Prucilla Law, Nov. 1, 1830. Sur. Thos. Law. 48.

Parcell, Wm. and Lucy White, dau. Polly, Dec 14, 1835. Sur. James. M. White. 8.

Paris, Elijah and Judith Harmon, g. Phebe Pucket, Dec. 4, 1816. Sur. Creed Meador.

Paris, Jeremiah and Mary Chandler, July 21, 1849. Sur. Benj. E. Pearson. 19.

Paris, Obediah and Sarah Simmons, dau. Jesse, Jan 3, 1849. Sur. Jas. W. Palmore.

Paris, Wm. S. and Elizabeth Greer, Oct. 1, 1835. 140.

Parish, John M. and Mary A. Zeigler, dau. John, Oct. 2, 1843. Sur. Joshua Zeigler.

Parker, Anderson and Polly Prilliman, May 17, 1833. Sur. Dennis Prillaman.

Parker, Henry and Elizabeth Doughty, July 7, 1791. Sur. John Jones.

Parker, James and Charlotte Cockran, dau. Charlotte, Sept. 9, 1818. Sur. Wm. Moore.
Parker, John and Susannah Webb, dau. Smith, Apr. 5, 1802. Sur. Caleb Tate.
Parker, John and Rhoda Rentfro, Oct. 16, 1786. Sur. Jesse Rentfro.
Parker, John and Eilzabeth Massey, dau. Obadiah, June 8, 1849. Sur. Smith Parker. 20.
Parker, Wm. and Polly Wray, dau. Viney, May 18, 1837. Sur. Drury Moore. 132.
Parker, Wm. and Jemima Saunders, Mar. 17, 1810. Sur. Geo. Sanders.
Parrott, Joseph and Susannah Thompson, Apr. 2, 1793. Sur. John Law.
Parrott, Luke and Mary Elizabeth Newbill, July 1, 1816. Sur. Joseph Rives. 7.
Parrott, Tharp (Thorp) and Elizabeth Sutherland, dau. Elizabeth, May 15, 1793. Sur. James Roberts.
Pasley, Callohill M., s. L., and Judy M. Smith, Sept. 26, 1848. Sur. Wm. Smith, Jr.
Pasley, John and Mary Ann Coleman, Dec. 10, 1845. Sur. Samuel Coleman. 132.
Pasley, John and Susannah Lumsden, May 4, 1831. Sur. Daniel Layman.
Pasley, Robt., Jr. and Fanny Dillion, Jan. 23, 1817. Sur. Jesse Dillion.
Pasley, Robt. and Frances N. Pasley, dau. S., Jan. 7, 1839. Sur. S. Pasley. 18.
Pasley, Samuel and Elizabeth Dudley, Nov. 16, 1840. Sur. Levi Dudley.
Pasley, Solomon, Jr. and Milly Kemp, Apr. 1817. Sur. John Kemp.
Pasley, Wm. and Elizabeth Dillion, May 12, 1812. Sur. Jesse Dillion.
Pate, Anthony and Frances McCormack, Aug. 30, 1828. Sur. Anderson McCormack. 140.
Pate, Esabue and Nancy Stone, May 8, 1832. Sur. Skelton Wright. 48.
Pate, John and Rhoda McCormack, dau. Anderson, Sept. 5, 1832. 48.

Pate, John and Rhoda Doran, dau. Hartman, Dec. 2, 1794. Sur. John Doran. 131.
Pate, Matthew and Polly Harrison, dau. Reuben, Sr., Apr. 4, 1811. Sur. Joel Franklin.
Pate, Meredith C. and Sarah Hartman, Oct. 31, 1850. Sur. John Hartman. 134.
Pate, Stephen and Suckey Martin, dau. Wm., July 17, 1792. Sur. Wm. Martin.
Patterson, Chas. and Lydia McCall, Apr. 2, 1827. Sur. Robt. H. McCall. 48.
Patterson, James and Sarah W. Wade, dau. John, June 7, 1834. Sur. Moses G. Carper.
Patterson, James and Margaret M. Innes, Oct. 12, 1796. Sur. Benj. Cook.
Patterson, John, s. Andrew, and Sicily Patterson, dau. Jonathan, Aug. 22, 1829. Surs. Jonathan and Andrew Patterson.
Patterson, Jonathan and Sally Bozwell, Dec. 27, 1810. Sur. Thos. Bozzell.
Patterson, Robt. and Susan Boone, Dec. 24, 1841. Sur. Jacob Boon. 18.
Patterson, Samuel and Jane Patterson, dau. Jonathan, Mar. 11, 1833. Sur. Samuel Patterson.
Patterson, Samuel, Jr. and Nancy Patterson, dau. Andrew, May 5, 1834. Sur. Samuel Patterson.
Patterson (or Pettison), Samuel and Jean Pinckard, widow of John, Mar. 12, 1788. Sur. Daniel Jett.
Paulevon (Paulivin), John and Keziah Belcher, dau. Phebe, Apr. 5, 1790. Sur. Francis Groves.
Payne, Daniel and Susannah Carter, dau. Barnet, Mar. 13, 1802. Sur. Henry Carter.
Payne, Dudley and Susan Thurman, dau. David, Apr. 9, 1835. Sur. Alexander Thurman. 3.
Payne (Penn), Floyd and Elizabeth Pollard, dau. Elizabeth Toney, Oct. 13, 1790. Sur. Wm. Turner.
Payne, Floyd and Ann Anderson, Aug. 9, 1826. Sur. John Arthur, Sr.
Payne, Geo. and Milly Young, dau. Joseph, Dec. 20, 1802. Sur. James Payne.
Payne, Henry and Ann Sence, Feb. 17, 1823. Sur. Wm. Lence.

Payne, Isham and Patsy Richardson, Nov. 8, 1815. Sur. Thos. McVey.
Payne, James and Sarah Webster, July 21, 1829. Sur. Daniel Webster. 48.
Payne, James and Naomi Ferguson, Mar. 10, 1828. Sur. John Ferguson. 140.
Payne, John and Agatha Beard, dau. Sally, Sept. 29, 1808. Sur. Samuel Beard.
Payne, John and Juliana Speer, Mar. 6, 1819. Sur. Isaac Speer.
Payne, John and Lucy Clarkson, dau. David, Oct. 7, 1806. Surs. Henry Debo and Wm. J. Edmunds.
Payne, Joseph M. and Elizabeth Webb, dau. Reuben, Apr. 4, 1836. Sur. Reed Payne. 140.
Payne, Jubal and Polly Harris, dau. Jubal, Dec. 17, 1839. Sur. Silas Payne. 86.
Payne, Jubal and Rhoda Basham, Aug. 20, 1808. Sur. Wm. Basham and Robt. Harrison.
Payne, Moses and Judith Beard, Jan. 27, 1808. Sur. Samuel Beard.
Payne, Robt. and Sarah B. Helm, Dec. 19, 1826. Sur. Jubal Early. 119.
Payne, Robt. and Elizabeth Wright, Oct. 4, 1813. 98.
Payne, Robt. P. and Elizabeth Payne, dau. Floyd, Mar 30, 1829. Sur. Calvin Bartholomew.
Payne, Silas and Mary Saunders, Jan. 5, 1847. 3.
Payne, Thos. and Mary A. Spencer, dau. Polly N. Newbill, Dec. 20, 1819. Sur. Jas. S. Newbill.
Payne, Thos. and Fanny Powell, dau. Robt., Jan. 14, 1799. Sur. Robt. Powell, Jr.
Payne, William and Sarah Payne, dau. Floyd, Dec. 3, 1828. Sur. Chas. B. Powell.
Peek (Peak), Abel and Lydia Jones, May 8, 1794. 52.
Peak, John and Elizabeth Carter, Sept. 2, 1797. 120.
Peak, Jacob and Polly Jones, Jan. 5, 1789. Sur. Abel Peak.
Pearcey, John and Lucinda Harkrider, Apr. 17, 1819. Sur. Jacob Harkrider. 98.
Pearcey, Nathan and Lucy Richardson, Jan 4, 1832. Sur. Luke Richardson. 140.

Pearson, Benj. E. and Matilda Robertson, Oct. 7, 1844. Sur. Thos. Pearson. 132.
Peerson, Doctor and Phoebe R. Brown, dau. John, Oct. 3, 1814. Sur. Joseph Rives. 8.
Peatt, Richard and Sarah Huckaly (Huckaly), Dec. 19, 1809. Sur. Thos. Highley. 117.
Peatross, Wm. L. and Ann F. Woods, Oct. 12, 1813. Sur. Robt. Wood.
Peckelsimer, Abraham Adam and Betsy Prator, July 25, 1800. Sur. Thos. Prater. 72.
Peckelsimer, David and Sarah Moore, dau. Sarah, June 14, 1802. Sur. Walter Bernard.
Peckelsimer, David and Elizabeth Sailor, Jan. 15, 1802.
Peckelsimer, John, Jr. and Charity Harger, dau. John, Sept. 7, 1803. Sur. Wilson Maddox.
Peckelsimer, Joseph, (from Montgomery Co.), and Susannah Trout, dau. Joseph, July 27, 1797. Sur. Jacob Trout.
Pickelsimer, Joseph and Christina Lazena, Mar. 18, 1793. Sur. Melcher Waggoner. 52.
Pickelsimer, Samuel and Catherine Logan, dau. Wm. and Marget, Mar. 18, 1793. Sur. Lemon Davis. 52.
Pickelsimer, Solomon and Polly Webb, Feb. —, 1804. Sur. Samuel Webb.
Peckner, Abram and Tena Hickman, dau. Barbaray, Aug. 18, 1790. Sur. Jacob Prillaman. 52.
Pedigay (Peregoy), Henry and Leah Cochrum, dau. Edward, Nov. 23, 1790. Sur. Thos. Cochran. 52.
Pedigo, Abel and Susannah Ross, dau. Daniel, Sept. 17, 1792. Sur. Wm. Ross. 52.
Pedigo, Churchill and Lucinda Cockran, Feb. 6, 1821. Sur. Spencer Cockran. 61.
Pedigo, John and Amy T. Neblett, gdau. Wm. Neblett, Aug. 2, 1824. Sur. Thos. Bondurant. 81.
Pedigo, Joseph and Sally Mitchell, Oct. 10, 1821. Sur. Wm. Mitchell.
Pedigo, Wm. and Lavinia Lemon, dau. Isaac, Sr., Jan. 29, 1825. Sur. Isaac Lemon. 130.
Peerey, Jas. Wm. and Cenia Clatcher, Sept. 3, 1813. Sur. Thos. Payne. 98.

Peggins, Geo. and Polly Blankenship, Aug. 26, 1824. Sur. Thos. Harmon.
Pelter, James and Luvisa Stanley, dau. Paten, Jan. 26, 1846. Sur. Madison M. Robertson.
Pelter, John and Elizabeth Lumsden, Apr. 6, 1835. Sur. Dudley Lumsden. 134.
Pelter, Pleasant M. and Julia Gilbert, Sept. 17, 1838. Sur. Samuel Gilbert.
Pettis, Mathew B. and Elizabeth Ferguson, Nov. 23, 1831. Sur. Josiah W. Dickinson. 53.
Pemberton, Edmond and Susannah Hundley, Feb. 15, 1819. Sur. Nehemiah Hundley.
Pendleton, Stephen and Elizabeth Willis, dau. Mark, Nov. 13, 1828. Sur. Henry Walker. 26.
Pennock, Wm. and Caty Boon, Oct. 3, 1803.
Pepple, Daniel (of Maryland), and Elizabeth Lewis, dau. Thos. and Elizabeth, May 18, 1789. Sur. Conrad Overlies. 52.
Perdue, Ada and Elizabeth Webb, June 10, 1813. Sur. Asa Ward. 8.
Perdue, Chas. R. and Lavinia F. Ward, dau. Asa, Oct. 5, 1846. Sur. Wm. R. Ward.
Perdue, Daniel and Rebecca F. Divers, Dec. 9, 1850. Sur. Christopher Divers. 86.
Perdue, Daniel, Jr. and Prudence Ward, dau. Daniel, Feb. 27, 1804.
Perdue, Daniel and Happy Ward, dau. Daniel, Sept. 24, 1792. Sur. Jesse Burns. 23.
Perdue, Edward and Elizabeth Bowman, Oct. 4, 1824. Sur. Asa Ward. 48.
Perdue, Eli and Mary A. W. Mitchell, dau. Wm., Feb. 15, 1848. Sur. Agnacious Mitchell.
Perdue, Eli and Sally Chitwood, Apr. 3, 1815. Sur. Wm. Chitwood.
Perdue, Isaiah and Milly Wingo, Oct. 10, 1815. Sur. James Wingo. 7.
Perdue, Jesse, Jr. and Dosha Arrington, Aug. 21, 1832. Sur. Thos. Poindexter.
Perdue, Jesse and Catherine Plyborne, Feb. 1, 1810. 8.

Perdue, John and Martha Martin, Nov. 25, 1825. Sur. Joseph Martin. 48.
Perdue, John and Elizabeth Wingo, dau. James and Kitty, Oct. 5, 1812. Sur. James Wingo. 8.
Perdue, John M. and Polly Ward, dau. Asa, Nov. 18, 1839. 18.
Perdue, John, Jr. and Asenath Ann Bennett, Jan. 27, 1840. Sur. Abner Bennett.
Perdue, Luke and Susannah Bowsman, Oct. 7, 1816. Sur. Geo. Bowman.
Perdue, Luke and Sarah Lynch, Sept. 6, 1847. Sur. Thos. Lynch. 18.
Perdue, Mark and Polly Bowsman, Mar. 11, 1815. Sur. Geo. Bowsman.
Perdue, Obediah and Caty Dillion, dau. Jesse, Oct. 4, 1847. 137.
Perdue, Obediah and Tempy Dillion, Sept. 23, 1825. Sur. Randolph Dillion. 48.
Perdue, Otey and Elizabeth Wray, Oct. 30, 1839. 18.
Perdue, Otey C. and Matilda Lumsden, Apr. 22, 1841. Sur. John W. Lumsden. 18.
Perdue, Ransom and Jane Angle, Oct. 27, 1835. 18.
Perdue, Silas and Nancy Powell, Sept. 5, 1842. Sur. Wm. Powell.
Perdue, Stephen and Elizabeth Sink, Dec. 21, 1838. Sur. Obediah Perdue. 18.
Perdue, Wm. and Ellender Jones, Apr. 26, 1794. 141.
Perdue, Wm. M. and Martha J. Arrington, Aug. 5, 1850. Sur. Chas. Arrington. 18.
Perdue, Wm. and Nancy Smith, dau. John, Oct. 6, 1806. Sur. John Smith. 8.
Perdue, Zachariah and Elizabeth Coon, Oct. 24, 1803. Sur. Henry Coon.
Pergrin, David and Susannah Brumley, May 3, 1799. Sur. Abraham Ritter. 89.
Perkins, James and Nancy Allen, dau. Winfred, Mar. 11, 1824. Sur. Chas. Allen. 12.
Perkins, John and Sarah Ann Richards, dau. Watman, May 4, 1839. Sur. Robt. Hodges. 3.
Perkins, Thos. and Nancy Manning, Sept. 20, 1858. Sur. Samuel Manning. 133.

Perkins, Wm. and Sicily Moss, Nov. 20, 1786. Sur. Thos. Prunty. 66.
Perren, Chas. and Catherine Jamison, 1795. 37.
Persinger, Geo. and Julia Ann Carper, Oct. 19, 1838. Sur. Moses G. Carper.
Peters, Aaron and Frances Flora, Jan. 26, 1856. 18.
Peters, Abraham and Elizabeth Bowman, Mar. 15, 1838. 18.
Peters, Christian and Charlotte Webster, Oct. 6, 1838. Sur. Wm. Webster.
Peters, Crisley and Mary Noftsinger, Feb. 20, 1796. Sur. John Nofsinger.
Peters, Daniel and Mary Brubaker, Jan. 7, 1850. Sur. Christian Brubaker.
Peters, David and Nancy Stover, dau. Henry, Dec. 29, 1845. Sur. Anderson Starkey. 18.
Peters, David and Christina Prupecker, Apr. 1, 1809. Sur. John Prupecker.
Peters, Geo. and Martha Wickman, Jan. 28, 1845. 18.
Peters, Henry and Tenor Kesler, Dec. 23, 1852. 96.
Peters, Jacob and Susannah Bowman, Jan. 7, 1805. Sur. John Bowman.
Peters, Jacob and Louisa C. Sink, July 5, 1841. Sur. Jacob Sink. 18.
Peters, Jacob and Barbara Gossett, Nov. 11, 1816. Sur. Stephen Peters. 130.
Peters, Joel and Elizabeth Barnhart, Aug. 22, 1833. 18.
Peters, Joel and Irena Bowman, Jan. 3, 1858.
Peters, John and Catherine Sink, Apr. 22, 1852. 11.
Peters, John B. and Mary A. Brown, Oct. 18, 1841. Sur. Cuthbert Weeks.
Peters, John and Elizabeth S. Gossett, Mar. 12, 1816. Sur. Abraham Gossett. 130.
Peters, Jonathan and Catherine Fisher, Mar. 22, 1817. Sur. Peter Fisher. 130.
Peters, Jonathan and Elizabeth Stover, Jan. 3, 1848. Sur. Henry Stover. 18.
Peters, Jordan N. and Sarah Cox, dau. Penima, Aug. 15, 1837. Sur. Moses W. Cox. 60.

Peters, Joseph and Dorinda Turner, Nov. 22, 1841. Sur. Lee Turner.
Peters, Joseph and Patsy Smith, dau. Gideon, Sept. 1, 1830. Sur. Samuel Grimmett. 61.
Peters, Landon and Mary Troup, dau. Henry and Dorothy, Oct. 6, 1817. Sur. Jacob Troup.
Peters, Matthew and Hannah Toney, dau. Wm., Sr., Jan. 20, 1791. Sur. Poindexter Toney. 52.
Peters, Michael and Mary Flora, Dec. 7, 1808. Sur. Joseph Flora. 180.
Peters, Moses and Rebecca Barnhart, Sept. 14, 1844. Sur. Abraham Barnhart. 18.
Peters, Samuel and Hannah Flora, Dec. 17, 1858. Sur. John Flora. 18.
Peters, Stephen and Elizabeth Palmer, Jan. 3, 1848. Sur. Samuel T. Palmer. 68.
Peters, Wm. and Alla Troup, dau. Henry and Dorothy, Dec. 12, 1818. Sur. Jacob Troup.
Peters, Wm. and Lydia Kemplin, Mar. 27, 1841. Sur. Jess Edward. 68.
Peters, Wm. and Ruth Smith, dau. Gideon, Mar. 21, 1829. Sur. John Powers.
Peters, Zachariah and Ally Hale, dau. Wm., Nov. 27, 1846. Sur. David Hale. 18.
Pew, Riley and Oriney McNeil, Sept. 10, 1833. Sur. John Floyd.
Phelps, John and Polly Ferguson, Feb. 16, 1804. Sur. John Ferguson.
Phelps, Richard and Bethany E. Thurman, dau. David, May 15, 1828. Sur. Wm. B. Thurman. 3.
Phillips, Geo. N. and Sally Smith, Aug. 6, 1806. Sur. Wm. Kemp. 8.
Phillips, John and Agnes Bradley, dau. Wm., Aug. 6, 1810. Sur. Joseph Ball.
Phillips, Wm. and Ellender Bradley, Nov. 10, 1817. Sur. Richard Bradley. 98.
Philpot, Samuel and Frances Kesterson, Oct. 21, 1803. Sur. Micajah Stone.

Picklesimer, Abraham and Polly Kingary, dau. Peter, Oct. 28, 1790. Sur. John Wimmer. 52.
Pinckard, Bailey and Nancy Waller, Nov. 22, 1811. Sur. Benj. Waller.
Pinckard, Baily W. and Rebecca Smith, Dec. 11, 1851. 14.
Pinckard, Benj. F. and Julia F. Hunt, dau. Chas., Oct. 3, 1843. Sur. Hartwell Carter.
Pinchard, Chas. G. and Sophia Ann Ferguson, Oct. 28, 1850. Sur. Lewis H. Turnbull. 134.
Pinckard, Cyrus E. and Amanda Luke, Feb. 13, 1843. Sur. Wm. Luke. 68.
Pinckard, John and Polly Waller, June 3, 1811. Sur. Benj. Waller.
Pinckard, Robt. and Jane Belcher, Sept. 19, 1829. Sur. Francis Belcher.
Pinckard, Robt., Jr. and Martha Lambert, Oct. 8, 1835. Sur. Elias Pinckard.
Pinkard, Wm. and Emaline Cooper, dau. George, Oct. 16, 1848. Sur. Peter Campbell. 80.
Plasters, Fleming and Jane Hall, Feb. 15, 1836. Sur. Joshua Hall. 129.
Plaister, Thos., s. Michael and Charity, and Mary Carter, dau. Ann, May 19, 1791. Sur. Isaac Lemon. 52.
Plaister, Wm. and Elizabeth Griffith, Feb. 1, 1795. Sur. Wm. Wright. 66.
Plunkett, Algeron S. and Sarah Neathawk, Oct. 11, 1858.
Plyborne, Jacob and Elizabeth Dillion, Mar. 10, 1826. Sur. John Dillion. 48.
Plyborne, John and Elizabeth Beckner, Oct. 1, 1832. Sur. Stephen Sink.
Plyborne, Ransom and Eveline Powell, dau. Wm. and Mary, Dec. 4, 1843. Sur. Courtland Cabaniss.
Poe, Wm. P. and Mary M. Hatcher, Aug. 22, 1851. 127
Poff, James and Polly Gray, Jan. 16, 1837. Sur. Edward Gray. 18.
Poff, Lewis and Perlina Webb, Jan. 8, 1851. 68.
Poff, Peter and Catherine Radford, Oct. 27, 1837. Sur. Lewis Radford. 68.
Poindexter, John M. and Elizabeth W. Helm, Apr. 15, 1837. Sur. M. G. Carper.

Poindexter, John W. and Nancy F. Witcher, Mar. 19, 1839. Sur. Wm. Parker. 8.

Poindexter, Stephen F. and Mary A. Dudley, Oct. 18, 1858.

Pollard, Chattin and Milly Greer, dau. Moses, Sept. 18, 1790. Sur. Daniel Brown. 52.

Pollard, Geo. and Jane Butler, dau. Elizabeth and Edward, Dec. 1, 1819. 130.

Pollard, Henry C. and Elizabeth L. Wood, June 17, 1852. 134.

Pollard, Moses and Polly Greer, Jan. 26, 1818. Sur. Samuel W. Greer. 130.

Polson, Absalom and Delilah Davis, dau. Joseph, Sept. 30, 1799. Sur. Solomon Grimmet.

Porter, David and Abagail Howell, dau. Joshua, Dec. 29, 1788. Sur. Joshua Howell.

Porter, Thos. and Rachael Hale, dau. Joseph, Oct. 23, 1789. Sur. John Hale. 66.

Poteet, Elijah and Jane Hughes, May 21, 1814. Sur. Benj. Wray. 130.

Poteet, Geo. and Nancy Custer, Aug. 1, 1814. Sur. Abraham Custer. 130.

Poteet, James and Sarah Arthur, Dec. 14, 1796. Sur. John Arthur.

Poteet, James and Mary Ann Kingery, dau. Henry, Mar. 15, 1847. Sur. John Bowman. 18.

Poteet, John and Susan P. B. Fowler, Sept. 25, 1838. Sur. Samuel S. P. Thompson.

Potter, Elias and Elizabeth Potter, Aug. 27, 1802.

Potter, Elias, s. Benj. and Sarah Roach, dau. Gideon, Nov. 26, 1794.

Potter Elisha and Hannah Toney, Jan. 20, 1791.

Potter, Elisha and Judah Dalton, dau. James and Elizabeth, June 24, 1791. Sur. John Kerby.

Potter, John and Phebe Lumsden, Apr. 15, 1813. Sur. Chas. Lumsden. 8.

Potter, Lewis and Cassandra Walker, dau. Elisha, Nov. 8, 1824. Sur. Nathaniel Walker.

Potter, Lewis and Nancy Hickerson, dau. Thomas, Aug. 15, 1786. Sur. Daniel Hickerman.

Potter, Moses and Frances Kirby, dau. Dicey Bartee, Jan. 14, 1789. Sur. John Bartee. 37.
Potter, Thos. and Susannah Shockley, dau. Levicy Rebeckah, Jan. 5, 1801. 37.
Powell, Archibald and Elizabeth Crow, July 28, 1811. Sur. Robt. Powell.
Powell, Booker and Elizabeth Jane Divers, dau. Elizabeth, Feb. 12, 1845. Sur. Silas G. Divers.
Powell, Chas. and Lucinda Hancock, Apr. 30, 1809. Sur. Lewis Hancock. 8.
Powell, Chas. Bcoker and Elizabeth Frith, July 29, 1852. 75.
Powell, Edward and Sarah Divers, May 16, 1818. Sur. Wm. Divers.
Powell, Edward and Jane Wingo, Jan. 3, 1831. Sur. James Williams. 48.
Powell, John W. and Polly Divers, Jan. 4, 1819. Sur. Aquila Divers.
Powell, John W. and Harriet H. Dudley, g. Thos. T. English, Jan. 3, 1848. 104.
Powell, Lewellin H. and Elizabeth H. Sample, dau. John, Oct. 26, 1840. Sur. Thos. S. Divers.
Powell, Ransom and Elizabeth Semmons, dau. Benj., Nov. 5, 1844. Sur. Thos. W. Murrell. 14.
Powell, Robt., Jr. and Polly Sutherland, dau. Philemon, Jan. 17, 1803.
Powell, Samuel A., s. Wm., and Hopy A. Dudley, dau. Patty, Jan. 7, 1833. Sur. Chas. B. Powell.
Powell, Thos. and Hessa Hall, Oct. 21, 1829. Sur. Currell Hale.
Powell, Wm. and Sophia Hancock, dau. Lew, Dec. 26, 1804. Sur. Benj. Hancock.
Powell, Wm. and Sarah R. Newbill, dau. Nathaniel, Sept. 26, 1814. Sur. Tyree G. Newbill.
Powell, Wm. and Julia A. Dillion, dau. Henry, Nov. 28, 1842. Sur. Henry C. Dillion. 86.
Powell, Wm. H. and Ann Jane Sample, Jan. 16, 1845. Sur. Robt. A. Scott. 14.
Prather, John D. and Sarah L. Hail, dau. Francis, Sept. 21, 1848. Sur. Valentine Ferris. 111.

Prather, John and Kitty Richardson, Dec. 3, 1831. Sur. Tazewell Richardson. 140.
Prater, Jourdan and Jane Atkins, dau. John, Jan. 18, 1826. Sur. John P. Bays.
Pratt, David (illegible).
Pratt, Richard and Sarah Hook, Dec. 19, 1809.
Pratt, Wm. and Julia Brockman, Jan. 13, 1817. Sur. Elijah Brockman. 98.
Pressel, Daniel and Macklin Reedie, Mar. 25, 1792. Sur. Daniel Reedie. 23.
Preston, Booker and Mary Ferguson, dau. Noah and Fanny, Apr. 18, 1832. Sur. Eli Ferguson. 140.
Preston, Bowker and Catherine Hook, dau. John, July 27, 1802. Sur. Henry Hook.
Preston, Caleb and Elizabeth Majors, Aug. 2, 1819. Sur. Henry Board. 48.
Preston, John and Elizabeth Barrett, dau. Geo., July 13, 1795. Sur. Wm. Robertson.
Preston, Moses and Sparkey Amos, Jan. 9, 1815. Sur. James Amos. 98.
Preston, Stephen and Polly Smith, July 18, 1807. Sur. Stephen Smith.
Price, Cyrus and Elizabeth Boone, Feb. 7, 1831. Sur. Weatherston S. Greer. 48.
Price, David and Sally Hill, dau. F., Nov. 5, 1797. Sur. John Hill.
Price, Peters G. and Malinda Callaway, dau. Henry, June 17, 1847. Sur. Robt. A. Scott.
Price, Robt. and Jane Keen, gdau. Elizabeth Keen, Apr. 14, 1840. Sur. Elisha Keen, Jr.
Price, Tazwell and Elizabeth A. Hancock, dau. Benj., Feb. 15, 1847. Sur. Robt. A. Scott.
Prillaman, Christopher and Elizabeth Wright, dau. Molly, June 18, 1796. Sur. Jacob Prillaman.
Prillaman, Daniel and Betsy Standley, Feb. 24, 1829. Sur. Peter Standley. 132.
Prillaman, David and Sally Helm, Jan. 16, 1821. Sur. Thos. Helms.

Prillaman, Dennis and Sally Walker, Sept. 27, 1809. Sur. Geo. Walker. 44.
Prillaman, Elisha and Mary Jane Turner, dau. Constantine, Feb. 5, 1849. Sur. Meshack Turner. 132.
Prillaman, Isaac and Ruth Prillaman, Jan. 5, 1824. Sur. Thos. Helms. 61.
Prillaman, John and Lucy Walker, July 30, 1810. 117.
Prillaman, Medad, s. Abraham, and Susan Jane Burd, dau. Wm., Sept. 3, 1853. 68.
Prindle, Wm. and Amy Gadd, dau. Wm. W., Feb. 12, 1825. Sur. Caleb Compton. 130.
Prim, David and Nelly Parker, Sept. 26, 1795.
Profit, Austin and Viney Newberry, dau. Sarah, Sept. 14, 1858. Sur. John A. Newberry.
Profit, Austin and Patsy Rakes, June 4, 1813. Sur. Elisha Rakes.
Proffit, David and Sarah Cockran, Oct. 21, 1813.
Proffit, Elisha, s. Austin, and Elizabeth Underwood, dau. Samuel, May 22, 1845. Sur. John Underwood.
Prunty (Primty), James and Martha Wimmer Turner, June 26, 1794. 52.
Prunty, Jesse and Nancy Finney, Mar. 18, 1802. Sur. John Finney.
Prunty, Jesse and Charlotte Temple Pinckard, dau. Mary, Jan. 18, 1845. Sur. Wm. Pinckard.
Prunty, John and Lucinda Pinckard, Mar. 25, 1828. Sur. John Pinckard.
Prunty, John and Cassathia Clardy, Sept. 21, 1816. Sur. Thos. Hale.
Prunty, Robt., Jr. and Judith Faris, May 6, 1816. Sur. Lankford Brizendine. 7.
Prunty, Robt. and Ann E. Finney, dau. Anna, May 17, 1845. Sur. Wesley A. Finney. 14.
Prunty, Thos. and Sally Rives, dau. Burwell, Aug. 10, 1804. Sur. Joseph Rives.
Prupecker, Abraham and Elizabeth Flora, Mar. 14, 1817. Sur. Jacob Flora. 130.
Prupecker, Christopher and Elizabeth Flora, Feb. 12, 1817. Sur. Joseph Flora.

Prupecker, Henry and Sally Eller, Jan. 24, 1810. Sur. Joseph Flora.
Prupecker, Henry and Susannah Fisher, May 22, 1827. 18.
Prupecker, Henry and Elizabeth Flora, dau. Jacob, Mar. 19, 1795. Sur. Joseph Flora. 89.
Prupecker, Jacob and Hannah Peters, Mar. 29, 1802. Sur. Stephen Peters. 72.
Prupecker, Joel and Elizabeth Fisher, dau. Peter, Oct. 31, 1825. Sur. Peter Fisher.
Prupecker, John and Phebe Harter, Aug. 10, 1798. Sur. Christian Harter.
Prupecker, Samuel and Elizabeth Wimmer, Apr. 21, 1822. Sur. Jacob Wimmer.
Puckett, Jacob and Lucy Helms, Mar. 10, 1852. 40.
Puckett, James and Sophia Clingenpeel, dau. Jonathan, Feb. 7, 1842. Sur. Abram Childress.
Puckett, Samuel and Susan Snyder, Dec. 24, 1849. Sur. Geo. Snyder. 96.
Puckett, Tazewell, s. Sarah and Jacob, and Elizabeth Helms, dau. Wm. and Barbary, Dec. 8, 1853. 96.
Puckleman, Abraham and Polly Kingery, Oct. 19, 1790.
Pugh, Fleming and Elizabeth Leffew, July 12, 1845. Sur. Thos. Leffew. 20.
Pugh, James and Mary Boyd, dau. Brigit Scott, Aug. 5, 1813. Sur. Brice Edwards.
Pugh, James and Mary Hall, dau. Jim, Dec. 2, 1853. 134.
Pugh, Richard, Jr. and Elizabeth Hood, dau. Martha, Aug. 14, 1834. Sur. David Wingo.
Pugh, Wm. and Elizabeth Ratcliff, Aug. 28, 1811. Sur. Richard Pugh. 130.
Pyrtle, Joseph and Rebecca Miller, Sept. 22, 1803. Surs. Joseph Miller and David Goode. 122.
Quarles, James Wm. and Elizabeth Rives, (of Bedford), dau. Frederick, Jan. 12, 1802. Surs. George Rives and Wm. Quarles.
Quigley, Elias and Susannah McCraw, July 27, 1822. Surs. John Gearhart and Ellias Leffew.
Quigley, James and Charity Bybee, May 20, 1797. Sur. Sherwood Bybee.

Radford, Geo. and Margaret Rigney, Dec. 18, 1832. Sur. Isaac Janney. 61.
Radford, Geo. and Catherine Woodcock, dau. Henry, Oct. 29, 1789.
Radford, James W. and Nancy Smith, dau. Samuel and Rosanah, Oct. 17, 1842. Sur. Creed Smith. 68.
Radford, James T. and Lydia Janney, dau. Isaac, Nov. 15, 1845. Sur. Lewis Radford. 68.
Radford, James and Jane Cannaday, Jan. 26, 1844. Sur. Stephen Thomas.
Radford, John and Nancy Crawford, dau. Rachael, May 25, 1799. Sur. Stephen Allen.
Radford, John and Gartry Truman, dau. Mary and Wm., Oct. 17, 1794. Sur. Geo. Blades.
Radford, Joshua and Elizabeth Smith, Sept. 25, 1811. Sur. Robt. Radford.
Radford, Lewis and Elizabeth Via, dau. Anderson, June 24, 1850. Sur. Sparel Via.
Radford, Lewis and Sarah Ascue, Feb. 16, 1819. Sur. Samuel Radford.
Radford, Robt., s. Lewis, and Harriet Moore, Sept. 20, 1843. Sur. Lewis Radford. 68.
Radford, Samuel and Ellen Radford, dau. Lewis, Nov. 12, 1839. Sur. Geo. Radford. 68.
Radford, Samuel and Joannah Underwood, May 28, 1818. Sur. Edmund Underwood.
Radford, Wm. and Ruth James, dau. Reuben, Oct. 9, 1848. Sur. James Underwood. 68.
Ragland, Wm. and Phebe Clabon, dau. Elizabeth, Nov. 21, 1796. Sur. Geo. Claibone.
Rains, Richard and Nancy Kester, Mar. 4, 1851. 96.
Rains, Wm. H. and Susannah L. Ashworth, Oct. 1, 1833. Sur. Daniel Vincent. 48.
Rakes, Anthony and Mary Oakes, dau. William, Feb. 20, 1807. Sur. Henry Rakes.
Rakes, Carter and Bitha Parker, Mar. 27, 1828. Sur. Drury Moore. 129.
Rakes, Chas., s. Samuel, and Mary Ann Griffith Feb. 16, 1841. Sur. Daniel Griffith. 60.

Rakes, German, and Mary Ann Allen, dau. Wm., Jan. 9, 1850. Sur. Wm. Allen.
Rakes, John Henry, s. Wm., and Elizabeth Maxey, dau. Arthur, Nov. 3, 1853. 68.
Rakes, Lewis and Mariah Wimphrey, dau. Richard R., Sept. 8, 1832. Sur. Carter Rakes. 61.
Rakes, Samuel and Lucinda Nowlin, dau. John, Dec. 18, 1815. Sur. Pleasant Nowlin.
Rakes, Samuel and Elizabeth Winfree, dau. Stephen, Mar. 18, 1818. Sur. Stephen Winfree.
Rakes, Samuel T. and Ruth Ann Thomas, Dec. 18, 1852. 31.
Rakes, Wm. B. and Elizabeth E. Hash, Dec. 23, 1858.
Rakes, Wm., s. Nancy, and Celia Leffew, Dec. 30, 1829. Sur. Isham High. 26.
Raley, Charles and Anne B. Goodwin, dau. John Henry, Oct. 21, 1797. Sur. Samuel Moody.
Ramsey, Armistead and Lucy Zeigler, Jan. 3, 1831. Sur. John Zeigler. 3.
Ramsey, Booker and Isabella P. Thornton, Oct. 20, 1852. 19.
Ramsey, Daniel and Nancy Goode, Sept. 26, 1823.
Ramsey, Hailey S. and Ester Zeigler, dau. Jacob, Feb. 22, 1803. Sur. Isaiah Ramsey.
Ramsey, John and Elizabeth Ann Martin, Dec. 2, 1799. Sur. James Martin. 72.
Ramsey, Joseph and Harriet E. Stanley, dau. Paten, Sept. 21, 1850. Sur. James Peters. 19.
Ramsey, Noton and Rachael Witcher, May 30, 1808.
Ramsey, Parks H. and Tabitha T. Russell, June 7, 1841. Sur. Benj. T. Bird.
Ramsey, Theodrick and Sarah Williams, dau. David, Mar. 19, 1811. Sur. John Williams.
Ramsey, Thos. and Winney Letteral, Nov. 9, 1791. Sur. Meshack Hodges.
Ramsey, Thos. and Nancy Stewart, dau. David, July 20, 1792. Sur. Meshack Hodges.
Ramsey, Thos. and Judy Mullins, Nov. 6, 1826. Sur. Bowker Mullins. 130.
Ramsey, Wm. and Rhoda McMillion, Mar. 17, 1786.

Ramsey, Wm. and Susannah Zeigler, dau. Jacob and Ester, Nov. 29, 1809. Sur. Haily S. Ramsey. 8.
Ramsey, Woodson and Sally Witcher, Apr. 10, 1797.
Randues, Benj. and Doshia Ross, Apr. 15, 1803.
Rasor, Geo. and Elizabeth Hudson, dau. John and Elizabeth, Nov. 5, 1804. Sur. Abel Hudson.
Ratcliff, Hugh Allen and Patsey Newberry, Aug. 3, 1829. Sur. Thos. Newberry.
Ratcliff, Ruben and Pheby Ratcliff, dau. Silas and Elizabeth, July 1, 1786. Sur. Thos. Dudley.
Ratliff, John and Eliza Scott, Dec. 12, 1847. Sur. John Scott. 60.
Ratliff, Wm. and Frances Moore, dau. James, Oct. 1, 1839. Sur. Peter Sigmon. 68.
Ray, James and Susannah Chamber, dau. John, Jan. 10, 1803. Sur. Wm. Stith.
Ray, Wm. and Pheby Leffew, dau. Enoch, Mar. 6, 1848. Sur. Elisha Hall. 42.
Read, Geo. and Peggy Griffith, Feb. 10, 1806. Sur. Jonathan Griffith. 130.
Read, John and Susannah Young, dau. Wm., Feb. 23, 1790. Sur. Wm. Young. 52.
Read, Wm. and Sarah Delaney, dau. Samuel and Mary, Feb. 20, 1790. Sur. Edward Abshire. 52.
Reagen, Benj. and Polly Price, dau. Jonathan, Jan. 20, 1802. Sur. Jonathan Price. 129.
Reall, Andrew and Mary Dirst, dau. Mary, Feb. 15, 1796. Sur. Tobias Miller.
Reed, Alfred and Elizabeth Olderman, Mar. 16, 1851. 18.
Reed, Hamilton and Lucy Roles, July 14, 1853. 68.
Reel, Andrew and Susan Peters, Oct. 16, 1839. Sur. Wm. Hixon.
Rheal, Geo. and Hannah Greer, dau. Wm., Mar. 22, 1787. Sur. Wm. Kelley. 66.
Reel, Henry and Patty Akers, dau. Wm., Apr. 27, 1790. Sur. Thos. Ferguson. 52.
Real, Henry and Elizabeth Lemon, dau. Isaac, Aug. 29, 1820. Sur. Benj. Lamon.
Reel, John and Mary Akers, May 26, 1810. Sur. James Akers. 122.

Reel, Michael and Ann Scott, dau. Wm., Jan. 2, 1833. Sur. John Kemp. 48.
Reese, Samuel and Sophia Booth, dau. Richard, Dec. 31, 1803. Sur. Richard Booth.
Reese, Silas G. and Catherine E. Callaway, Nov. 5, 1833. Sur. James Callaway. 48.
Reese, Wm. and Mary Smith Booth, dau. Richard, Nov. 17, 1797. Sur. Richard Booth.
Reges, Townley and Charity Williams, Feb. 4, 1799. Sur. John Guilliams.
Rentfro, Jesse and Lucy Bates, July 13, 1787. Sur. Wm. Rentfro. 52.
Rentfro, Turpin and Sarah Troupe, (Troupt), Apr. 7, 1794. Sur. Moses Rentfro. 52.
Repeto (Rippito), Wm. and Fanny Jones, Mar. 6, 1792. Sur. Joshua Rentfro. 52.
Reynolds, Archibald and Betsey Ann Martin, dau. John Aug. 27, 1808. Sur. John Martin, Jr.
Reynolds, Chas. B. and Elizabeth Guerrant, Mar. 1, 1827. Sur. Peter Guerrant, Sr. 48.
Reynolds, Corbin M. and Lucy Callaway, Apr. 25, 1844. Sur. Chas. B. Reynolds. 104.
Reynolds, James and Mary Ross, Mar. 5, 1795. 52.
Reynolds, Thos. and Madeline G. D. Wade, dau. Isaac, Dec. 4, 1844. Sur. Aburtis Hill. 18.
Rhodes, Chas. W. and Mary B. Ferguson, May 6, 1833.
Rhodes, Chas. W. and Elizabeth Donahaven, Oct. 22, 1844. Sur. Wilson Donahower. 18.
Rice, David and Sally Hill, Nov. 16, 1797.
Rice, James L. and Martha J. Walker, dau. Robt. M., Oct. 18, 1844. Sur. Wm. Rice. 14.
Rice, Thos., s. Thos., and Mary Palmer, dau. Booker, July 12, 1853. 10.
Rice, Wm. and Charlotte Kemp, dau. James, Aug. 20, 1845. Sur. Wm. W. Laprad.
Rich, David and Sally Pridy, dau. Nancy, Dec. 29, 1789. Sur. Moses Brock.
Richards, Benj. and Polly Williams, dau. Cedric, Dec. 3, 1804. Sur. Joseph Williams.

Richards, Bolling and Mary P. Delancy, dau. Mahala Webb, Nov. 20, 1832. Sur. Christopher Richards. 60.
Richards, Chas. and Sarah Richards, dau. Susannah, July 20, 1827. Sur. Joab Hodges.
Richards, Christopher and Nancy Moore, Feb. 9, 1826. Sur. Jacob Moore.
Richards, David and Polly Hodges, July 21, 1818.
Richards, Edmund and Sally Warren, dau. Zachariah, Mar. 22, 1802. Sur. Wilson Maddox. 72.
Richards, Gabriel and Martha Dearin, dau. Joel, Oct. 4, 1858. Sur. Elijah Hodges. 133.
Richards, Isaiah and Hannah Gearhart, dau. Peter, Aug. 26, 1796. Sur. Valentine Gearhart.
Richards, Joel and Lucy Warren, dau. Elijah, Dec. 19, 1812. Sur. Robt. C. Jones. 8.
Richards, Pleasant and Ann Cooper, Sept. 29, 1826. Sur. Wm. Cooper.
Richards, Powhatan and Harriet Lavinder, Feb. 3, 1849. Sur. Sur. Wm. Lavender. 134.
Richards, Robt. and Cynthia Hodges, Aug. 4, 1829. Sur. Wiley Hall. 132.
Richards, Waitman and Sally Hodges, dau. Robt., Jan. 11, 1797. Sur. Wilson Maddox.
Richardson, Aaron and Sallie Bennett, Oct. 6, 1788. Sur. Wm. Bennett. 37.
Richerson, Benj. and Celia Basham, dau. Wm., June 17, 1800. Sur. Wm. Basham. 21.
Richardson, Benj. and Ellen Holt, dau. Ambrose, Dec. 19, 1789. Sur. Daniel Richardson. 37.
Richardson, Chas. and Margaret Meador, June 18, 1823. Sur. Chesley Cooper. 130.
Richison, David and Mary Talley, dau. Happy, Sept. 7, 1797. Sur. Samuel King.
Richardson, Edmund and Obedience Cooper, dau. Eiles and Sarah, Jan. 22, 1816. Sur. Thos. Cooper.
Richardson, Edmond and Elizabeth Cooper, dau. Arthur, Dec. 16, 1799. Sur. Nathaniel Cooper. 21.
Richardson, Geo. and Elizabeth Cooper, Dec. 14, 1840. Sur. Iles Cooper.

Richardson, Geo. S. and Sarah J. Hazelwood, Feb. 2, 1852. 144.
Richardson, John and Jane Smith, June 18, 1825. Sur. John Smith. 61.
Richardson, John George and Dolly F. Early, dau. Elizabeth Conaway, Sept. 17, 1810. Sur. Aaron Franklin.
Richardson, Lot and Mary Feathers, dau. Peter and Susan, Oct. 9, 1845. Sur. Nathan Pearey.
Richardson, Randolph and Elizabeth Meador, dau. Hezekiah, Jan. 28, 1832. Sur. Luke Richardson. 140.
Richardson, Richard and Sarah Hubble, Feb. 24, 1789. Sur. David Duease.
Richardson, Sparrel and Nancy J. Harris, Jan. 7, 1843. Sur. Jubal Harris.
Richardson, Tazwell and Polly Ferguson, Dec. 17, 1832. Sur. John Ferguson, Jr.
Richardson, Turner and Eleanor Payne, Dec. 27, 1825. Sur. Joseph Payne.
Richardson, Turner and Harriet Payne, dau. B. W., June 17, 1834. Sur. Reed Payne.
Richeson, Wm. and Nancy Wright, Mar. 24, 1806. Sur. Joseph Wright.
Richardson, Wm. and Mary Adney, dau. Thos., Feb. 18, 1800. Sur. James McVey, Jr.
Richardson, Wm. P. and Mary M. Hopkins, Apr. 17, 1847. Sur. Wm. Hopkins. 86.
Richeson, Bowker and Nancy Cheatham, dau. Leonard, Jan. 25, 1805. Sur. Jasper Franklin.
Richeson, Edmond and Elizabeth Moody (Woody), Dec. 16, 1799.
Richeson, Edward and Mary Betz, Jan. 5, 1818. Sur. Mathias Crook. 98.
Richeson, Luke and Nancy Meador, Jan. 22, 1823. Sur. Geo. Meador.
Richeson, Richard and Rachael Kelly Wright, Jan. 30, 1797. Sur. Wm. Kelly.
Richeson, Skelton and Naomi Ferguson, dau. John, June 14, 1813. Sur. John Plyborn. 130.
Richey, John and Catherine Hunley, Nov. 17, 1796. 89.
Riddle, Geo. and Elizabeth Martin, Oct. 25, 1808. Sur. Wm. Ferguson.

WINGFIELD'S WORKS 195

Ridgeway, Edmund and Malinda Cooper, dau. Milly, July 14, 1821. Sur. Anderson Cooper. 130.
Ridgeway, Edward and Martha Merryman, Jan. 7, 1853. 18.
Rigney, Creed J. and Elizabeth Price, dau. Sarah, Dec. 14, 1840. Sur. Daniel Noble.
Rigney Wm. and Sophia Stephens, Nov. 4, 1832. Sur. Thos. Wood. 48.
Rigney, Wm. and Ameriah Potter, Sept. 19, 1791. Sur. Benj. Potter.
Rinehart, Jacob and Susannah Brower, Jan. 6, 1806. Sur. Enoch Brower. 130.
Ritter, Abraham and Catherine Kelly, dau. Wm., Mar. 7, 1791. Sur. John Kelly. 52.
Ritter, John and Eva Miller, Aug. 7, 1787. Sur. Wm. Kelly. 66.
Ritter, John and Delilah Wilson, dau. John and Elizabeth, Mar. 18, 1793. Sur. Joseph Ritter. 52.
Ritter, Joseph and Mary Kelly, May 10, 1787. Sur. Wm. Rentfro. 52.
Rives, Doctor B. F. and Gilley E. Keen, Apr. 8, 1846. Sur. Moses G. Carper. 104.
Rives, Joseph and Frances Prunty, dau. Robt., Feb. 15, 1814. Sur. Chas. Lumsden. 8.
Rives, Wm. W. and Sarah Ann Hatcher, Sept. 15, 1845. Sur. Doctor B. F. Rives.
Roason (Rosson), Wm. and Elizabeth Webster, Aug. 8, 1792. Sur. Edward Toney. 23.
Roberson, James and Joan B. Meador, —, 1851. 86.
Roberson, John and Sarah Boyd, Nov. 23, 1799. Sur. Abram Harris. 21.
Robertson, Leach and Mary F. Powell, dau. Mary, Jan. 5, 1846. Sur. Wm. T. Powell.
Robinson, Wm. and Nancy Skinner Duvall, dau. Benjamin, Aug. 19, 1786. Sur. Marren Duvall. 66.
Roberts, James and Mary Nancy Underwood, dau. Samuel, Dec. 27, 1790. Sur. James Stinnet.
Roberts, John and Elizabeth Mitchell, June 3, 1805. Sur. James Mitchell. 8.
Roberts, John and Elizabeth Smith, Dec. 4, 1815. Sur. Wm. R. Smith.

Roberts, Wm. and Polly Allen, July 12, 1819. Sur. James Allen.
Robertson, Berry and Milly Dudley, Dec. 23, 1825. Sur. James Dudley.
Robertson, David and Mary Hunter, June 6, 1803. Sur. John Hunter. 72.
Robertson, Edward and Mary Coger, dau. Peter and Polly, Oct. 13, 1804. Sur. Wm. Coger.
Robertson, Geo. and Susannah Woody, Nov. 1798. Sur. Martin Woody.
Robertson, Granville and Mary B. Ferguson, May 6, 1833. Sur. Stephen Ferguson. 48.
Robertson, Granville and Sarah Powell, Oct. 4, 1858.
Robertson, Henry and Martha Arnold, Mar. 6, 1802. Sur. Elisha Arnold.
Robertson, Hezekiah and Catherine Carrow, Aug. 16, 1858.
Robertson, James and Frances English, dau. Nancy, May 7, 1831. Sur. John W. Smith.
Robertson, John and Hannah Smith, Sept. 3, 1804. Sur. John Smith.
Robertson, John R. and Julia Ann Dudley, Oct. 18, 1858.
Robertson, John and Aggy Hudson, Oct. 6, 1828. Sur. Joel Hudson.
Robertson, Jordan and Elizabeth Chewning, Jan. 5, 1846. Sur. Nathaniel Chewning.
Robinson, Littleberry and Nancy Watts, Nov. 28, 1805. Sur. Benj. Watts.
Robertson, Mills and May Taylor, Apr. 2, 1832. Sur. John Boon. 48.
Robertson, Richard and Polly Camp, dau. John, Dec. 24, 1790. Sur. Thos. Camp.
Robertson, Richard and Sarah Divers, Nov. 9, 1840. Sur. Silas G. Divers. 86.
Robertson, Samuel J. and Elizabeth Divers, Mar. 16, 1840. Sur. Silas Divers. 86.
Robertson, Smithson D. and Sarah M. Robertson, dau. John, Mar. 1, 1847. Sur. James Robertson. 86.
Robertson, Stephen and Martha A. Palmer, Nov. 25, 1828. Sur. John P. Palmer. 140.

Robertson, Thos. B. and Charlotte Divers, Feb. 7, 1842. Sur. Silas G. Divers. 86.
Robertson, Thos. and Naomi Wade, dau. Fanny, Feb. 7, 1803. Sur. Samuel McCornell.
Robertson, Thos. and Miriam Hall, dau. Hiram, Dec. 24, 1826. Sur. Hezekiah Hall. 48.
Robertson, Wm. and Rebecca Brizendine, Apr. 19, 1813. Sur. Leroy Brizendine. 8.
Robertson, Wm. and Nancy H. Ferguson, July 7, 1834. Sur. Daniel Ferguson.
Robertson, Wyatt and Cynthia E. Ferguson, dau. Daniel, Mar. 3, 1834. Sur. Albert G. Ferguson. 140.
Robeson, Albert M. and Janetta Smelser, Sept. 26, 1836. 18.
Robins, Absalom and Mary Ogle, Mar. 13, 1787. Sur. Herculus Ogle. 66.
Robins, Daniel C. and Keziah Alee, dau. Nicholas, Feb. 21, 1788. Sur. David Alee.
Robins, Jacob and Rachael Robbins, Nov. 15, 1790. Surs. Wm. Robins, Jacob and Mary Robbins, Nathaniel and Ann Robbins. 52.
Robins, Wm. and Dolly Jefferson, dau. Fred, Dec. 26, 1826. Sur. Wm. Jefferson.
Robins, John and Sarah Boid, Nov. 23, 1813. Sur. Abraham Harris.
Rodgers, Andrew and Polly Starkey, Oct. 23, 1806. Sur. John Rodgers.
Rodgers, Benj. and Prucilla Doss, Dec. 21, 1795. Sur. Joshua Doss.
Rodgers, Josiah and Martha Clack, dau. Spencer Clack, Jan. 22, 1786. Sur. Richard Litteral.
Rodgers, Josiah and Chole Hill, Apr. 16, 1806. Sur. Wm. Armstrong.
Ronnels, Thos. and Mary Love, Mar. 2, 1797. 89.
Ross, Benj. and Peggy Dunn, dau. Thos., Jan. 2, 1807. Sur. Christopher Woodall.
Ross, David and Sally Anderson, dau. John, Oct. 20, 1802. Sur. John Anderson. 122.
Ross, McD. and Minerva T. Williams, Mar. 10, 1852. 127.
Ross, David and Jane Lyon, Aug. 2, 1819. Sur. Peter Lyon.

Ross, David and Mary Wood, Sept. 7, 1795. Sur. Stephen Wood. 93.
Ross, Robt. B. and Lucinda M. Turner, Mar. 12, 1846. Sur. Meshack Turner. 18.
Ross, Thos. and Nancy Harris, Jan. 22, 1819. Sur. David Ross.
Rowland, Andrew and Margaret Hartzell, Jan. 25, 1793. Sur. Philip Hartzell. 32.
Roy, John and Jane A. Dick, Apr. 15, 1852. 127.
Ruble, Swinfield and Polly Staton, July 11, 1793. 52.
Ruble, Owen Thos. and Alley Wade, Dec. 24, 1801. Surs. Stephen Smith and Owen Ruble.
Ruble, Thos. and Elizabeth Ross, dau. Daniel, Oct. 17, 1786. Sur. Wm. Ross.
Rucker, Mathew and Celia Ferguson, Dec. 12, 1838. Sur. Samuel A. B. Law. 86.
Rucker, Tinsley S. and Catherine Mills, Oct. 4, 1834. Sur. Wm. Miller, Sr.
Rucker, Wm. and Celia Leffeur, Dec. 30, 1829.
Ruddell, Andrew and Julia Cowley, Aug. 15, 1848. Sur. Bryant Cowley. 86.
Ruddock, Richard and Eve Rinehart, Mar. 1, 1824. Sur. Ezekiel Aldridge. 130.
Rudy, Samuel and Sally McGuire, dau. Sally, Sept. 2, 1795. Sur. James Slone.
Running, Adam and Rachael Wright, dau. Isaac, Sept. 21, 1788. Sur. Daniel Hoff. 52.
Rush, John and Elizabeth Peters, May 2, 1814. Sur. John Peters. 130.
Russell, Benj. and Sarah Ann Ship, Dec. 18, 1832. Sur. Lewis Oyler. 48.
Russell, James and Sarah Greer, May 26, 1814. Sur. John Greer. 130.
Russell, Richard and Polly Mitchell, Oct. 3, 1803. Sur. Henry Mitchell.
Rutledge, David and Priscilla Mullins, dau. Judith, Mar. 3, 1828. Sur. Austin W. C. Farley. 26.
Ryan (Ryner), Adam and Katy Stover, dau. Jeremiah, Dec. 25, 1785. Sur. John Coop. 52.

Ryherd, Jacob and Peggy Dehaven, Mar. 7, 1803. Sur. Abraham Dehaven.
Saint Clair, John F. and Nancy Helm, Jan. 7, 1839.
Sale, Thos. and Ellender H. Cooper, Oct. 22 1836. Sur. Josiah R. Willis.
Salsbury Elijah and Keziah Ray, dau. Benj., Mar. 29, 1808. Sur. Richard Pugh. 130.
Salsbury, Thos. and Lucy Maxey, dau. Phebe, Jan. 7, 1801. Sur. John Maxey. 141.
Salmon, Rowland and Frankey Carter, Mar. 12, 1795. 52.
Sammons, Wm. and Elizabeth Griffith, Dec. 26, 1798. Sur. Benj. Griffith. 21.
Sample, John and Elizabeth Turnbull, Jan. 1, 1803. Sur. Geo. Turnbull. 106.
Sanders, Andrew J. and Ann Peters, Jan. 16, 1851. 96.
Sanford, Thos. and Rachel Doran, Dec. 7, 1794. 22.
Saul, Albert and Martha H. Williams, Oct. 5, 1846. Sur. Morris W. Williams. 132.
Saul, Creed and Sophronia Holburt, Feb. 3, 1845. Sur. Greenberry Griffith. 18.
Saul, Dr. James and Esther Gibson, Mar. 6, 1821. Sur. John Ferguson. 49.
Saul, James D. and Mary Willis, dau. Susan, Aug. 23, 1849. Sur. Tazewell Saul. 18.
Saul, James D. and Docia Brammer, Sept. 23, 1839. Sur. Wm. Brammer. 132.
Saul, John and Ann Brammer, Jan. 1, 1849. Sur. James D. Saul. 47.
Saul, John H. and Elzira Sink, dau. Polly, Feb. 7, 1848. Sur. Tazewell Saul. 18.
Saul, John and Anne Luke, Sept. 15, 1804. Sur. Faithful Luke. 122.
Saul, Samuel, Jr. and Polly Baker, Mar. 5, 1810. Sur. Samuel Saul, Sr. and Moses Hawkins.
Saul, Samuel and Sibbinia S. Kingery, Oct. 16, 1843. Sur. Thos. Kingery. 58.
Saul, Tazewell, s. John, and Catherine Anderson, Sept. 14, 1853. 134.

Saul, Thos. and Jerusha M. Feazel, Nov. 27, 1839. Sur. Wm. Luke 132.
Saul, Wm. L. and Mary Kingery, dau. Thos., Aug. 4, 1853. 68.
Saunders, Abner and Polly Gilbert, Aug. 7, 1828. Sur. Joseph Wright. 3.
Saunders, Alexander and Jane Shavers, Jan. 26, 1837. Sur. Jesse Shavers.
Saunders, Berry and Polly Cunningham, dau. Joseph, Aug. 31, 1812. Sur. Randolph Cunningham. 15.
Saunders, Booker and Ann David, dau. Abraham, Dec. 12, 1842. Sur. John W. Ferguson.
Saunders, Chas. and Lucy Hatcher, g. Polly and Robert Cunningham, Dec. 17, 1810. Sur. John Arthur.
Saunders, E. Philip and Jemima Greer, g. Thomas and Ann Demos, Nov. 23, 1786. Sur. Elisha Lyons.
Saunders, Fleming and Frances Greer, June 25, 1828. Sur. Peter Moore. 140.
Saunders, Jacob and Margaret Marrs, ..., 1815. 130.
Saunders, Jesse and Joannah Payne, Mar. 6, 1809. Sur. Frayl Payne.
Saunders, John and Mahala Moris, Sept. 14, 1831. 95.
Saunders, John and Martha Dillion, dau. Rebecca, Dec. 29, 1831. Sur. Robt. P. Dillion. 140.
Saunders John and Patey P. Meador, dau. John, Feb. 24, 1801. 21.
Saunders, John R. and Nancy Leftwich, dau. Sarah, Aug. 4, 1845. Sur. Isaac Prillaman. 134.
Saunders, John I. and Ann E. Booth, Mar. 5, 1850. Sur. Edward H. Saunders. 47.
Saunders, John Q. and Susan Nancy Webster, July 17, 1851. 96.
Saunders, Julius H. and Pricilla W. Carter, g. Joseph Miles, Apr. 26, 1824. Sur. Edward Miles.
Saunders, Robt. and Rebecca Martin, Nov. 8, 1819. Sur. John Martin. 98.
Saunders, Robt. H. and Sarah L. Claiborne, Dec. 21, 1850. Sur. Fleming Saunders. 47.
Saunders, Samuel H. and Mary D. Asbury, Dec. 11, 1823. Sur. Geo. Asberry.
Saunders, Stephen and Laura Helms, Nov. 11, 1852. 68.

Saunders, Wm. and Biddy Bradshaw, dau. Allen, Mar. 4, 1816. Sur. Seth Bradshaw. 98.
Scarborough, David and Sarah Mullins, Dec. 30, 1822. Sur. Wm. Standley. 49.
Scarborough, Fredrick and Judith Chumbly, Sept. 7, 1835. Sur. Patrick Cumpton. 3.
Scarborough, Samuel and Nancy Mullins, Apr. 21, 1825. Sur. Bowker Mullins. 48.
Scott, Burnett and Susan Burnett, dau. James, June 11, 1835. Sur. Abram Childress.
Scott, Earl S. and Martha J. Hunter, June 24, 1844. Sur. John Hunter. 132.
Scott, Hullum and Mary Ann Wysong, dau. Henry and Catherine, Jan. 28, 1831. Sur. Sanford Scott. 48.
Scott, Hugh and Martha Parrott, Jan. 4, 1792. Sur. John Mattox.
Scott, James and Nancy Brown, Apr. 27, 1811. Sur. Jennings Brown.
Scott, James and Emily Jones, Aug. 24, 1853. 60.
Scott, Jesse and Elizabeth Jones, dau. John L., Sept. 13, 1837. Sur. John Scott. 68.
Scott, John and Frances Moore, Dec. 4, 1828. Sur. Christopher Richards.
Scott, John D. and Mary Southall, dau. Turner, Dec. 21, 1840. Sur. Abram Childress. 86.
Scott, Josiah A. and Frances Custard, Oct. 26, 1840. Sur. Samuel B. Fisher. 86.
Scott, Michael and Nancy Purtle, dau. Jane Adams, Nov. 21, 1818. Sur. Wm. Harrison.
Scott, Michael W. and Sarah K. Steagall, dau. Wm., Oct. 19, 1839. Sur. Rivers Steagall. 132.
Scott, Robt. A. and Veriller J. Chewning, Apr. 20, 1843. Sur. Doctor B. T. Rives.
Scott, Robt. A. and Isabella Nininger, July 29, 1847. Sur. Jeremiah Griggs.
Scott, Sandford and Sarah Ferguson, Jan. 1, 1827. Sur. Jeremiah Ferguson. 49.
Scott, Tazewell and Frances J. Mason, Feb. 2, 1850. Sur. Henry A. Mason. 132.

Scott, Wm. P. and Martha Hodges, dau. Ann, Feb. 11, 1850.
Sur. John Scott. 68.
Scott, Wm. P. and Janetty Jones, dau. John, Nov. 28, 1842.
Sur. Laskin Sigmon. 68.
Scott, Wm. B. and Julia Jones, Nov. 4, 1835. Sur. Henry Jones. 140.
Scott, Wm. and Lucy Moore, dau. Jacob, Jan. 3, 1832. Sur. John Scott. 60.
Scott, Wm. T. and Mary Ann Lavinder, dau. Chilton, Nov. 28, 1838. Sur. Michael W. Scott.
Scruggs, John and Amelia Menefee, Mar. 11, 1786. Sur. Wm. Menefee. 66.
Seabrough, (Scarborough), Robt. and Catherine Beheler, Aug. 29, 1793. 52.
Seay, Joseph R. and Susan W. Spencer, dau. Mary, Feb. 17, 1824. Sur. Thos. Payne. 101.
Sebert, Chas. and Catherine Lemon, Mar. 2, 1789. Sur. Daniel Spangler.
Sellers, Samuel and Ellender Duease, dau. Wilburn, Oct. 7, 1789. Sur. David Iddings. 52.
Sellers, Thos. and Elizabeth Harvy, dau. Evan and Abigail, Dec. 3, 1787. Sur. Samuel Kirby 52.
Semonis, Abraham and Polly Hickman, Nov. 16, 1803.
Semones, John and Patsy Hutcherson, Jan. 5, 1824. Sur. Wm. Hutcherson. 48.
Semones, Thos. and Betsy Brown, May 7, 1839. Sur. Benj. Hunt. 3
Semones, Wm., Jr. and Elizabeth Ann Matthews, July 5, 1824. Sur. John Matthews. 48.
Sence, Adam and Sally Simmons, Sept. 23, 1797. Sur. Wm. Simmons. 21.
Sence, Wm. and Rutha Priest, Jan. 21, 1830. Sur. Palmer Pearson. 140.
Sermones, Isaac and Jiels Mason, Oct. 13, 1829. Sur. John Oxley. 26.
Sevenny, Joseph and Phebe Belcher, July 4, 1791. Sur. Benj. Cock.
Shanks, David and Sarah Boone, Dec. 6, 1848. Sur. Thos. Boon. 100.

Shaon, Richard R. and Susan Robertson, Nov. 27, 1853. Sur. John Robertson.

Sharrocks, Wm. B. and Martha Menefee, Dec. 16, 1807. Sur. Geo. Menefee. 130.

Shasteen (Chasteen), Valentine, s. Wm. and Sary, and Mary Robins, dau. Jack and Mary, Sept. 24, 1791.

Shattain (Stratton), Geo. and Rebecca Statton, dau. Geo., Aug. 13, 1791. Sur. Jesse Moore. 52.

Shavers, Jacob and Nancy Fisher, July 20, 1852. 18.

Shavers, Jesse and Rebecca Beverly, Dec. 16, 1805. Sur. Harold Beverly.

Shaver, Michael and Hannah Miller, June 13, 1791. Sur. Tobias Millar. 52.

Shelton, Abraham C. and Mary Leigh Claiborne, niece of Nathaniel C., Feb. 1, 1819. Sur. C. Tate.

Shelton, Joseph C. and Adaline W. Faris, dau. Nancy and Valentine, Dec. 18, 1849. Sur. John P. Hale. 20.

Shelton, Thos. and Sarah Crump, May 8, 1834. Sur. Wm. Crump. 12.

Shelton, Wm. H. and Eleanor Greer, Jan. 9, 1797. Sur. Moses Greer.

Shepherd, Joel and Eleanor Dowdy, Nov. 21, 1833. Sur. John Dowdy. 48.

Sherrum, Wm. and Mary Wyatt, Nov. 18, 1809. Sur. Andrew Wyatt.

Sherwood, Thos. and Elizabeth Davis, dau. Jonathan, Nov. 28, 1789. Sur. Jonathan Davis, Jr. 37.

Sherwood, Wm. and Jinny Davis, Mar. 27, 1786. Sur. Jonathan Davis.

Shewman, John and Catharine Minnix, Oct. 3, 1807. Sur. Charles Minnix. 117.

Shilling, Geo. P. and Sarah Miles, dau. Arthur, Jan. 25, 1849. Sur. Geo. Teel. 96.

Shilling, Jacob and Rosanna Shockley, Dec. 2, 1787. Sur. John King.

Shirwood, Thos. and Susannah Hybs, (Bybee), June 15, 1808. 113.

Shively, Daniel, Jr. and Sarah Thomas, Oct. 20, 1853.

Shively, Fleming and Celia Ann Janney, May 17, 1850. Sur. Sparrel P. Janney. 68.
Shively, Isaac and Nancy Foster, May 10, 1822. Sur. John Foster.
Shively, Isaac and Elizabeth Sigmon, Nov. 28, 1831. Sur. Thos. Sigmon. 60.
Shiveley, Jacob and Elizabeth Huff, Feb. 20, 1847. Sur. Jacob Huff. 68.
Shiveley, John W. and Naomi Sigmon, dau. Jacob, Oct. 17, 1844. Sur. John C. Sigmon. 28.
Shoat (Choat), Austen and Theodoskey Webb, 1787. 48.
Shockey, Daniel and Sarah King, dau. Anthony, Aug. 22, 1830. Sur. Anthony King. 48.
Shoemaker, Isaac and Nancy Lonney, Aug. 6, 1806. Sur. Peter Lonney.
Shoemaker, Wm. and Sophie Nichols, Dec. 5, 1835. Sur. Isaac Shoemaker.
Short, Calvin R. and Sarah Janney, May 5, 1834. Sur. Moses Janney. 61.
Short, Cornelius and Mournin Stanley, dau. Jane, Aug. 5, 1831. 129.
Short, Edward and Caroline Payne, dau. Thos., Jan. 5, 1847. Sur. Clinton Richardson.
Short, Samuel and Sirenna P. Young, Dec. 16, 1839. Sur. Austin Barnes. 132.
Short, Thos. and Happy Frame, ..., 1797.
Shorter, James and Tamsey B. Ramsey, Dec. 5, 1832. Sur. Joseph Eades. 12.
Shorter, James and Agnes Shelton, Sept. 21, 1852. 10.
Shorter, Wm. and Ruby Ramsey, dau. Theodrick, Dec. 16, 1835. Sur. Booker R. Shorter. 3.
Showalter, Abraham and Frances McCormack, Jan. 11, 1802. Sur. Wm. McCormack. 106.
Showalter, Cornelius and Elizabeth Huddleston, Nov. 27, 1851. 11.
Showalter, Geo. and Sally Ann Fralin, Feb. 5, 1838. Sur. John Fralin.
Showalter, Henry, s. Henry, and Catherine Gossett, Dec. 25, 1807. Sur. Joseph Gossett.

Showalter, John and Kitty Abshire, Oct. 4, 1813. Sur. Wm. Abshire. 130.
Showalter, John and Elizabeth Showalter, June 26, 1816.
Showalter, Joseph and Milla Wright, Feb. 4, 1822. Sur. Wm. Wright. 130.
Showalter Nicholas and Elizabeth Griffith, dau. Jonathan, Sept. 16, 1818. Sur. Henry Showalter. 130.
Showalter, Randolph and Susan Huddleston, Sept. 25, 1851. 18.
Showalter, Stephen and Margaret Ann Bush, Jan. 13, 1853. 18.
Shrewsbury, John and Susanna Hatcher, Oct. 19 1826. Sur. Edmund Hatcher.
Shumate, Ballus and Louisa Holloway, May 2, 1845. Sur. Hugh Halloway. 132.
Shumate, Daniel and Lucy Luttrell, Aug. 7, 1809. Sur. Willis Luttrell. 8.
Shumate, Hardin and Mary A. Parcell, Dec. 10, 1850. Sur. Isaac Parcell. 132.
Shy, Edward and Elizabeth Wray, Sept. 18, 1810. Sur. Benj. Wray. 130.
Sigmon, Jacob and Sarah Huff, dau. Sarah, Sept. 2, 1844. Sur. Thos. Sigmon. 28.
Sigmon, Jacob and Polly Keys, dau. James, Feb. 24, 1834. Sur. Wm. Sigmon. 60.
Sigmon, John, Jr. and Ann Hancock, dau. Francis, Sept. 30, 1839. Sur. James Reuben. 68.
Sigmon, John C. and Mary Shively, Feb. 16, 1848. Sur. Sparrell P. Janney. 68.
Sigmon, John and Rachael Richards, Jan. 1, 1810. Sur. Isaac Richards. 122.
Sigmon, Joseph and Elizabeth Willis, Sept. 7, 1829. Sur. Isaac Shiveley.
Sigmon, Larkin and Elizabeth Keys, dau. James, Nov. 24, 1842. Sur. Wm. B. Sigmon. 68.
Sigmon, Peter and Catharine Willis, Apr. 5, 1819. Sur. Moses Jinney.
Sigmon, Peter, Jr., s. Peter, Sr., and Catharine, and Mary Willis, Nov. 2, 1829. Sur. David Willis, 132.
Sigmon, Robt. and Eilzabeth Gipson, dau. Mary, Dec. 6, 1839. Sur. Peter Sigmon. 68.

Sigmon, Wiatt Jackson and Rachael Sigmon, Feb. 15, 1842. Sur. Wm. Sigmon, Sr. 68.
Simmons, Arthur and Polly Ferguson, dau. Nancy, Apr. 17, 1815. Sur. Thos. Ferguson.
Simmons, Chas. and Mary E. Hughes, Jan. 8, 1852. 18.
Simmons, Elijah, s. Chas., and Rhoda Anderson, dau. Chas., Jan. 14, 1805. Sur. Caleb Anderson.
Simmons, Elisah and Matilda Payne, Jan. 1, 1842. Sur. Moses Payne. 86.
Simmons, Ezekiel and Patty Cooper, dau. Nathaniel, July 20, 1797. Sur. Thos. Simmons.
Simmons, Fletcher and Lucy Ann Hughes, Jan. 6, 1851. 18.
Simmons, James and Mary Richardson, Jan. 23, 1847. Sur. Turner Richardson. 86.
Simmons, Geo. W. and Elizabeth Flowers, dau. Samuel, Mar. 6, 1843. Sur. Wm. Flowers.
Simmons, Jesse and Susan Prater, dau. Jonathan, May 23, 1821. Sur. Chas. H. Hopkins.
Simmons, Jesse and Nancy F. Basham, July 5, 1858.
Simmons, Joel and Margaret Payne, dau. Elizabeth, Feb. 1, 1850. Sur. Greer H. Payne. 18.
Simmons, John C. and Elizabeth Richardson, Dec. 14, 1840. Sur. Wm. C. A. Meador 86.
Simmons, John and Susannah Morgan, Oct. 19, 1818. Sur. James Mitchell. 130.
Simmons, Jonathan, (rest illegible), Sept. 5, 1828.
Simmons, (Summers), Moses and Aggy Meadow, Jan. 2, 1797. Sur. Jesse Meadows.
Simmons, Moses and Catherine Sense, Aug. 6, 1811. Sur. Rowland Wheeler. 98.
Simmons, (or Simmerson), Paul and Polly Donehaur, Aug. 31, 1812. 130.
Simmons, Samuel D. and Julianna H. Woods, June 4, 1849. Sur. Stephen Wood. 86.
Simmons, Skelton and Elizabeth Meador, Jan. 29, 1824. Sur. Moses Simmons. 130.
Simmons, Stephen and Betsy Saunders, dau. Geo., July 21, 1820. Sur. John Martin. 130.
Simmons, Thos. and Lucy Basham, Sept. 17, 1799. 21.

Simmons, Thos. A. and Sarah A. Short, dau. Geo., Nov. 26, 1850. Sur. John Brown. 86.
Simmons, Wm. and Polly Chambers, dau. Thos. Ferguson, Jan. 12, 1815. Sur. Josiah Ferguson. 98.
Simones, Jacob H. and Arbeler Hiets, Nov. 24, 1842. Sur. Samuel B. Ashworth. 104.
Simones, Wm. W and Jemima Bernard, dau. Priscilla, Apr. 8, 1841. Sur. John K. Bernard.
Simpkins, Garrett and Susannah Roberts, dau. Anne, Aug. 31, 1786. Sur. John Roberts. 103.
Simpson, Daniel S. and Marie Jane Bernard, Aug. 16, 1845. Sur. Wm. Langdon Bernard.
Simpson, Thos. and Elizabeth Anderson, Apr. 2, 1827. Sur. Flayl Payne.
Sims, Ignatius A. J. and Caroline Y. Cannaday, dau. James, Jr., Dec. 4, 1841. Sur. Wm. A. Cannaday.
Siner, Adam and Sally Simmons, Sept. 23, 1797.
Siner, Jesse and Sethey Barton, May 1, 1799. Sur. Wm. McCormack. 21.
Sink, Abraham and Elizabeth Fisher, Dec. 15, 1845. Sur. Jacob Fisher. 18.
Sink, Benj. and Catherine Peters, Sept. 23, 1852. 18.
Sink, Caleb and Lydia Bowles, Jan. 23, 1847. Sur. Elias Sink. 18.
Sink, Cornelius and Emily Leffew, dau. Sarah, Jan. 4, 1845. Sur. James R. Mitchell. 18.
Sink, Daniel and Ann McKensie, Apr. 3, 1809. Sur. Wm. Dillion.
Sink, Daniel and Emily Ferguson, dau. Frances, Mar. 18, 1841. Sur. Peter Angle. 18.
Sink, David and Elizabeth Layman, Sept. 12, 1846. Sur. Robt. A. Scott. 18.
Sink, David and Delily Dillion, dau. Jesse, Aug. 16, 1813. Sur. Wm. Dillion. 8.
Sink, David and Asenath Arthur, Aug. 22, 1807. Sur. John Arthur.
Sink, Eson and Nancy Chitwood, Sept. 27, 1831. Sur. Joel Chitwood. 48.
Sink, Henry and Betsy Snider, Apr. 15, 1805. Sur. John Snidor.

Sink, Henry and Julia T. Hutts, Dec. 4, 1848. Sur. John D. Taylor. 19.
Sink, Henry and Sophia Clingenpeal, Mar. 6, 1811. Sur. Joseph Clingenpeel. 130.
Sink, Jesse and Julia Ann Wray, June 26, 1837. Sur. Charley Wray. 18.
Sink, John and Martha Bowman, Jan. 21, 1839. Sur. John Bowman. 18.
Sink, Jonathan and Susannah Altic, Jan. 3, 1820. Sur. Daniel Altick. 130.
Sink, Leonard, s. Mar, and Sarah Jane Saul, dau. James D., Dec. 1, 1840. Sur. James D. Saul. 18.
Sink, Otey and Elizabeth Snider, dau. John, Nov. 23, 1835. Sur. Abram Bousman. 140.
Sink, Peter and Susannah Beckner, May 6, 1816. Sur. Jacob Beckner. 130.
Sink, Peter and Parmelia Fisher, Nov. 15, 1858.
Sink, Samuel T. and Polly Ann Matthew, Oct. 4, 1824. Sur. Daniel Vinson. 48.
Sink, Stephen and Lydia Dillion, dau. Wm., Nov. 23, 1834. Sur. John Plybon, Jr.
Sink, Wm. and Polly Hodges, Oct. 20, 1825. Sur. Robt. Hodges. 48.
Slaton, Geo. and Jane Handy, Nov. 6, 1797. Sur. John Handy.
Slaton (Staten), Reuben and Martha Smith, dau. Elizabeth, Dec. 2, 1795. Sur. Matthew Knowles. 66.
Slaughter (Sleator), John and Mary Handy, Feb. 10, 1787. Sur. John Handy. 66.
Slaughter, Young and Mary Sullivant, Jan. 23, 1819. Sur. James Sullivant.
Slaughter, Young and Lucy Smith, Nov. 4, 1811. Sur. Ivry Smith.
Slayton, Robt. and Minerva Ashwell, Aug. 2, 1858.
Sleator, Edmund Smith and Susanah Dishong, June 22, 1799. Sur. Drury Hodges. 21.
Sledd, Wm. and Sophia Ann Howell, Feb. 15, 1841. Sur. Moses Howell. 68.
Slone, Allen and Milly Pate, May 17, 1823. Sur. Henry Ashworth. 48.

Slone, Clemens B. and Margaret Griffith, dau. Isaac, June 25, 1827. 48.
Slone, Clifford and Peggy Doran, dau. Hartman, July 31, 1789 Sur. Thos. Stone. 77.
Slone, Commodore and Ann McCormack, dau. Anderson, Feb. 22, 1831. Sur. Anthony Pate.
Slone, James and Polly Starkey, dau. Jonathan, Feb. 10, 1807. Sur. John Culp. 130.
Slone, James and Sarah McGuire, Sept. 8, 1797. Sur. Daniel Thomas. 89.
Slone, Jesse and Deborah Thomas, dau. David and Deborah, June 5, 1790.
Slone, Jehu John and Sally Kemplin, Apr. 15, 1822. Sur. Jacob Slone. 130.
Slone, John and Agnes Pate, Aug. 25, 1852. 11.
Slone, Patrick and Malinda Owens, Nov. 25, 1819. Sur. Leonard Hutts.
Slone, Patrick and Elizabeth Hambrick, Mar. 24, 1834. Sur. Elizabeth Chitwood. 68.
Slone, Reuben and Polly McGrady, dau. Lorthen M., Sept. 24, 1789. Sur. Patrick Slone. 77.
Slone, Samuel and Charlotte McCormack, dau. Anderson, Jan. 12, 1838. Sur. Anthony Pate. 140.
Slone, Thos. and Ann Spur, Apr. 4, 1818. Sur. Elijah Spur. 130.
Slone, Thos. and Sarah Griffith, Aug. 22, 1805. Sur. Geo. Griffith. 130.
Slone, Tubal C. and Jane Pate, May 10, 1832. Sur. Allen Slone.
Slone, Wm., Jr. and Rhoda Doran, dau. Hartman Doran, July 26, 1792. Sur. Thos. Sloan.
Slone, Wm. B. and Edith Akers, Nov. 25, 1850. Sur. Henry Silas Akers. 134.
Sloy, John and Mary Miller, Nov. 4, 1805. Sur. Moses Greer, Jr.
Smith, Benj. and Liby R. Crump, dau. Geo., Jan. 25, 1823. Sur. Wm. Haynes
Smith, Benj. and Elizabeth Drake Oakes, July 20, 1786. Sur. John Drake. 66.

Smith, Benj. and Nancy Sutherland, dau. Philemon, Nov. 23, 1801. Sur. Stephen Smith.
Smith, Chas. R. and Elizabeth Law, July 1, 1822. Sur. Wm. Crump. 49.
Smith, Chas., s. Peyton, and Jane Pinkard, dau. Jane Patterson, Nov. 8, 1790. Sur. Jas. Pinckard.
Smith, Chas. and Julia Ann Davis, Oct. 7, 1837. Sur. Thos. Davis. 132.
Smith, Creed and Mary Radford, Nov. 3, 1834. Sur. Samuel Radford. 60.
Smith, Daniel and Ruth Hickson, Jan. 17, 1789. Sur. Daniel Hickson. 52.
Smith, David W. and Elizabeth Ferguson, Jan. 7, 1788.
Smith, Ebenezer and Sarah Knowles, dau. Joshua, June 14, 1793. Sur. Matthew Knowles. 52.
Smith, Ervin and Liddy Mannen, dau. Davis, Aug. 25, 1808. Sur. John Webb. 117.
Smith, Fleming and Harriet Boles, Nov. 14, 1839. Sur. Jeremiah Bowles. 132.
Smith, Geo. Anderson and Milly Jones, dau. Rachael, Mar. 6, 1787. Sur. John Edwards. 66.
Smith, Geo. and Mary Boulton, dau. Thos., Jan. 11, 1800. Sur. Susannah Bolton.
Smith, Gideon and Nancy Rakes, Sept. 30, 1808. Sur. Henry Rakes. 122.
Smith, Guy and Hannah Hill, dau. Swinfield, Oct. 26, 1795. Sur. Stephen Smith.
Smith, Guy and Arabelle Richeson, dau. Jonathan, Jan. 20, 1793. Sur. Pratt Hughes.
Smith, Henry and Nancy Going, Dec. 13, 1806. Sur. David Young.
Smith, Henry P. and Frances P. Crump, dau. Geo., Jan. 29, 1831. Sur. Samuel Smith. 3.
Smith, Henry and Polly Wright, dau. Wm., Aug. 4, 1800. Sur. Wm. Wright. 21.
Smith, Henry and Susannah Holland, dau. John W., May 16, 1829. Sur. Thos. J. Holland. 26.
Smith, Henry and Elizabeth Powell, dau. Robt., May 10, 1790. Sur. John Smith. 37.

Smith, Isaac and Nancy Ickson (Johnson), Sept. 26, 1798. Sur. Geo. Johnson. 21.
Smith, James and Aditha Boile, Sept. 4, 1790. Sur. Levi Loid.
Smith, James and Quintina Wright, Sept. 28, 1850. Sur. John A. Smith. 96.
Smith, James and Elizabeth Clarkson, Feb. 2, 1802. Sur. David Clarkson.
Smith, James and Susannah Knowles, dau. John, Oct. 26, 1829. Sur. Thos. Smith.
Smith, James and Lucy Greer, dau. Nathan, Sr., Dec. 5, 1814. Sur. Nathan Greer, Jr.
Smith, John C. M. and Nancy Jamison, Sept. 5, 1842. Sur. John Jameson. 68.
Smith, John and Nancy Gray, Mar. 21, 1818. 130.
Smith, John and Judith Via, Apr. 8, 1823. Sur. Benj. Lemon.
Smith, John and Nancy W. Johnson, June 9, 1853. 68.
Smith, John A. and Christina Kinsey, Nov. 10, 1825. Sur. Jacob Kinsey. 48.
Smith, John and Prudence Coleman, Oct. 20, 1836. Sur. Wm. Coleman.
Smith, John and Rosanna Rolf, dau. Mary, Dec. __, 1806. Sur. John Webster. 130.
Smith, John W. and Polly Webb, Nov. 8, 1813. Sur. Thos. Helms.
Smith, John and Mary J. Brown, dau. John, Nov. 25, 1845. Sur. Geo. W. Argabrite.
Smith, Juny and Elizabeth Law, May 9, 1808. 8.
Smith, John and Frances Hatcher, dau. Benj., of Bedford Co., Jan. 4, 1790. Sur. Christopher Divers.
Smith, Leroy and Milley Guthery, Mar. 25, 1792. Sur. Penelope Guttery.
Smith, Luke and Polly Nafe, dau. Jacob, Nov. 4, 1828. Sur. Jacob Nafe. 48.
Smith, Mark and Lucy Johnson, Apr. 2, 1838. Sur. Nathan Johnson. 18.
Smith, Peter and Hannah Richardson, dau. James and Martha, Apr. 1, 1789. Sur. David Iddings. 52.
Smith, Peter and Susan Prillaman, June 28, 1830. Sur. John Prillaman. 124.

Smith, Peyton and Polly James, Jan. 17, 1805. Sur. Fielding Jones.
Smith, Philemon and Nanny Abshire, dau. Luke, Feb. 10, 1795. Sur. Edward Abshire. 89.
Smith, Ralph and Judith W. Cook, dau. Abraham, Jan. 2, 1815. Sur. Cabell Tate. 135.
Smith, Robt. and Mary Smith, 1795. 37.
Smith, Robt. and Phebe H. Hancock, dau. Benj. Apr. 20, 1826. Sur. Stephen Ashworth. 48.
Smith, Samuel and Mary Peters, Dec. 18, 1823. Sur. Wm. Peters. 61.
Smith, Samuel and Judith Colman, Jan. 4, 1816. Sur. John Coleman. 130.
Smith, Samuel and Elizabeth Woods, dau. Frances, Nov. 4, 1828. Sur. Hugh M. Huston. 48.
Smith, Samuel and Jennie Holland, Oct. 10, 1811. Sur. John Ashworth.
Smith, Samuel and Lucinda Faris, dau. Valentine, Sr., Nov. 4, 1843. Sur. Valentine Faris, Jr.
Smith, Samuel and Malinda L. Holland, Dec. 16, 1844. Sur. John M. Holland, Jr. 18.
Smith, Samuel D. and Matilda V. Walker, Mar. 2, 1853. 1.
Smith, Stephen H. and Mary L. McCall, Nov. 24, 1834. Sur. Wm. McCall. 134.
Smith, Stephen and Elizabeth White, dau. Henry Page, Feb. 23, 1799.
Smith, Stephen and Sarah Smith, dau. John W., Nov. 19, 1828. Sur. John W. Smith. 26.
Smith, Thos. and Elizabeth Knowles, dau. John, Mar. 2, 1818. Sur. Wm. Lemmon.
Smith, Tucker and Mekin Shumaker, Mar. 25, 1852. 18.
Smith, Wiatt and Mary Holland, Oct. 12, 1810. Sur. Peter Holland. 8.
Smith, Wm. and Elizabeth Ferguson, Jan. 7, 1788. Sur. Alex Ferguson. 37.
Smith, Wm. and Nancy Ferguson, dau. Nancy, Nov. 6. 1828. Sur. Wright Smith. 140.
Smith, Wm. and Ann Carmichael, Apr. 5, 1819. Sur. Wm. Carmichael.

Smith, Wm. and Sally Law, dau. John, Jan. 31, 1799. Sur.
Wm. Law. 21.
Smith, Wm. and Ann Preston, dau. Ann Robertson, Nov. 9,
1796. Sur. Jesse Preston. 82.
Smith, Wm. H. and Sarepta Turner, Dec. 2, 1850. Sur. Andrew
H. Turner. 132.
Smith, Wm. and Nancy Henderson, dau. Samuel, Dec. 30, 1808.
Sur. Wm. Henderson. 130.
Smith, Wm. and Mary Kemp, June 6, 1829. Sur. Solomon
Pasley. 48.
Smith, Willis and Lucy J. Peters, dau. Willis, Dec. 28, 1847.
Sur. Wm. Foster. 68.
Smith, Wright and Sarah Smith, dau. Wm., Dec. 18, 1830.
Sur. John Craghead. 3.
Snead, Richard and Patsy Adams, dau. Wm., Mar. 5, 1792.
Sur. Nathaniel Ross. 52.
Snead, Richard and Seney Turner, dau. Isaiah and Frances,
Dec. 29, 1801. Sur. Stephen Turner. 141.
Snead, Wm. and Elizabeth Adams, dau. Wm., Mar. 5, 1792. Sur.
Swinfield Rubel. 52.
Sneifer (Snuffer), Geo. and Alsy Huff, July 8, 1798. 89.
Snidor, Daniel and Caty Hartman, Nov. 8, 1809. Sur. John
Hartman.
Snider, David and Susannah Gearhart, dau. Margaret, Aug. 1,
1803. Sur. Peter Gearhart. 72.
Snider, Geo. and Mariah Howvin, Mar. 3, 1853. 11.
Snider, Jacob and Susannah Huff, dau. John, Mar. 1, 1808.
Sur. John Huff. 117.
Snider, John and Peggy Crowl, Aug. 17, 1808. Sur. Daniel
Lemon. 130.
Snider, John and Lucy Helm, Oct. 1, 1827. Sur. James Littrell.
Snidor, Michael and Elizabeth Akers, Mar. 9, 1849. Sur.
McDonough Ferguson. 96.
Snuffer, John and Hannah Huff, July 1, 1816. Sur. John Huff.
Snuffer, Peter and Elizabeth Cannaday, dau. Elizabeth, Apr.
6, 1846. Sur. Isaac Y. Cannaday. 60.
Souter, Jacob and Anne Prillaman, dau. Jacob and Priscilla,
June 18, 1788. 52.

Southall, Turner and Julia Ann Palmer, dau. John P., Dec. 13, 1841. 86.
Spalden, Fleming and Mary Fearis, dau. Athanasius, Feb. 2, 1793. Sur. John Peter Hudson.
Spangle, Geo. and Elizabeth Langdon, dau. John D., Feb. 9, 1786. Sur. Daniel Spangler. 103.
Spangler, John and Christina Myers, Feb. 5, 1787. Sur. Floyd Nichols and John Fuson. 52.
Sparks, Samuel and Susannah Jones, Dec. 6, 1798. Sur. John Jones.
Spaulding, John and Elizabeth Dobbins, Sept. 18, 1822. Sur. John Dobbins. 122.
Speece, Martin L. and Elizabeth Fisher, Aug. 7, 1843. Sur. Joel Fisher. 18.
Spencer, John and Rachael Key, Nov. 20, 1827. Sur. Wesley Keys. 48.
Speer, Elijah and Nanny (Mainey) Slone, Aug. 2, 1819. Sur. Jehu Slone.
Spitler, Jacob and Frances Lemon, Sept. 7, 1818. Sur. Joseph Clingenbill.
Spitler, Michael and Polly Peters, dau. Michael, Aug. 25, 1802. Sur. Michael Peters. 129.
Spoon, John and Polly Crowl, dau. Mary Bolf, Jan. 8, 1806. Sur. Michael Crowl.
Spradling, Benj. and Sally Loyd, dau. Cornelius, May 9, 1818. Sur. Joseph Wright.
Spradlin, Green and Susan Basham, dau. John, Oct. 25, 1847. Sur. James Meador. 86.
Spradling, Henry and Mary Martin, Aug. 20, 1797. 21.
Spradlin, James and Lucinda Meador, Jan. 24, 1837. Sur. Paschal Meador.
Spradlin, John and Louisa Meador, dau. David, Dec. 11, 1837. Sur. Clement Dickerson.
Spradling, John and Rhoda Meador, dau. Luney, May 23, 1818. Sur. Moss Meador.
Spradlin, Wright and Frances Weaver, Nov. 5, 1833. Sur. Jacob Weaver. 48.
Spradling, Wright and Polly Spradling, Oct. 31, 1825.

Spradling, Pleasant and Agnes Allen, May 20, 1824. Sur. Jonathan Ward. 48.
Staley, Isaac and Lavinia Murphy, dau. Liddia, June 29, 1829. Sur. Abraham Staley. 48.
Stanback, Benj. and Peggy Payne, dau. Isham, May 31, 1841. Sur. Silas Payne. 86.
Standifer, Luke and Mary Ann Price, dau. Joseph Showers, Jan. 15, 1787. 52.
Standley, Clayton and Elizabeth Mullins, Jan. 3, 1842. Sur. Nicholas Kemplin. 68.
Standley, Costilla and Dorothy Walden, Oct. 24, 1829. Sur. Wm. Walden. 132.
Standley, Creed and Frances Campbell, Apr. 15, 1844. Sur. Thos. Campbell. 132.
Standley, Creed and Polly Ann Ward, dau. Samuel and Mary, Apr. 2, 1849. Sur. Wm. Saul. 132.
Standley, Daniel P. and Mary Emily Prillaman, dau. Elizabeth, Sept. 25, 1848. Sur. Geo. Standley. 132.
Standley, Geo. and Mary Jane Jones, Dec. 5, 1842. Sur. John M. Gregory. 132.
Standley, James and Aley Standley, dau. Wm., Nov. 12, 1805. Sur. Wm. Standley.
Standley, John and Franky Warren, May 3, 1800. 72.
Standley, John and Olly Baker, Jan. 21, 1823. Sur. Bowker Mullins.
Standley, Jonathan and Nancy Martin, Dec. 22, 1819. Sur. Jeremiah Bowles.
Standley, Joseph and Polly Mullins, Aug. 25, 1806. Sur. Wm. Mullins.
Standley, Larkin and Judith Prillaman, Sept. 5, 1814. Sur. Daniel Prillaman.
Standley, Luke and Jane Standley, Jan. 22, 1813. Sur. Thos. Standley.
Standley, Moses and Jinney Warren, Mar. 29, 1806. Sur. Benj. Warren.
Standley, Owen, s. Catherine Blatcher, and Elizabeth Thornton, dau. Stanton, May 25, 1840. 132.
Standley, Peyton and Lucinda King, dau. Samuel, Feb. 8, 1826. Sur. Geo. Standley.

Standley, Richard and Mary Ann Howser, Nov. 28, 1821.
Standley, Richard and Elizabeth Warren, Sept. 21, 1802. 72.
Standley, Samuel and Martha Lowel, Feb. 21, 1837. Sur. Swinfield Standley. 132.
Standley, Wm. F. and Mourning Doss, Apr. 4, 1825. Sur. Joseph Standley. 48.
Stanley, Geo. W. and Catherine Greer, Dec. 23, 1851. 20.
Stanley, Thos. and Delilah Hill, Apr. 27, 1801. Sur. Wm. Mullins. 72.
Starkey, Anderson and Catherine Owen, Oct. 3, 1831. Sur. Belinda Slone. 48.
Starkey, Austin and Tempey Spradling, dau. Edward and Luley, Oct. 18, 1819. Sur. Pleasant Spradling.
Starkey, Briant and Pamelia Blankenship, Feb. 28, 1805. Sur. Elijah Starkey.
Starkey, Edward and Julia Ann Smith, dau. Henry, Sept. 25, 1849. Sur. James Martin. 18.
Starkey, John and Polly Starkey, dau. Joshua, Jan. 30, 1797. Sur. Benj. Epperson.
Starkey, Joel and Harriet Kingery, dau. Henry and Polly, Jan. 2, 1843. Sur. Addison Kingery. 18.
Starkey, John and Polly Plybon, Oct. 20, 1799. Sur. James Callaway, Jr. 21.
Starkey, John and Elizabeth Ferguson, dau. Alexander, Feb. 3, 1829. Sur. Stephen Ferguson. 140.
Starkey, John, s. Austin, and Catherine Oyler, dau. Aron, June 29, 1843. Sur. Catherine Oyler.
Starkey, Joshua and Lucy Mason, Apr. 7, 1828. Sur. Kemuel C. Gilbert, Jr.
Starkey, Joshua and Susannah Fellows, dau. Peter and Caty, Mar. 22, 1798. Sur. John Starkey. 21.
Starkey, Wm. and Elizabeth Webb, dau. Samuel and Rebeccah, Apr. 7, 1788. Sur. Jacob Webb.
Starkey, Wm. and Mary Webb, July 29, 1819. Sur. Samuel Ulman.
St. Clair, John T. and Nancy Helm, Jan. 7, 1839. Sur. Samuel Helm.
Steagall, David Pinkard and Jane Warren, Aug. 4, 1828. Sur. John Dearen. 48.

Steagall, Henry and Mary J. Bondurant, dau. Thos., Oct. 14, 1844. Sur. Robt. Prunty. 14.
Steagall, Wm. and Mary Hodges, dau. Abednego, Nov. 24, 1804. Sur. Rives Hodges.
Stearnes, Owen D. and Temperance Ward, May 15, 1846. Sur. Asa Ward. 19.
Stearnes, Lewis and Sarah Cabaniss, dau. Nancy, June 4, 1828. Sur. Tracy G. Todd. 26.
Stephens, Gilbert and Hannah Poteet, dau. Wm. and Kizziah, June 6, 1791. Sur. John Gillaspy. 52.
Stephen, John Derben and Polly Bates, Dec. 24, 1804. Sur. Isaac Bates. 122.
Stephens, John and Sarah Musgrove, g. Nicholas Allen, Oct. 3, 1791. Sur. Achilles Smith.
Stephens, Owen and Hessie Proffit, Aug. 19, 1835. Sur. David Prophet. 129.
Stephenson, Benj. and Ruth Shey, May 26, 1792. Sur. Patrick Sloan.
Stephens (Stevens), Edward and Mary Knowles, Apr. 2, 1804. Sur. John Knowles. 122.
Stephens, Elijah and Polly Delany, Aug. 5, 1812. 130.
Stewart, (Stuart), Brice and Polly Hodges, dau. Robt., Jan. 30, 1798. Sur. Watemon Richards.
Stewart, Isaac and Polly Krook, Oct. 12, 1811. Sur. Mathias Krook.
Stewart, James , s. James, Sr., and Phebe Jones, dau. Robt. Feb. 24, 1804. Sur. John Bird. 66.
Stewart, John and Agnes, Warren, dau. Zachariah, Apr. 15, 1805. Sur. Edmund Richards.
Stewart, Josiah and Elizabeth Stewart, Apr. 2, 1787. Sur. John Stewart.
Stewart, Samuel G. and Mary Jane Arrington, dau. Samuel, May 3, 1847. Sur. Robt. Bush. 18.
Stewart, Wm. and Frances Lyon, Jan. 27, 1821. Sur. Elisha Lyon.
Stickerman, Thos. and Sarah Young, July 24, 1858.
Still, Murphy and Phoebe Rieves, July 23, 1795. Sur. Abram Dehaven. 93.

Stinnett, John and Betsy Justice, dau. John, Jan. 2, 1788. Sur. Wm. Stinnett.
Stinnett, Wm. and Nancy Carter, dau. Baley, July 13, 1789. Sur. John Carter. 52.
Stockton, Chas. and .Polly Wingfield, dau. John, Dec. 5, 1814. Sur. Peter C. Stockton.
Stockton, Peter C. and Sally Wingfield, dau. John, June 1, 1812. Sur. Lewis Wingfield. 8.
Stockton, Peter C. and Cynthia Arnold, Jan. 24, 1823.
Stockton, Wm. L. and Sarah E. Keen, dau. Thos., Sept. 15, 1841. Sur. John H. Choice.
Stokes, Demarcus and Harriet A. Dunn, Dec. 19, 1844. Sur. Thos. Dunn.
Stokes, Wm. and Isabel Hale, Dec. 25, 1798. 21.
Stone, Ingram and Sarah Massey, Aug. 22, 1839. Sur. Obediah Massey. 132.
Stone, John and Polly Massey, Mar. 31, 1838. Sur. Obediah Massey. 132.
Stone, Richard and Marget Montgomery, Sept. 6, 1803. 122.
Stone, Solomon and Mary J. Draper, dau. Martin, Feb. 2, 1849. Sur. John H. Draper.
Stone, Stephen and Jane Fisher, Jan. 21, 1817. Sur. Andrew Turner.
Stone, Wm. and Jane Standley, Oct. 6, 1828. Sur. Thos. Standley. 132.
Stone, Wm. and Mary Ann Turner, Nov. 18, 1806. Sur. John Turner. 44.
Stoner, John and Polly Kingery, Apr. 3, 1799. 89.
Stovall, James R. and and Mary J. Wingfield, dau. Wm., Nov. 11, 1847. Sur. Wm. Wingfield. 80.
Stover, Abraham and Matilda Kingery, May 13, 1839. Sur. Joel Starkey. 18.
Stover, Henry and Ann Starkey, Apr. 8, 1822. Sur. Jesse Starkey.
Stover, Jacob and Sallie McGhee, Mar. 16, 1788. Sur. Holdin McGhee.
Stover, Jacob and Catherine Fisher, Dec. 6, 1858.
Stover, John and Catherine Rankin, Jan. 29, 1829. 18.

Stover Obediah and Massey Standley, Jan. 12, 1809. 44.

Stover, Thos. W., s. Catherine, and Mary J. Baley, dau. Henry and Elizabeth, Sept. 9, 1853. 18.

Street, Anthony and Polly Kemp, Feb. 17, 1816. Sur. Wm. Kemp.

Street, Moses H. and Judith Hubbard, dau. Moses, Dec. 27, 1832. Sur. Samuel Smith.

Street, Park and Mary Jane Smith, g. John W. Cook, July 28, 1829. Sur. Jordan Robertson.

Street, Wm. A. and Nancy M. Holland, dau. John M., Aug. 17, 1835. Sur. David S. Keen. 3.

Stripe, Jacob and Susanna Clinginbill, Nov. 5, 1821. Sur. Joseph Clinginbill.

Stuart, Robt. and Polly Goff, Aug. 14, 1806. Sur. Asa Dillion.

Stuart, Wm. and Caty Short, dau. Winford, Sept. 3, 1806. Sur. John Starkey. 130.

Stuart, Wm. and Altamina Deyerle, Dec. 19, 1848. 18.

Stultz, Abner and Dorothea B. Lesseuer, Sept. 30, 1858. Sur. Martel Lessuer. 132.

Stump, Cebret and Rhody Boles, May 6, 1844. Sur. Skelton Stump. 68.

Stump, John and Martha J. Webb, Dec. 23, 1853. 68.

Stump, Silas and Jane Nicholas, Apr. 30, 1840. Sur. Skelton Stump. 68.

Stump, Skelton and Sarah Bowles, Nov. 6, 1843. Sur. Burwell Millirons. 134.

Stump, Tompkins and Permelia Bishop, Sept. 9, 1848. Sur. David Thomas. 68.

Sullivant, Samuel and Sarah Bell, dau. James and Frances, Dec. 17, 1792. Sur. John Bell.

Sullivant, Walter and Martha Craghead, Dec. 18, 1797. Sur. Thos. Camp.

Sumpter, Edmund and Elizabeth Kingery, Mar. 16, 1795. Sur. Sur. Jacob Kingery. 89.

Sumpter, Geo. and Caty Prillaman, June 6, 1808. Sur. John Prillaman. 117.

Sumpter, Richard and Mary Kingery, Nov. 12, 1800. Sur. Jacob Kingery.

Sumpter, Richard and Catherine Sowder, dau. Anna, Feb. 10, 1824. Sur. John Sowder. 130.
Sutherland, Jacob P. and Sarah J. Rives, dau. Joseph, Feb. 2, 1844. Sur. Doctor B. F. Rives. 14.
Sutherland, Ransom and Elizabeth Newbill, dau. Nathaniel P., June 12, 1812. Sur. Nathaniel Newbill.
Sutherland, Ransome B. and Matilda E. Semonis, dau. Benj. Oct. 18, 1845. Sur. Thos. W. Murrell. 14.
Sutherland, Wm. M. and Angeline Semones, Dec. 30, 1844. Sur. Ranson B. Sutherland.
Swanson, Gabriel and Matilda Arnold, dau. Maryan, Oct. 20, 1802. Sur. Jonathan Charter. 129.
Sweeny, Jonathan and Dicey Parker, Sept. 5, 1828. Sur. James Key. 130.
Sweeny, Joseph and Pheba Belcher, July 4, 1791. Sur. Benj. Cook.
Swinney, Samuel and Winney Hammock, Mar. 11, 1811. Sur. Levi Hammock. 122.
Swinney, Joel and Nancy A. Moore, Nov. 1, 1824. Sur. Benj. Moore.
Sydnor, Beverly and Ann L. Burwell, dau. J. S., Nov. 25, 1828. Sur. Wm. Penick. 24.
Tabscott, James and Zepporah Price, dau. Showers, Aug. 4, 1836. Sur. Benj. Price.
Tapscott, John and Nancy Hill, dau. Isaac, Nov. 23, 1810. Sur. Barber Hill.
Tapscot, Samuel and Winney Hill, Dec. 14, 1812. Sur. Wilson Turner. 130.
Taliaferro, Richard M. and Polly Hale, Dec. 5, 1812. Sur. John Hale.
Taliaferro, Tazewell and Millie Nowlin, Sept. 1, 1852. 75.
Taliaferro, Tazewell and Amanda Callaway, Aug. 31, 1836. Sur. Henry Dillard.
Taswell, Peter and Abagail Sherwood, dau. Robt., Apr. 13, 1789.
Tate, Edmund and Kitty Turnbull, Aug. 6, 1807. Sur. Caleb Tate. 92.
Tate, Edmund and Mary J. Callaway, Mar. 15, 1843. 104.
Tate, Jesse Netherland and Julia Ann Heptinstall, Nov. 20, 1827. Sur. Thos. Heptinstall. 3.

Tate, Jesse N. and Mary Carter, Aug. 2, 1832. Sur. Geo. D. Odineal.
Tate, Joel and Catherine Zeigler, dau. John, Jan. 22, 1844. Sur. John M. Parish.
Tate, John G. and Jinnetty W. Heptinstall, May 21, 1827. Sur. Wm. G. Heptinstall.
Taylor, Christopher and Julia Ferguson, Jan. 7, 1822. Sur. Thos. Ferguson. 48.
Taylor, David P. and Ann Moore, dau. Joseph, June 24, 1817. Sur. Peter Moore.
Taylor, Edmund and Mildred Jackson, dau. Mildred, Mar. 14, 1829. Sur. Wm. Meador. 140.
Taylor, Geo. W., s. Susan, and Martha Short, dau. Martha, Jan. 23, 1850. Sur. Wm. Mason. 19.
Taylor, Jesse and Susannah Beheler, Oct. 14, 1839. 18.
Taylor, Joel and Wilmuth Gilbert, Oct. 3, 1814. Sur. Michael Gilbert. 8.
Taylor, John D. and Emily P. Callaway, Jan. 12, 1839. Sur. Stephen Turnbull.
Taylor, John M. and Cassandra Barnes, dau. Permelia, Oct. 14, 1841. Sur. Wm. Moore. 132.
Taylor, Lewis B. and Harriet K. Carper, Sept. 23, 1833. Sur. Moses G. Carper. 48.
Taylor, Mark and Polly Fowler, May 20, 1812. 130.
Taylor, Obediah and Mary Choice, dau. Anne, Oct. 10, 1791. Sur. Silas Cyrus Choice.
Taylor, Samuel and Elizabeth Conner, Feb. 29, 1792. Sur. Wm. Conner. 52.
Taylor, Seaton and Milly Abshire, June 29, 1814. Sur. Peter Abshire. 130.
Taylor, Skelton and Letitia M. Helm, dau. Samuel, Feb. 13, 1843. Sur. Wm. M. Greer. 118.
Taylor, Thos F. and Ann C. Wright, dau. Wm., Sept. 2, 1844. Sur. John O. Taylor.
Teal, Abraham and Sooky Wright, Sept. 18, 1823. Sur. Geo. Wright. 130.
Teal, Adam and Caty Baker, dau. Geo., Nov. 19, 1790. Sur. Caty Thomas. 52.

Teel, Calvin, dau. Tabitha, and Angeline Wray, dau. Lucinda and Jacob, Oct. 13, 1853. 96.
Teal, Geo. and Catey Showalter, Feb. 7, 1801. Sur. John Showalter. 21.
Teel, Joseph and Mahala Showalter, Dec. 5, 1842. Sur. John Showalter.
Teel, Melon and Charlotte Teel, July 3,1837. Sur. Terry Teel.
Teel, Mankin and Amelia Ferguson, dau. John, Mar. 8, 1822. Sur. Davis Ferguson. 130.
Teal, Peter and Jemima Ray, Oct. 6, 1800. Sur. James Ray. 21.
Teal, Peter and Jane Mills, dau. Arthur, Dec. 15, 1827 Sur. Wm. Mills. 140.
Teal, Terry and Elizabeth Mary Boone, Jan. 22, 1839. Sur. Jacob Abshire.
Teal, Wm. and Polly Gearhart, Oct. 9, 1827. Sur. Bluford Hawkens. 48.
Tench, Clark W. and Frances Brewer, dau. Arthur, June 22, 1849. Sur. Wm. A. Finney. 80.
Tench, Edmund W. and Elizabeth Ferguson, June 7, 1841. Sur. John H. Ferguson. 18.
Tench, Henry W. and Temperance Brewer, Apr. 24, 1843. Sur. Andrew W. Tench.
Terry, Carter and Tabitha Kidd, dau. John, Dec. 30, 1822. Sur. Chas. Hunt.
Terry, Champ and Judith Cook, Dec. 27, 1790. Sur. John Choice.
Terry, Henry B. and Polly Rakes, Feb. 4, 1828. Sur. Elisha Rakes. 61.
Thomas, Chas. Pleasant, Jr., and Polly Cannaday, Jan. 31, 1828. Sur. John Cannaday. 61.
Thomas, Cornelius and Elizabeth Slaughter, Apr. 7, 1806. Sur. John Slaughter. 44.
Thomas, David and Nancy Jane Hoffman, dau. John, Aug. 2, 1847. Sur. John Jones. 68.
Thomas, David and Sarah McGuire, Sept. 8, 1797. Sur. James Stone.
Thomas, Ephraim and Caty Teal, dau. Adam and Mary, Jan. 19, 1791, Sur. David Thomas. 52.
Thomas, James and Sarah Goode, Nov. 12, 1840. Sur. Jacob Goode. 132.

Thomas, Peter J. and Mary Jane Griffith, Mar. 10, 1853. 60.
Thomas, Pleasant and Frances Kennett, Nov. 11, 1839. Sur. Samuel Thornton. 132.
Thomas, Pleasant and Polly Kennaday, Mar. 6, 1800. Sur. James Kennedy. 66.
Thomas, Woodley and Mary Ann Aliff, Sept. 16, 1851. 68.
Thomas, Zachariah and Mary Young, Aug. 8, 1794. 20.
Thomason, Bartlett and Mildred Anderson, Dec. 11, 1843. Sur. Jesse Anderson. 104.
Thomason, Creed T. and Alley W. Saunders, dau. Phillip, Dec. 18, 1833. Sur. Wm. M. H. Haley. 140.
Thomason, David and Elizabeth Pridy, dau. Nancy, July 25, 1789. Sur. Hezekiah Branson. 37.
Thomason, James and Minerva Anderson, dau. Joseph, Dec. 20, 1836. Sur. James Anderson.
Thomason, Wm. and Polly Oyler, dau. John, July 14, 1830. Sur. Smithson G. Holly. 140.
Thomerson, Robt. W. and Elizabeth Bowles, Dec. ...., 1853. 132.
Thompson, David W. and Mary Riddle, Mar. 16, 1796.
Thompson, Dickerson and Susannah Dorety, dau. Elizabeth Parker, June 21, 1797. Sur. Stephen Allen.
Thompson, Geo. W. and Nancy Ann Cannaday, Oct. 28, 1852. 1.
Thompson, Giles M. and Harriet K. Helm, dau. Sparrell, Nov. 22, 1847. Sur. John C. Carper.
Thompson, James and Nancy F. Pollard, dau. Nancy, Nov. 18, 1817. Sur. Moses Pollard. 130.
Thompson, John and Nancy Radford, Dec. 24, 1836. Sur. Moses Janney. 68.
Thompson, John and Rhoda Bowles, Feb. 8, 1803. Sur. Geo. Bowls.
Thompson, Joseph and Elizabeth Hedge, June 18, 1790. Sur. Prat Hughes. 52.
Thompson, Pyrant and Jane Ingram, Dec. 19, 1828. Sur. Alexander Ingram.
Thompson, Samuel and Sarah Greer, Nov. 20, 1797. Sur. Joseph Calloway. 21.
Thompson, Samuel S. P. and Jane W. Webb, July 3, 1843. Sur. Moses G. Carper.

Thompson, Thomas and Catherine Price, March 10, 1818. Sur. James Thompson. 130.

Thompson, Wm. and Polly Brown, June 10, 1802. 72.

Thompson, Wm. and Frances Bowles, May 7, 1791. Sur. Stephen Smith. 52.

Thompson, Waddy and Catherine James, dau. Spencer, Sept. 2, 1799. Sur. Braxton James.

Thornton, Allen and Elizabeth Warren, dau. Ambrose, Apr. 8, 1799. Sur. Starling Thornton.

Thornton, John and Lucy P. Ashworth, dau. Susannah, Jan. 13, 1834. Sur. John H. Ashworth. 3.

Thornton, Littleberry and Sally Stewart, Mar. 24, 1807. Sur. James Sewart.

Thornton, Page and Rebecca Frith, dau. Thos., Feb. 11, 1839. Sur. Wm. Scarberry. 132.

Thornton, Samuel G. and Mary J. Claughton, Aug. 22, 1844. Sur. Robt. A. Scott. 118.

Thornton, Starling and Sally Moseley, Aug. 29, 1803. Sur. David Richeson.

Thorp, Richard and Parthena B. Ray, Dec. 6, 1841. Sur. John B. Lyon. 86.

Thrasher, Paul M. and Susannah Wood, dau. Stephen, Jan. 16, 1841. Sur. Samuel G. Wood. 86.

Thurman, David and Ann A. Livesay, dau. Susannah, Oct. 25, 1839. Sur. Lewis M. Livesay.

Thurman, Henry and Sarah Lumsden, May 5, 1850. Sur. Robt. Thurman. 18.

Thurman, Henry and Quintilla Adams, July 8, 1811. Sur. Elias Wraye. 130.

Thurman, John and Wilmoth Lumsden, Mar. 5, 1838. Sur. Dudley Lumsden. 18.

Thurman, Philip and Jane T. Powell, dau. Robt., Oct. 22, 1807. Sur. Chas. Powell. 57.

Thurman, Robt. P. and Elizabeth M. Law, dau. Jesse, June 2, 1845. Sur. Robt. A. Scott. 14.

Thurman, Wm. and Elizabeth Austen, ..., 1797.

Tinsley, Allen B. and Eleanor Wright, dau. Geo., Dec. 26, 1842. Sur. James S. Wright.

Tinsley, John and Mahala Jeter, dau. John, Dec. 16, 1817. Sur. Wright McCormack. 98.
Tinsley, Reubin L. and Jane M. Woods, Dec. 18, 1839. Sur. John S. Burwell. 132.
Tinsley, Stuart and Nancy Price, dau. Joseph, June 25, 1830. Sur. Pleasant Price. 48.
Tinsley, Tipton S. and Elizabeth H. Calhoun, June 20, 1848. Sur. Peter Saunders. 104.
Tinsley, Wm. and Lucy Webb, dau. Joseph, Oct. 13, 1817. Sur. Joseph Webb. 130.
Tinsley, Willis and Ammanilla Good, Sept. 4, 1809. Sur. Reuben Tinsley.
Tinsley, Willis and Permelia Doughton, Feb. 23, 1835. Sur. John Doughton.
Toney, Carey and Betsy Doran, dau. Harkman, Aug. 27, 1789. Sur. Thos. Slone. 77.
Toney, Edmund and Linna Chasteen, Feb. 6, 1795. Sur. James Toney. 52.
Toney, James and Milly Doran, Mar. 3, 1806. Sur. John Doran. 130.
Toney, Jesse and Frony Sink, Dec. 16, 1806. Sur. Stephen Sink.
Toney, Poindexter and Mary Rawson, dau. Chas., Apr. 24, 1788. Sur. Geo. Griffith. 52.
Tosh, Wm. and Caroline Toney, Dec. 15, 1858.
Townes, Robt. and Jane McCreery, g. W. A. Burwell, Nov. 6, 1813. Sur. John S. Burwell. 8.
Townsley, Wm. and Rebecca Serug, dau. John, Sept. 3, 1810. Sur. Philip Ascue. 117.
Trail, Jacob and Locky Cumpton, Oct. 5, 1838. Sur. Micajah Cumpton. 68.
Trail, James and Martha W. Evans, dau. Thos., Dec. 5, 1845. Sur. John Ulman.
Trail, Marville and Sally Moore, Dec. 27, 1826. Sur. Jacob Moore.
Trail, Thos. and Sally Brothers, July 26, 1820. Sur. Wm. Brothers.
Trail, Wm. and Margaret Jones, May 6, 1842. Sur. Jekiel Jones. 68.
Traling, John and Elizabeth Shorewater, ..., 1816. 130.

Traylor, Field and Julia Ann Rigney, dau. Elizabeth Chitwood, Jan. 31, 1835. Sur. Creed J. Rigney. 68.
Trent, Jesse Berry, s. Archibald, and Delila Basham, dau. Jonathan, Dec. 2, 1850. Sur. Jesse Trent. 18.
Trent, Jesse and Lucinda Southall, dau. Mary, Mar. 26, 1850. Sur. Fernew Southall. 18.
Trent, John and Jane Craighead, dau. Polly, Aug. 13, 1824. Sur. Wm. Heptinstall.
Trent, Noah and Jemima Cundiff, June 14, 1843. Sur. Wilson Cundiff. 104.
Trent, Wm. and Ellander Fintch, June 15, 1845. 18.
Trent, Wm. and Christin Bowles, Apr. 14, 1853. 96.
Troup, Henry and Dolly Wade, Jan. 16, 1794. 52.
Troup, Jacob and Caty Willis, Aug. 18, 1829. Sur. Allen Howry.
Troup, John and Elizabeth Hale, dau. Wm., Dec. 11, 1835. Sur. Lewis Hale.
Trout, Abraham and Mary Law, Nov. 16, 1808. 117.
Trout, David and Nancy Murphy, Mar. 13, 1802. Sur. Butler Murphy.
Trout, (Trent), Joseph and Sarah Jones, dau. David and Sarah, Oct. 3, 1798. Sur. Jacob Miller. 48.
Truman, Anderson and Sally Blades Hancock, dau. Lew Hancock, Dec. 31, 1804.
Tuggle, John, Jr., s. John, and Mary Prillaman, dau. David, Nov. 25, 1844. Sur. Thos. H. Prillaman.
Turnbull, Hay and Susan M. Mitchell, Nov. 26, 1837. Sur. Wm. Turnbull.
Turnbull, James and Ann M. Booth, dau. Mary B., Aug. 3, 1846. Sur. Edward C. Booth.
Turnbull, Lewis H., s. Stephen and Abiah, and Elizabeth J. Booth, dau. Mary B., Sept. 16, 1843. Sur. Thos. T. Jones.
Turnbull, Lewis and Abiah Taylor, Oct. 5, 1801. Sur. Henry Taylor.
Turnbull, Stephen and Louisa M. Callaway, Dec. 23, 1845. Sur. James Callaway. 134.
Turnbull, Wm. and Elizabeth S. Hale, Jan. 25, 1833. Sur. Moses G. Carper. 61.
Turnbull, William and Ruth Hairston, dau. Ruth, Nov. 5, 1792. Sur. Wm. Anderson. 52.

Turner, Andrew H. and Frances Holland, dau. John M., Apr. 5, 1824. Sur. John Holland. 48.
Turner, Andrew H. and Martha Prillaman, Aug. ....., 1852. 1.
Turner, Anselm W. and Elizabeth Lazenby, Nov. 10, 1834. Sur. John Lazenby.
Turner, Bartley and Maria Boon, Dec. 2, 1833. Sur. Jacob Boon. 48.
Turner, Constant and Mary Lavinder, Sept. 24, 1838. Sur. John Lavinder. 132.
Turner, Edmund and Alzira Abshire, Dec. 23, 1852. 96.
Turner, Elijah H. and Sarah A. Heptinstall, dau. Thos., Nov. 1, 1847. Sur. Wm. B. Heptinstall.
Turner, Elkanah B. and Elizabeth C. Wingfield, dau. Christopher, Oct. 27, 1840. Sur. John S. Wingfield. 132.
Turner, Geo. and Elizabeth Greer, Dec. 2, 1805. Sur. Joseph Greer.
Turner, Geo. C. and Emeline Menefee, Aug. 2, 1847. Sur. Wiley Menefee.
Turner, Geo. W. and Lucy A. Luke, Dec. 13, 1858.
Turner, Greenville and Deborah Webster, Aug. 19, 1811. Sur. Reuben Webster. 130.
Turner, Isaiah and Elizabeth Cannaday (Candy), Dec. 9, 1797. Sur. James Prunty.
Turner, Isham and Elizabeth Young, dau. Catherine and Redley, May 16, 1792. Sur. Merlin Young.
Turner, James and Mary Mclarry (Mailery), dau. Richard, Dec. 21, 1790. Sur. Michael Coats. 52.
Turner, James and Lydda Rentfro, dau. Joshua, Jan. 13, 1787. Sur. Joshua Rentfro. 52.
Turner, James A. and Mary Oyler, Feb. 22, 1853. 18.
Turner, James M. and Mary A. James, Nov. 24, 1853. 127.
Turner, Jeffery, s. Jubal, and Nancy A. Mason, dau. John, Dec. 7, 1839. Sur. Lewis Mason.
Turner, Jeremiah and Rachael Ross, dau. Daniel, Apr. 21, 1792. Sur. Thos. Ruble. 52.
Turner, John and Betsey Price, dau. Joseph Showers, June 13, 1786. Sur. Luke Standifer.
Turner, John and Nancy Abshire, Sept. 23, 1823. Sur. Abraham Abshire. 130.

Turner, John T. B. and Jane Wright, dau. Lute, Feb. 4, 1839. Sur. Fleming J. T. Wright.
Turner, Jonas and Recky M'Clary, dau. Richard, Dec. 25, 1792. Sur. Coats Kinsey. 52.
Turner, Josiah, Jr. and Malinda Ingram, Sept. 1, 1848. Sur. James Ingrum.
Turner, Josiah H., s. Wm., and Sarah Turner, dau. Isaiah, Dec. 4, 1843. Sur. Meshack Turner. 132.
Turner, Josiah and Elizabeth Reel, dau. Michael, Nov. 19, 1808. Sur. John Reel. 44.
Turner, Lewis and Cynthia Turner, May 5, 1817. Sur. Isaiah Turner.
Turner, Micajah and Judith Smith, Oct. 7, 1816. Sur. Francis G. Harwood.
Turner, Obediah and Frances Lavinder, Nov. 4, 1822. Sur. John Lavender. 130.
Turner, Richard and Lucinda Boyd, dau. Wm., Dec. 28, 1842. Sur. Jesse Boyd.
Turner, Stephen and Lucy Snead, Feb. 15, 1803. Sur. Richard Snead.
Turner, Stephen and Ruth Prillaman, Nov. 28, 1832. Sur. John Prillaman.
Turner, Washington and Eve Brubaker, Nov. 25, 1845. Sur. Christian Brubaker. 18.
Turner, Wm. and Sally Abshire, Mar. 11, 1823. Sur. Abraham Abshire. 130.
Turner, Wm. D. and Juliet Price, Nov. 11, 1833. Sur. Merit Price. 48.
Turner, Wm. H. and Margaret Jane McGhee, dau. Martin, Apr. 1, 1850. Sur. John Martin. 80.
Turner, Wilson, Jr. and Elizabeth Noftsinger, g. Jacob Abshire, Mar. 8, 1824. Sur. Greenville Turner. 130.
Turpin, Geo. and Jane Ferguson, Feb. 11, 1839. Sur. Henry Smith, Jr. 18.
Turpin, Thos. and Sally Charter, dau. Thos., Oct. 10, 1806. Sur. Walter Eady.
Turtle, John and Sally Easley, dau. Wm., Mar. 5, 1788. Sur. Joseph Parrott. 37.

Tyree, Geo. W. and Elvira Hutchinson, Jan. 3, 1848. Sur. Wm. Hutcherson.
Tyree, Hiram and Betsy Woody, Mar. 5, 1810. Sur. Martin Woody. 8.
Tyree, John and Ann Keen, Apr. 10, 1821. Sur. Thos. S. Keen.
Tyree, Martin and Elizabeth Hunt, Nov. 4, 1833. Sur. Daniel B. Hunt.
Tyree, Meredith and Rebecca Dillion, dau. Meriday, Mar. 7, 1831. Sur. John A. Deering. 48.
Tyree, Wm. B. and Pamelia Woody, Nov. 7, 1832. Sur. Randolph Woody. 48.
Ullman, Joseph and Rebecca Webb, Oct. 12, 1825. Sur. Joseph Webb. 48.
Ullman, Sebastian and Sally Webb, Aug. 25, 1797. Sur. Samuel Webb. 21.
Ullman, Samuel and Elizabeth Webb, Dec. 23, 1820. Sur. Joseph Webb.
Ullman, John and Chloe Hodges, Dec. 24, 1838. Sur. Abednego Hodges.
Umphlet, Pressly and Mary Ann Barton, Dec. 23, 1839. Sur. John Barton.
Underwood, Alexander and Sintha Radford, Jan. 7, 1841. Sur. Samuel Radford. 68.
Underwood, Alexander and Eleanor Radford, Dec. 11, 1837. Sur. Lewis Radford.
Underwood, Burwell, s. Jesse, and Martha Smith, dau. Rosanah, Feb. 15, 1845. Sur. John Terry. 68.
Underwood, David, s. Mary, and Jane McGhee, dau. Mary, Sept. 13, 1824. Sur. Samuel Underwood.
Underwood, James and Huldah Radford, dau. Joshua, Feb. 1, 1845. Sur. James T. Radford. 68.
Underwood, Jesse and Nancy Manning, Dec. 23, 1817. Sur. David Manning.
Underwood, Jesse and Ellender Greer, Dec. 19, 1812. Sur. Chas. Greer.
Underwood, Jesse, s. Daniel, and Elizabeth Foster, Aug. 30, 1842. Sur. Daniel Underwood. 60.
Underwood, John and Jane Prater, Dec. 31, 1838. Sur. Creed Underwood. 68.

Underwood, John and Hannah Janney, dau. Isaac, Dec. 8, 1836. Sur. David Willis.
Underwood, John and Nancy Roberts, Jan. 9, 1817. Sur. Jacob Wright.
Underwood, John and Sarah Lemon, Nov. 27, 1795. Sur. Samuel Underwood. 66.
Underwood, Joseph and Ellen Justice, dau. John, Mar. 9, 1789. Sur. John Heard. 66.
Underwood, Joseph and Elizabeth Greer, dau. Chas., Mar. 29, 1823. Sur. Andrew Allen.
Underwood, Joshua, s. Wm. and Mary Underwood, dau. Joseph, Aug. 26, 1844. Sur. Sur. James T. Radford. 68.
Underwood, Richard, s. Jesse, and Adeline Radford, Feb. 5, 1849. Sur. Geo. Radford. 68.
Underwood, Robt. and Martha Hancock, dau. Frances, Dec. 10, 1839. Sur. Reuben James. 68.
Underwood, Samuel and Rebecca Hollins, dau. John, Sept. 13, 1833. 61.
Underwood, Seth and Sarah Worley, dau. John, Jan. 13, 1797. Sur. James Candy.
Underwood, Wm. and Rachael Allen, Oct. 11, 1837. Sur. Creed Smith. 68.
Underwood, Wm. and Sealey Mannen, dau. Davis, Mar. 21, 1808. Sur. Payton Ellyson.
Uplinger, Cornelius and Judith Darby, Feb. 12, 1833. Sur. Samuel Worts. 48.
Vance, John and Elizabeth Law, Jan. 4, 1818. Sur. Robt. Law. 8.
Vance, John W. and Lucinda Saunders, dau. Wm., Dec. 19, 1831. Sur. Jordan Robertson. 8.
Vance, Peter and Fanny Thomas, Oct. 20, 1811. 122.
Vansel, Samuel and Mary Picklesimer, dau. Jacob, Feb. 2, 1791. Sur. Malcolm Waggoner. 103.
Van Maple, John and Susannah Pergram, Jan. 18, 1814. Sur. John Peatt.
Vanover, Cornelius and Nancy Moody, Oct. 10, 1795. Sur. Edmund Moody.
Vanover, John and Polly Taylor, ..., 1811. 130.
Vaughn, David and Patsey Newton, Nov. 14, 1812. Sur. Joseph Starkey.

Vaughn, Joseph and Nancy Akers, July 11, 1808. Sur. Thos. Highley. 130.
Vealy, Peter and Jane Newman, ..., 1816. 130.
Vest, Chas. and Theney Manning, dau. David and Nancy, Dec. 4, 1809. Sur. John Vest. 117.
Vest, Chas. and Elizabeth Vier, dau. John, Jan. 9, 1812. Sur. Littleberry Vest.
Vest, John D. and Polly Rakes, Mar. 2, 1810. 112.
Vest, John and Mary Smith, dau. Rosamot, Dec. 11, 1834. Sur. Creed Smith. 60.
Vest, Littleberry and Polly Moore, Jan. 7, 1805. Sur. James Whorley.
Vest, Littleberry and Sally James, dau. Wm., Jan. 3, 1817. Sur. Joshua James.
Vest, Mosby and Mary Robert, Feb. 17, 1803. 122.
Vest, Mosby and Sarah Cockran, June 3, 1835. Sur. Isham Cockran. 129.
Vest, Philip and Sally Goodson, dau. Thos., Dec. 6, 1808. Sur. Daniel Shelor. 112.
Vest, Rowland, s. John, and Delila Vest, dau. Bery, Feb. 9, 1830. Sur. John Vest.
Via, (Vier) David and Nancy King, dau. Lida, Apr. 28, 1804. Sur. Josias Viar.
Via, James and Sarah Hale, Nov. 4, 1803. Sur. Thos. Hale. 72.
Via, James and Hetty Edwards, Oct. 30, 1826.
Via, James and Rachael Martin, Nov. 2, 1839. Sur. Peter Cannaday. 60.
Via, Josiah and Rachael Hale, Oct. 4, 1844. Sur. Daniel Griffith. 65.
Via, Peter and Nancy Justice, Aug. 4, 1845. Sur. Sparrel H. Griffith.
Via, Peter and Margaret Martin, dau. Matthew, Oct. 29, 1833. Sur. Wm. Martin. 60.
Via, Robt. and Frances Parker, Dec. 15, 1819. Sur. Wilkins Wray.
Via, Samuel, s. Josias, and Hetty Edwards, dau. Brice, Oct. 30, 1826. Sur. James Via. 61.
Via, Anderson and Jane Vest, dau. Berry, Apr. 29. 1824. Sur. Abraham Jones.

Viar, Claudius and Nancy Mitchell, dau. James, Nov. 17, 1823. Sur. Wm. Mitchell.
Via, Josias and Rachael Hale, dau. Benj., Jan. 2, 1800. Sur. John Vier. 66.
Vinson, Chas. and Sally McElwane, dau. Nancy, Apr. 22, 1799. Sur. Wm. Kelly. 89.
Vinson, Thos. Francis and Mary New, Nov. 7, 1798. Sur. John Vinson. 21.
Vinson, John and Nancy McKlewain, dau. John and Franky Kelly, Feb. 2, 1799. Sur. Wm. Kelly.
Vinson, Daniel and Milly Ashworth, Apr. 5, 1824. Sur. Lewis Ashworth. 48.
Vinyard, John and Tincey Muse, Oct. 16, 1807. Sur. Tables Vineyard. 130.
Wade, Benj. H. and Mary Louisa Taylor, Dec. 18, 1852. 47.
Wade, Bradley and Magdalen Gibson, Mar. 4, 1850. Sur. Nicholas Cassell. 68.
Wade, Bradley and Rachael Lemon, Feb. 5, 1810. Sur. Isaac Lemon.
Wade, Henry and Polly Gallaspie, dau. Evan, Aug. 15, 1820. Sur. Wm. Gillaspie. 130.
Wade, Henry H. and Julia E. Patterson, Nov. 27, 1834. Sur. John H. Wade. 60.
Wade, Issac and Elizabeth Haynes, Feb. 4, 1842. Sur. Nicholas Cassell. 68.
Wade, Jefferson and Mary Jane Smith, Dec. 29, 1847. Sur. John A. Smith.
Wade, John and Alley Hale, Mar. 7, 1814. Sur. John Hale. 122.
Wade, John and Phebe Akers, Dec. 18, 1834. 134.
Wade, John and Hannah Jones, dau. Henry, Jan. 30, 1792. Sur. John Hale. 52.
Wade, Lewis and Elizabeth B. Hale, July 21, 1826. Sur. Francis Hale. 61.
Wade, Reuben and Lucy Martin, dau. Hugh, Jan. 30, 1804. Sur. John Mullins.
Wade, Robt. and Ann Standifer, June 6, 1808. Sur. Luke. Standifer.
Wade, Robt. and Sarah Haynes, dau. Drewry, Feb. 7, 1850. Sur. Isaac Wade. 68.

Wade, Royal and Rachael Jones, Feb. 24, 1791. Sur. John Hale. 52.
Wade, Zackfield, Jr. and Mary F. Boone, dau. John, Nov. 25, 1839. Sur. Skelton Taylor.
Waggoner, Daniel and Polly Coltrite, Jan. 12, 1821. Sur. Jacob Fishburne. 130.
Waggoner, Henry and Jane Beheler, Dec. 5, 1826. Sur. Geo. Beheler. 48.
Waggoner, Melcher and Elizabeth Picklesimer, dau. John, Mar. 11, 1789. Sur. Christian Chas. Lange. 52.
Waid, Chancellor and Delilah Gallaspy, Sept. 1, 1835. Sur. Evin Gallaspy. 134.
Waid, Chandler and Jane Troup, Mar. 5, 1844. Sur. John Troup.
Waid, Chas. and Elizabeth Hale, Sept. 1, 1814. Sur. Thos. Hale. 130.
Waid, Edmund and Sophronia Waid, Dec. 18, 1838. Sur. John P. Waid.
Waid, James S. and Eliza Ann Hiett, Dec. 18, 1837. Sur. Joseph Hiett.
Waid, Jesse and Elizabeth M. Perdue, Feb. 22, 1842. Sur. Obediah Perdue.
Waid, John F. and Polly Cassell, July 17, 1833. Sur. James C. Tate. 60.
Waid, John and Elizabeth Ferguson, Mar. 22, 1823. Sur. Chas. Ferguson.
Waid, Powell M. and Susan Ferguson, Dec. 20, 1842. Sur. James S. Waid. 132.
Waid, Robt. and Elizabeth Waid, Aug. 20, 1849. Sur. Lewis Wade.
Waid, Wm. and Elizabeth Ferguson, Nov. 24, 1840. Sur. Moses G. Carper.
Waid, Wm. R. and Anna Beckner, dau. Jonathan, July 25, 1843. Sur. John M. Holland, Jr. 18.
Waldron, Burwell and Carolina McGhee, July 19, 1837. Sur. Nelson McGhee. 132.
Walden, Wm. and Margaret King, Dec. 31, 1792. 52.
Waldren, John and Elizabeth F. Austin, dau. Miles, Oct. 15, 1853. 75.

Walker, Arnold and Jane H. Martin, Apr. 19, 1843. Sur. Thos. Pearson.

Walker, Burwell and Frances Shorter, dau. John, Dec. 20, 1831. Sur. Booker Shorter.

Walker, Burwell and Susannah Walker, Jan. 13, 1806. Sur. Joel Walker. 122.

Walker, Dandy and Judy Green, Oct. 26, 1806. Sur. Esom Edmons. 8.

Walker, Geo. and Sally Webb, 1811. 130.

Walker, Henry W. and Mary Belcher, dau. Francis, Feb. 4, 1839. Sur. Joshua Zeigler.

Walker Henry and Cynthia Ferguson, Mar. 3, 1823. Sur. Standifer Ferguson. 49.

Walker James A. and Elizabeth D. Booth, July 25, 1827. Sur. Benj. Booth.

Walker, James and Phoebe Estes, dau. Bottom, Feb. 11, 1803. Sur. Bird Estes.

Walker, John and Elizabeth Sailer Jan. 15, 1802. Sur. Joseph Davis. 72.

Walker, John H. and Nancy Foster, Nov. 19, 1831. Sur. Joseph Edds. 3.

Walker, Lewis and Betsy A. Hudson, Mar. 9, 1825. Sur. Wm. Hudson. 48.

Walker, Moses and Frances Glass, Apr. 10, 1830. 3.

Walker, Nathaniel and Susannah Lacy, dau. John, Dec. 21, 1824. Sur. Henry Arum. 90.

Walker, Robt. M. and Clarissa J. Allen, dau. Jeremiah, Sept. 7, 1840. Sur. Jeremiah Allen.

Walker, Wm. and Mary Hartman, dau. Mary, Sept. 13, 1794. Sur. James Prunty. 120.

Walker, Wm. and Catherine Zeigler, dau. Jacob, Jan. 25, 1817. Sur. Wm. Bozewell. 7.

Walker, Wilson and Nancy Brizendine, Aug. 23, 1828. Sur. Banister Brizendine. 48.

Waller, Christopher and Frances Lambert, May 4, 1810. Sur. Robt. Lark.

Waller, Wm. and Elizabeth Hibbs, May 10, 1811. Sur. John Pinkard.

Walrone. Isaac and Caty Saul, Jan. 23, 1830. Sur. Wm. Luke.

Walton, Dr. L. and Serena Law, dau. Jesse, Aug. 18, 1838. Sur. Chas. Richards. 3.

Walton, Wm. and Nancy Griffith, dau. Benj., Sept. 29, 1800. Sur. Benj. Griffith. 21.

Ward, Asa and Susannah Sink, May 2, 1814. Sur. Stephen Sink. 8.

Ward, Benj. and Elizabeth Perdue, Sept. 15, 1804. Sur. Meshack Perdue.

Ward, Daniel and Fanny Blankenship, May 20, 1809. Sur. Legan Blankenship. 8.

Ward, David and Sarah Ann Feazel, Nov. 13, 1845. Sur. Aaron Feazel. 134.

Ward, Jesse and Anna Greer, Sept. 30, 1799. Sur. Philip Sanders. 21.

Ward, Jonathan and Annie Plyborne, Aug. 10, 1815. Sur. Jesse Dillion, Jr.

Ward, Samuel and Mary Altick, Dec. 2, 1816. Sur. David Altick. 7.

Ward, Samuel, Jr., s. Samuel, Sr., and Julia Ann Campbell, Dec. 23, 1845. Sur. Elijah Campbell. 134.

Ward, Whittenton W. and Celia Perdue, dau. Happy, Nov. 21, 1825. Sur. Elijah Lyon. 48.

Ward, Wm. and Mary Ann Jones, Sept. 9, 1811. Sur. James Jones.

Warden, David and Theodosia Hardwick, Apr. 26, 1791. Sur. Joseph Dyche. 52.

Warner, Daniel and Charlotte Greer, Apr. 23, 1831. Sur. Samuel W. Greer.

Warren, Drury and Susanna Cooley, Oct. 15, 1810. 8.

Warren, Elijah and Sarah Mason, dau. Robt., Feb. 27, 1787. Sur. Thos. Warden. 66.

Warren, Jesse and Rhoda Richards, dau. Edward, Feb. 13, 1790. Sur. Elijah Warren. 37.

Warren, John A. and Sally Parberry, Sept. 24, 1839. Sur. Wm. S. Niblett.

Warren, John W. and Polly Tyree, Dec. 27, 1836. Sur. Hiram Tyree.

Warren, Joseph and Sarah Allen, Nov. 26, 1805. Sur. Geo. Wright. 122.

Warren, Lankston and Drusiller Preator, dau. Thos., Oct. 5, 1791. Sur. Jesse Warren.

Warren, Lot and Lucy Mitchell, Apr. 30, 1813. Sur. Elijah Cooley. 71.

Warren, Thos. and Mary McWilliams, dau. Hugh, Dec. 16, 1786. Sur. Drury Warren. 66.

Warriner, Woodson and Eva Alley, Feb. 5, 1820. Sur. Joseph Warriner. 61.

Warwick, Wyatt and Polly Belcher, dau. Frances, Nov. 25, 1805. Sur. Isham Belcher.

Washington, Solomon and Nancy Prillaman, Apr. 29, 1819. Sur. Isaac Prillaman.

Watkins, Geo. and Elizabeth Kinsey, dau. Jacob, July 11, 1838. Sur. Cornelius Kinsey.

Watson, Ezekiel and Sally Agee, Mar. 5, 1811. Sur. Jesse Agee.

Watson, James and Mary Lyon, Aug. 29, 1792. Sur. Zachariah Blankenship.

Wattson, James and Lydia Willis, dau. Phebe and John, July 2, 1789. Sur. Alexander Watson. 52.

Watson, John and Eleanor Martin, Mar, 7, 1796. Sur. James Martin. 37.

Wattington, Herbert C. and Alice A. Short, Aug. 31, 1846. Sur. Robt. Short. 132.

Watts, Francis and Lydia Robertson, May 6, 1808. Sur. Litteberry Robertson.

Weatherford, Chas. A. and Nancy Crump, Apr. 10, 1843. Sur. Wm. Crump.

Weaver, Adam and Caty Koon, Aug. 16, 1813. Sur. Henry Koon. 130.

Weaver, Bailey and Minerva Ann Loving, May 30, 1835. Sur. Chrisholm Griffith.

Weaver, Jacob and Elizabeth Sink, Jan, 3, 1803. Sur. Stephen Sink. 106.

Weaver, James O. and Susannah Fisher, July 10, 1849. Sur. Joel Fisher. 18.

Weaver, John and Matilda Murray, Dec. 3, 1803. Sur. Rhodham Brown.

Weaver, Stobull W. and Elizabeth Thurmon, Dec. 21, 1846. Sur. Wm. Thurmon. 18.
Weaver, Wm. H. and Sarah Thurman, Nov. 1, 1847. Sur. Wm. Thurman. 18.
Weaver, Wm. H. and Mary N. Law, dau. Samuel B., Mar. 14, 1842. Sur. Samuel T. Law. 18.
Webb, Aaron and Lucy Fitzgerald, June 27, 1793. 52.
Webb, Aaron A. and Lydia Quisenberry, Aug. 11, 1806. Sur. Henry Gatewood. 8.
Webb, Bird L. and Martha E. Pinkard, Nov. 17, 1858.
Webb, Creed T. and Mahala F. Booth, Feb. 5, 1827. Sur. Moses G. Carper.
Webb, Cuthbert, s. Elizabeth, and Mary Jones, Mar. 7, 1791. Sur. Theodrick Webb. 52.
Webb, Daniel and Mary Burton, Dec. 24, 1803. Sur. John Robertson. 72.
Webb, Eli and Mahala Delancy, Mar. 13, 1830. Sur. Lewis Moore.
Webb, Geo. W. and Jamima A. Kasey, Feb. 17, 1853. 18.
Webb, Jacob and Elizabeth Fitzgerald, June 4, 1787. Sur. Theodrick Webb. 52.
Webb, Jacob and Elizabeth Webb, Apr. 4, 1791. Sur. Cuthbert Webb. 103.
Webb, Jacob and Hannah Jones, dau. Thos., Oct. 3, 1805. Sur. John Wray.
Webb, James and Elizabeth Billups, dau. Ed., Feb. 12, 1802. Sur. Thos. Harrison.
Webb, John and Fanny Biggers, Mar. 5, 1810. Sur. Theodoric Webb and James Biggers. 117.
Webb, John and Leuse Wilson, Sept. 15, 1798. Sur. John Wilson. 89.
Webb, John F. and Seline Noell, July 13, 1853. 55.
Webb, Joseph and Babara Thompson, Oct. 4, 1790. Sur. Andrew Thompson. 52.
Webb, Josiah and Jane Bowles, Aug. 3, 1835. Sur. Henry Willard.
Webb, Littleberry and Suckey Webb, dau. Adam and Conny Helm, Nov. 5, 1800. Sur. Thos. Helm. 72.

Webb, Robt. J. and Catherine Greer, Aug. 23, 1834. Sur. Moses G. Greer.

Webb, Smith and Nancy Clowers, July 6, 1797. Sur. Jacob Clowers. 21.

Webb, Theodrick F. and Nancy Tate Greer Callaway, dau. James, Jan. 17, 1821. Sur. Samuel W. Greer. 130.

Webb, Theodrick and Permelia Webster, dau. John, Feb. 17, 1792. Sur. Jacob Webster. 52.

Webb, Theodrick and Christy Copeland, Oct. 24, 1789. Sur. Richard Copeland. 52.

Webb, Wm. and Mary Dillion, Dec. 27, 1820. Sur. John Dillon. 48.

Webb, Wm. and Violet Moore, Feb. 6, 1815.

Webster, Adam R. and Susannah Akers, Apr. 20, 1844. Sur. James B. Akers. 134.

Webster, Daniel and Rhoda Arthur, dau. John, Jan. 25, 1803. Sur. Geo. Webster. 106.

Webster, David and Lucinda Hawkins, Jan. 16, 1819. Sur. Bluford Hawkins. 130.

Webster, David and Phebe Akers, dau.. James, Nov. 13, 1830. Sur. Owen Gillaspee. 48.

Webster, Henry and Elizabeth Webster, dau. Samuel and Susannah, Aug. 12, 1800. Sur. James Webster.

Webster, Jacob and Fanny Walker Woodson, dau. Shadrach, May 3, 1790. Sur. Shadrack Woodson. 89.

Webster, James and Martha Henderson, dau. Samuel, Jan. 25, 1806. Sur. Jesse Webster. 130.

Webster, James and Elizabeth McKinsay, Oct. 29, 1801. Sur. James McKinsay.

Webster, James and Polly Akers, Oct. 15, 1834. Sur. Samuel Akers.

Webster, James and Lucy Webster, Aug. 7, 1826. Sur. Daniel Webster.

Webster, Jesse and Polly Henderson, Apr. 6, 1807. 130.

Webster, Jesse and Aby Fisher, June 6, 1852. 11.

Webster, John R. and Catherine Peters, Jan. 23, 1839. Sur. John B. Peters. 68.

Webster, John and Jane Webster, Mar. 20, 1794. F2.

Webster, John and Deborah Webster, Feb. 3, 1834. Sur. James Webster. 68.
Webster, B. and Elizabeth Akers, dau. James, May 25, 1840. Sur. David S. Webster.
Webster, Lewis and Catherine Jamison, dau. John, Nov. 28, 1836. Sur. Samuel Jameson. 134.
Webster, Luke and Catherine Hawkins, Apr. 28, 1821. Sur. Geo. McVey 130.
Webster, Nathaniel and Catherine Greer, Nov. 15, 1841. Sur. John H. Greer. 134.
Webster, Nathaniel and Mary Oxley, Dec. 18, 1851. 134.
Webster, Samuel and Sarah Billups, dau. Edward, Feb. 14, 1801. Sur. Thos. Harrison.
Webster, Wm. and Elizabeth Reynolds, Nov. 10, 1807. 130.
Webster, Wm. H. and Rebecca Akers, Sept. 26, 1840. Sur. Richard M. Taliaferro.
Weddel, Joseph and Susannah Bowman, Mar. 15, 1849. 18.
Weeks, Archibald and Lane D. Cabaniss, Nov. 5, 1831. Sur. Nelson Abshire. 48.
Welch, Isaiah and Eleanor Campbell, Mar. 15, 1822. Sur. Robt. H. Calhoun. 130.
Welch, James and Rhoda Willis, dau. Josiah, Dec. 31, 1792. Sur. Isaiah Willis. 52.
Wells, John D. and Mary F. Bernard, dau. Benj., Aug. 8, 1848. Sur. Joseph G. Bernard.
Wells, Richard and Mary J. Cannaday, May 20, 1850. Sur. Ferdinand Cannaday. 111.
Wells, Thos. W. and Sally Kinsey, dau. Jacob, Dec. 29, 1840. Sur. John Kinsey.
West, John and Hester Wright, Oct. 10, 1798. Sur. Wm. Ferguson. 72.
West, Nathaniel and Polly Mills, Mar. 8, 1819. Sur. Wm. Mills. 98.
West, Thos. and Margaret Hook, dau. John, Feb. 11, 1801. Sur. Henry Hook.
Wheat, John and Sarah Hudson, Sept. 2, 1800. Sur. Wm. Farmer. 141.
Wheeler, Robt. and Miriam Payne, Feb. 5, 1821. Sur. Joseph Payne. 49.

White, Benj. and Suckey Bartee, Oct. 8, 1786. Sur. Wm. Bartee. 66.

White, Henry P. and Barbara Zeigler, Nov. 1, 1824. Sur. Michael Zeigler.

White, Jacob A. and Eliza Robins, 1851. 132.

White, James and Martha A. M. Allen, Dec. 30, 1840. Sur. Robt. M. Walker.

White, James M. and Nancy Belcher, Feb. 7, 1829. Sur. Geo. Belcher.

White, Obediah and Lucy Akers, Apr. 28, 1806. Sur. Wm. Akers.

White, Wm. and Elizabeth Pratt, Aug. 4, 1806. Sur. Obediah White.

Whitlow, Banister and Nancy Richards, Dec. 6, 1834. Sur. Chas. Richards. 3.

Whitlow, Henry and Nancy Scott, May 31, 1823. Sur. Nicholas Whitlow. 49.

Whitlow, Nicholas and Elizabeth Scott, Jan. 1, 1825. Sur. Michael Scott. 48.

Whitlow, Wm. and Nancy Shoemaker, Feb. 1, 1839. Sur. Moses G. Carper.

Whitenight, Benj. and Martha Wimmer, July 17, 1794. Sur. Jacob Wimmer. 52.

Whitneck, Wm. and Bidzy Lambeth, Nov. 3, 1828. Sur. Edward Lambeth. 48.

Whitworth, Philemon and Rebecca Woody, dau. Henry, Feb. 13, 1801. 72.

Whitworth, Roland and Polly A. Kennett, Nov. 1, 1858.

Whorley, Edmund and Martha Moore, dau. Wm., Mar. 16, 1833. Sur. Elisha Boyd. 61.

Whorley, Geo. and Mary H. Via, July 19, 1838. Sur. Josias Via. 61.

Whorley, Trail and Dochy Burrell, 1796. 21.

Wickham, Nathaniel, Jr. and Mary B. Short, Jan. 25, 1829. Sur. Reuben Short.

Wigginton, Geo. and Mary G. Clay, Aug. 14, 1846. Sur. Ezekiel Clay. 104.

Wigginton, Henry and Mary Bird, dau. John and Jane, Nov. 4, 1844. Sur. Wm. B. Mitchell. 133.

Wigginton, James M. and Juliana Law, Dec. 4, 1848. Sur.
    Thos. Law. 18.
Wildman, Elisha, s. Israel, and Mary E. Gilbert, dau. Samuel,
    Feb. 12, 1848. Sur. Wm. W. Wildman.
Wilkes, Gilbert and Eleanor Charter, Apr. 2, 1798. Sur. Jonathan
    Charter.
Wilkes, James and Susannah Ross, dau. Mauring, Sept. 18,
    1801. Sur. Thos. Charter. 141.
Wilkes, Jesse and Julia Pratt, dau. Mary, Aug. 3, 1801. Sur.
    Walter Addy. 141.
Wilks, Jonathan and Mary Gregory, dau. Bichael, May 5, 1831.
    Sur. Elisha Mitchell.
Wilks, Minor and Lucy Walker, June 23, 1797. Sur. Wm. Estes.
Wilks, Thos. and Jane New, sdau. Mary Vest, Feb. 13, 1817.
    Sur. Thos. Dudley. 7.
Wilkinson, Wm. and Joan Vest, Sept. 9, 1802. 122.
Willard, Henry and Harriet Richards, Dec. 9, 1836. Sur.
    Abednego Hodges.
Willard, Wm. and Hannah Tyree, Jan. 5, 1835. Sur. Samuel Clay.
William, Abraham and Jane Goode, Dec. 1, 1848. Sur. David
    Goode, Sr. 18.
Williams, Benj. and Elizabeth F. English, dau. Parmenas, Nov.
    29, 1845. Sur. Wm. D. Smith. 14.
Williams, Benj. F. and Anna C. Perkins, dau. Temple, Nov. 28,
    1836. Sur. David C. Perkins.
Williams, Isaac and Lucy Highley, Dec 25, 1813. Sur. Thos.
    Highley. 130.
Williams, James and Clarissa Richards, Feb. 25, 1845. Sur.
    Christopher Richards. 68.
Williams, Jesse and Ann Key. Feb. 17, 1821. Sur. Thos. Keys.
    130.
Williams, John and Polly Richards, Sept. 17, 1804. Sur. Isaac
    Richards. 122.
Williams, John and Elizabeth Pearson, dau. Thos., June 23, 1837.
    Sur. Joseph A. Pearson.
Williams, Johnson and Judith Thornton, dau. Polly, July 6, 1821.
    Sur. James Keys.
Williams, Lewis and Malinda Green, Mar. 25, 1846. Sur. Jabez
    B. L. McCormack. 68.

Williams, Lewellen and Winfred Lovell, Nov. 17, 1803. Sur. Markham Lovel.

Williams, Morrison W. and Mary A. Pearson, dau. Thos., Oct. 6, 1846. Sur. Benj. E. Pearson. 132.

Williams, Robt. and Harriet Menefee, Oct. 15, 1832. Sur. Joseph Harter. 53.

Williams, Shrewsbury and Elizabeth Ramsey, dau. Thos., Feb. 5, 1816. Sur. Theodrick Ramsey.

Williams, Thos. and Martha Dowdy, dau. Zekel and Jane, Dec. 23, 1807. Sur. Jabez Dowdy. 130.

Williams, Thos. and Sarah Price, dau. Joseph, June 10, 1829. Sur. Stewart Tinsley. 48.

Williams, Thos. and Juliet Turner, Aug. 2, 1847. Sur. Stewart Tinsley. 19.

Williams, Wm. and Jane Welch, Sept. 17, 1821. Sur. James Welch.

Williams, Wm. B. and Mildred C. Tate, Jan. 23, 1833. Sur. James C. Tate.

Williamson, Henry and Elizabeth Callicoat, Nov. 20, 1813. Sur. Micajah Dillion. 8.

Williamson, James and Keziah Pasley, dau. Robt., Sr., June 4, 1821 Sur. John Pasley. 49.

Williamson, James and Frances Wingo, Jan. 5, 1829. Sur. Moses Greer, Jr. 49.

Williamson, James and Lucy Ward, dau. Stephen, Feb. 11, 1808. Sur. Stephen Wood. 8.

Williamson, Jonathan and Nancy Hiatt, Nov. 27, 1828. Sur. Geo. Woody. 3.

Williamson, Jonathan and Nancy Jackson, Nov. 7, 1797. 89.

Williamson, Lawson and Sophia Stockton, July 18, 1829. Sur. Wm. Copeland.

Williamson, Wm. and Christine Millirons, Oct. 5, 1819. Sur. Coleman Hamlin. 130.

Willis, David and Susannah Winfree, dau. Mary, Aug. 29, 1826. Sur. Stephen Winfree. 61.

Willis, Fleming and Mary C. Overfelt, Dec. 2, 1858.

Willis, Fleming and Mary Elizabeth Ferguson, Dec. 21, 1843. Sur. Henry Taliaferro. 14.

Willis, Fleming and Mariah Greer, May 26, 1846. Sur. Richard
    M. Taliaferro.
Willis, Hardin and Miriam Chitwood, Aug. 24, 1828. Sur. Thos.
    Slone. 26.
Willis, James and Sally Custer, Dec. 27, 1840. Sur. Henry
    Custer. 18.
Willis, John and Mary Winfree, Nov. 9, 1825. Sur. Runnell
    Winfrey. 61.
Willis, Jubal and Violet Jones, dau. Thos., Oct. 27, 1820. Sur.
    John Jones.
Willis, Lee, g. F. Saunders, and Ann Webb, dau. Hannah, Mar.
    5, 1827.
Willis, Mark and Lucy Garrett, (Garrell), Feb. 23, 1803. Sur.
    John Highly.
Willis, Peter B. and Lucinda Saul, Feb. 20, 1851. 11.
Willis, Wm. and Rozzy Pigg, dau. James, May 21, 1788. Sur.
    Thos. Prunty.
Willis, Wm. and Sophia Snidor, Nov. 10, 1827. Sur. Spencer
    James. 48.
Wills, Robt. and Mary L. Turner, Dec. 6, 1858.
Wilson, Andrew and Sarah Webb, Oct. 5, 1820. Sur. Abraham
    Jones.
Wilson, Geo. W. and Susan M. Claiborne, dau. N. H., June
    7, 1837. Sur. Matthew W. Pettigrew.
Wilson, Samuel and Elizabeth Croxall, dau. Richard, Feb. 2,
    1791. Sur. Wm. Hoff. 103.
Wilson, Solomon and Rachael Martin, dau. Moses, Jan. 22,
    1817. Sur. James Martin. 122.
Wilson, Thos. and Milly Smith, Sept. 7, 1795. Sur. John Smith.
Wilson, Wm. P. and Ann Cora Basham, dau. Lucinda, Jan. 11,
    1849. Sur. John Crecy.
Wimmer, Jacob and Polly Margaret Caper, dau. Elizabeth
    Wimmer, Nov. 23, 1799. Sur. Thos. Caper.
Wimmer, Jacob and Elizabeth Capper, Oct. 30, 1794. Sur. Wm.
    Key. 89.
Wimmer, Jacob and Elizabeth Mills, Mar. 23, 1818. Sur. Miles
    Lamberth. 130.
Wimmer, Jacob and Lucy Moore, Feb. 12, 1852. 96.

Wimmer, John and Polly Akers, Oct. 18, 1823. Sur. Henry
Akers.
Wimmer, John and Elizabeth Willis, Dec. 6, 1824. Sur. Caty
Boon. 130.
Wimmer, John and Hannah Lemon, Sept. 2, 1793. Sur. Jacob
Wimmer. 52.
Winfree, Richard R. and Darkes Rakes, dau. Chas., June 8,
1812. Sur. Brice Edwards. 44.
Winfrey, Stephen and Elizabeth Carter, July 22, 1834 Sur.
Dabney Carter.
Winfrey, Stephen and Agnes Foster, Apr. 30, 1846. Sur. Joseph
Sigmon. 68.
Wingfield, Austin and Nancy F. Cook, Dec. 23, 1826. Sur. Chas.
M. Wingfield.
Wingfield, Christopher and Nancy Stockton, dau. Richard, Feb.
1, 1815. Sur. Chas. Stockton.
Wingfield, James Lewis and Elizabeth Parberry, dau. Ann.,
Dec. 15, 1807. Sur. Jas. Parberry, Jr.
Wingfield, John S. and Harriet N. Bondurant, dau. Jane B., Feb.
11, 1847. Sur. Wm. Copeland. 80.
Wingfield, John and Lucy Hill, (Hix), Jan. 7, 1828. Sur. Austin
Wingfield.
Wingfield, Oliver P. and Delilah Smith, Apr. 3, 1843. Sur.
Edmund W. Tench. 18.
Wingfield, Pinckney Green and Harriet B. Cooper, Sept. 2, 1850.
Sur. Gideon B. Cooper. 132.
Wingfield, Wm., Jr. and Elizabeth W. Prunty, dau. Jesse, Oct.
4, 1824. Sur. Copeland Stockton.
Wingfield, Wm. H. and Sarah V. Bondurant, Oct. ----, 1853. 132.
Wingfield, Wm. and Polly Brooks Tench, Jan. 6, 1817. Sur.
John Kidd.
Wingo, Davis and Sarah Housman, Oct. 10, 1848. Sur. Geo.
Houseman.
Wingo, David M. and Susan A. Pugh, Sept. 6, 1832. Sur. Richard
Pugh.
Wingo, Drewry and Elizabeth Williamson, Aug. 1, 1814. Sur.
John Ashworth. 8.
Wingo, James and Charity Solmon, Jan. 8, 1795. 52.

Wingo, John and Nancy Gilbert, July 26, 1808. Sur. Michael Gilbert. 8.
Wingo, Thos. and Susan Jenkins, dau. Gentry, Dec. 5, 1842. Sur. Samuel Dillion.
Wingo, Thos. and Milly Perdue, Dec. 23, 1846. 18.
Wingo, Warren and Mary Crum, Aug. 7, 1848. Sur. Jesse Ward. 18.
Winston, Ferdinand A. and Lucinda Hickman, dau. Solomon Winston, Sept. 23, 1858. Sur. John Bowman.
Winston, Roma and Salome Hickman, dau. Joseph, Sr., Feb. 4, Sur. Joseph Hickman, Jr. 130.
Winters, Lewis and Anne Prillaman, dau. Jacob, Feb. 16, 1799. Sur. Christian Prillaman.
Witcher, Armistead and Frances Ann James, dau. John, Mar. 28, 1834. Sur. John Craghead.
Witcher, Daniel C. and Mary Glass, dau. John, Aug. 29, 1836. Sur. Dudley Glass. 3.
Witcher, John and Polly Graves, dau. David, Sept. 29, 1821. Sur. Lewis Potter, Jr.
Witcher, Vincent and Nancy Newbill. Mar. 5, 1810. Sur. John G. Newbill.
Witcher, Wm. and Lucy Graves, Feb. 9, 1818. Sur. David Graves.
Wolf, Jacob and Hannah Kingery, dau. Henry, Mar. 2, 1801. Sur. Henry Kingery. 21.
Woodall, Wm. and Polly Hale, Mar. 13, 1809. Sur. Wm. Clay. 3.
Woodall, Willis and Cary Johnson, Apr. 16, 1804. Sur. Wm. H. Shelton.
Woodcock, John and Lucy Hawkins, Aug. 20, 1793. 131.
Woodcock, Mark and Susannah Simmons, dau. Thos., Mar. 5, 1803. Sur. Thos. Woodcock.
Woodcock, Thos. and Mary Standifer, July 3, 1786. Sur. Israel Standifer.
Woodcock, Wm. and Rhoda Simmons, dau. Chas., May 16, 1804. Sur. Joel Simmons.
Wood, Alexander and Susannah Boyd, Oct. 8, 1834. Sur. Hugh Boyd, Jr.
Wood, Berry and Delilah Proffit, July 11, 1836. Sur. Austin Prophet. 60.

Wood, Citizen S. and Jane M. Hale, Mar. 15, 1821. Sur. Wm. Williams. 49.

Wood, David and Jane Shilling, Mar. 21, 1848. Sur. John K. Shilling. 96.

Wood, Edward and Nancy Nowling, Dec. 4, 1841. Sur. Thos. Martin. 32.

Woods, Geo H, .and Abagail Sample, Feb. 16, 1824. Sur. Wm. B. Williams.

Woods, Hawkins and Jane Campbell, Dec. 3, 1814. Sur. Wm. Campbell.

Woods, John and Elizabeth Thompson, Oct. 12, 1814. Sur. Andrew Thompson.

Woods, John and Anne Hairston, Oct. 12, 1792. 52.

Woods, Josiah P. and Elizabeth J. Early, dau. J., Apr. 24, 1843. Sur. Peter Saunders. 104.

Woods, Josiah and Delilah Boyd, dau. Sarah, Aug. 24, 1835. Sur. Abraham Moore.

Woods, Lewis G. and Elizabeth F. Claughton, Apr. 7, 1845. Sur. Richard A. Claughton.

Woods, Nathan and Delilah Boyd, Aug 31, 1836. Sur. Abraham Moore.

Woods, Robt. and Ann E. Tate, May 28, 1829. Sur. Wm. B. Williams. 48.

Woods, Samuel H. and Cecelia Patterson, dau. Andrew, Mar. 20, 1822.

Woods, Stephen, Jr. and Nancy Cabaniss, May 1, 1837. Sur. Cassimer Cabaniss. 134.

Woods, Stephen and Lydia Holland, Feb. 2, 1812. 8.

Wood, Thos. and Sally Pasley, dau. Robt., Dec. 17, 1802. Sur. Henry Dillion. 106.

Woods, Wiley P. and Polly Saunders, Jan. 14, 1817. Sur. Samuel Hale.

Woodson, David and Margaret Ritter, Oct. 7, 1795. Sur. Abraham Ritter.

Woodson. Jacob B. and Pamelia Smith, dau. Benj., Feb. 29, 1832. Sur. Samuel Smith. 62.

Woody, Geo. and Lydia Williamson, dau. I., Oct. 24, 1825. Sur. Braxton Williams. 48.

Woody, Geo. and Rachael Mitchell, dau. John and Ann., Feb. 13, 1797. Sur. Benj. Mitchell.

Woody, Henry, Jr. and Catherine Hughes, May 18, 1824. Sur. John Dillion. 48.

Woody, Henry, Jr. and Judith Webb, Nov. 6, 1806. Sur. Samuel Webb.

Woody, Henry S. and Mary J. Jamerson, Nov. 6, 1843. Sur. Marshall Jamerson.

Woody, Jeffrey and Susan A. E. Stockton, dau. Peter C., Jan. 24, 1835. Sur. Wm. F. Cook.

Woody, John and Frances Harger, Apr. 2, 1821. Sur. John Harger. 130.

Woody, Mitchell M. and Sarah Jamison, Nov. 5, 1838. Sur. Lewis Jamison.

Woody, (Moody), Moses and Polly Bigley, May 21, 1798. Sur. Hugh French. 21.

Woody, Thos. and Ann Harger, dau. John, Mar. 21, 1814. Sur. Caleb Tate. 130.

Woody, Wiley and Mary L. Richards, 1852. 132.

Woody, Wyatt and Polly Robinson, Aug. 21, 1799. Sur. Martin Woody. 72.

Woolsey, David and Elizabeth Butler, Aug. 3, 1801.

Wooten, Joseph and Sarah Wilson, dau. John, Dec. 25, 1805. Sur. Ezra Wilson. 130.

Worley, Daniel and Mary Russell, Feb. 5, 1829. Sur. Seth Russell. 48.

Worley, Finch and Elizabeth Cunningham, Dec. 14, 1804. Sur. John Worley.

Worley, Joel S. and Judith S. Law, dau. Daniel, May 1, 1828. Sur. Wm. T. Perkins. 3.

Worley, Matthew, s. Dennis, and Susannah Talley, Mar. 15, 1813. Sur. John Jones. 130.

Worley, Samuel and Mary Worley, dau. Moses, Apr. 19, 1809. Sur. Joel Hutson. 117.

Worley, Samuel and Nancy Mills, Nov. 24, 1827. Sur. Jesse Mills.

Wort, Robt. and Catherine Kelly, Mar. 16, 1841. 18.

Wray, Adam and Polly Agee, dau. Jesse and Elizabeth, Mar. 22, 1813. Sur. Samuel Woody. 15.

Wray, Benj. and Frances Hartwell, May 7, 1832. Sur. Peter Angle. 48.
Wray, Benj. and Mary Angle, dau. Daniel, Sr., Dec. 6, 1847. Sur. Peter Angle. 18.
Wray, Benj. and Patsy Goode, Mar. 5, 1806. Sur. David Goode. 130.
Wray, Bird and Rebecca Seay, dau. Abram B., Oct. 18, 1832. Sur. Abraham B. Seay.
Wray, Chesley and Betsey Lemon, dau. Daniel, Mar. 5, 1810. Sur. Squire Chitwood.
Wray, Daniel and Fanny Abshire, Feb. 25, 1818 Sur. Edward Abshire. 130.
Wray, Daniel and Elizabeth Campbell, Nov. 13, 1813. Sur. James Stone. 130.
Wray, Daniel and Naomi Johnson, Nov. 16, 1840. Sur. Nathan Johnson.
Wray, Elias and Dolly Thurman, Mar. 25, 1806. Sur. John Thurman. 130.
Wray, Elijah and Elizabeth McHenny, Oct. 5, 1801. Sur. Samuel McHenry. 21.
Wray, Isaac and Mary Carlton, Apr. 5, 1805. Sur. Geo. Wright.
Wray, Joconas and Lucinda Seay, dau. John, Feb. 2, 1829. Sur. Edward T. Seay. 48.
Wray, James, Jr. and Sally R. Forbes, dau. J., Oct. 20, 1809. Sur. Wm. Forbes.
Wray, James Otey, s. Sally Reeves, and Louisa Forbes, dau. John R., Mar. 17, 1843. Sur. Wiley B. Forbes.
Wray, John and Barbara S. Lloyd, Dec. 18, 1810.
Wray, John and Susannah Kinsey, Feb. 4, 1805. Sur. John Wright. 130.
Wray, John and Sarah Starkey, dau. Catherine, Feb. 26, 1850. Sur. Benj. Betz. 18.
Wray, John, Jr. and Frances Wright, dau. Geo., Jan. 2, 1836. Sur. Wm. Turner.
Wray, John and Ellender Abshire, dau. Abraham, Jan. 28, 1841. Sur. John H. Wade. 18.
Wray, Jonas and Betsey Angle, Aug. 10, 1829. Sur. Henry Angle. 48.
Wray, Jonas and Elizabeth Angle, Nov. 16, 1837. 18.

Wray, Josiah T. and Mary M. Heptinstall, dau. Thos., Feb. 6, 1849. Sur. Jesse Bradley.
Wray, Joseph and Sarah Martin, June 25, 1845. 18.
Wray, Lott and Julia Beckner, dau. Jonathan and Mary, Apr. 4, 1845. Sur. Peter Angle, Jr. 18.
Wray, Meredith and Susan Beckner, Oct. 26, 1846. Sur. Jonathan Beckner. 18.
Wray, Perry C. and Martha W. Huddleston, Sept. 6, 1841. Sur. Abram Huddleston. 18.
Wray, Preston and Polly Abshire, Dec. 1, 1825. Sur. Abraham Abshire.
Wray, Stephen and Susannah Harter, June 7, 1794. 52.
Wray, Squire and Mary Wray, Jan. 15, 1801. 21.
Wray, Wesley and Mary Williams, Jan. 14, 1834. Sur. John Haines. 132.
Wray, Wilkins and Mary Powers, Mar. 2, 1824. Sur. John Powers.
Wray, Wm. and Polly Hixon, Apr. 17, 1817. Sur. Patrick Graham.
Wright, Abram O. and and Elizabeth F. Cundiff. Jan. 26, 1853. 80.
Wright, Ambrose and Vicey Hatcher, Feb. 19, 1816. Sur. John Hale. 130.
Wright, Anselm and Kitty C. Forbes, dau. Agnes, Oct. 27, 1826. Sur. John R. Forbes.
Wright, Armistead B. and Pamelia Doran, Jan. 7, 1833. Sur. Geo. Doran.
Wright, Asa and Polly Huddleston, Oct. 19, 1841. Sur. Perry C. Wray.
Wright, Berry and Polly Kelly, Oct. 1, 1810. Sur. Thos. McKinzey. 130.
Wright, Daniel and Lucy Tuning, Aug. 5, 1816. Sur. Nathaniel Tuning.
Wright, Enoch and Susannah Abshire, dau. Abraham, Oct. 3, 1808. Sur. Philemon Smith. 130.
Wright, Ezekiel and Elizabeth Bowles, May 20, 1812. 130.
Wright, Gabriel and Florina Wray, dau. James, Nov. 2, 1829. Sur. Bird Wray. 48.

Wray, Geo. and Keziah Simmons, Apr. 5, 1813. Sur. Anthony Simmons. 130.
Wright, Geo. and Susannah Abshire, Dec. 18, 1813. Sur. Edward Abshire. 130.
Wright, Geo. and Polly Abshire, dau. Luke, June 9, 1792. Sur. John Abshire. 23.
Wright, Geo. W. and Polly Teal, Feb. 16, 1828. Sur. Abraham Teal. 26.
Wright, Goodman and Elizabeth Jamison, Oct. 27, 1835. Sur. John Jamison. 68.
Wright, Hiram and Elizabeth Brockman, Mar. 6, 1809. Sur. Elijah Brockman. 130.
Wright, Isaiah and Peggy Ferguson, Nov. 20, 1797. Sur. Nelson Chapman.
Wright, Jacob and Hannah Underwood, Jan. 18, 1809. Sur. Joseph Underwood. 112.
Wright, James Grant, Jr. and Susannah Overfelt, Apr. 13, 1840. Sur. John Overfelt. 18.
Wright, James, s. Berry, and Polly Doran, dau. John, Nov. 6, 1832. Sur. John Gearhart.
Wright, James, of Bedford Co., and Judith P. Wright, dau. Peter, June 13, 1846. Sur. Fleming J. T. Wright. 19.
Wright, James, g. Stephen Kasler, and Elizabeth Gearhart, dau. Hiram, Jan. 31, 1844. Sur. Isaac Boon. 18.
Wright, James G. and Tabitha Angel, Jan. 21, 1852. Sur. Theo. F. Webb.
Wright, James and Peggy Young, Oct. 9, 1786. Sur. David Morgan. 66.
Wright, Jesse and Elizabeth Crawford, dau. Rachael, Mar. 21, 1799. Sur. Geo. Wright.
Wright, John and Elizabeth Kelley, Sept. 2, 1805. Sur. John Vincent. 130.
Wright, John and Elizabeth Abshire, Feb. 8, 1800. Sur. Lodowick Abshire.
Wright, John B. and Jemima Abshire, dau. Susannah, Dec. 29, 1831. Sur. Barnabas Arthur. 48.
Wright, John and Teresa Abshire, Apr. 25, 1836. Sur. Isaac Abshire.
Wright, John A. and Mary Elizabeth Pearson, Apr. 11, 1849. 18.

Wright, Joseph and Judith Agee, dau. Polly, Feb. 23, 1824. Sur. Isaac Agee. 130.
Wright, Joseph and Clary Drake, Oct. 28, 1793. 41.
Wright, Joseph and Cynthia Belcher, July 18, 1808. Sur. Woodson Bagley.
Wright, Joseph and Martha Pagin, June 15, 1829. 140.
Wright, Josiah and Peggy Ferguson, Nov. 20, 1797. Sur. Nelson Chapman.
Wright, Moses and Nancy Wright, Nov. 30, 1816. Sur. Hiram Wright.
Wright, Pendleton and Nancy Wright, Jan. 13, 1825. Sur. John Wright. 130.
Wright, Solomon, Jr. and Phebe Wright, Dec. 27, 1817. Sur. Solomon Wright, Sr.
Wright, Thos. and Susanna Pasley, dau. Robt., Sr., Mar. 10, 1821. Sur. Citizen S. Woods.
Wright, Wesley A. and Jane S. Holland, dau. John M., Nov. 4, 1844. Sur. Abram T. Holland.
Wright, Wm. A. B. and Barbara Jamison, Oct. 18, 1841. Sur. John Jamison. 18.
Wright, Wm. and Ann Nunley, Mar. 26, 1840. Sur. Thos. Nunley. 18.
Wright, Wm. and Sarah Greer, Oct. 1, 1823. Sur. Samuel W. Greer.
Wright, Wm. and Ellender Johnson, dau. Geo., Feb. 18, 1803. Sur. Geo. Johnson. 106.
Wright, Wright and Polly Scott, dau. Jane, Feb. 9, 1809. Sur. James B. Scott.
Wrightsman, John and Mary Fisher, Feb. 13, 1851. 18.
Wyatt, Elijah and .... Canterbury, Dec. 27, 1794. 22.
Wyatt, John and Susannah Law, dau. John, Jr., Aug. 9, 1802. Sur. Wm. Farmer. 106.
Wyatt, Solomon and Hannah Reese, June 12, 1797. Sur. Edward Wyatt. 141.
Wyatt, Thomas and Mary Reese, Dec. 4, 1797. Sur. John Reese. 141.
Wysong, Henry and Catherine Dodd, dau. Rebecca, Jan. 24, 1811. Sur. Abraham Dodd. 112.

Wysong, Henry, Jr., s. Henry, Sr., and Catherine Oyler, dau. Vallentine, Apr. 4, 1814. Sur. Henry Wysong, Sr. 6.

Wysong, Jacob and Polly Hopkins, July 27, 1811. Sur. Isaac Hopkins.

Wysong, Jacob and Mamy Cotterel, dau. Mamy and James, Feb. 24, 1801. Sur. Jesse Chappel. 21.

Wysong, Joseph, Jr. and Susannah Kitchen, dau. Caleb, Aug. 26, 1808. Sur. Valentine Oyler and John Coleman.

Wysong, Lewis and Eleanor Wright, Mar. 21, 1842. Sur. James Wright. 18.

Wysong, Lewis P. and Mirah Simmons, g. and bro. Fletcher Simmons, Dec. 16, 1847. Sur. John F. Kennett. 19.

Wysong, Valentine and Mary Altick, Dec. 21, 1798. Sur. John Altick. 21.

Yates, Wm. and Milly Board, Nov. 30, 1798. Sur. Wm. Sperlock. 72.

Yeats, John D. and Stelly Moore, Sept. 7, 1858.

Yeats, Jubal S. and Stelly Moore, Sept. 7, 1846. Sur. John N. Moore.

Yeatts, John M. and Caren Moore, May 28, 1850. Sur. Jubal D. Yeatts.

Young, Andrew and America Ramsey, dau. Thos. Ramsey, Feb. 1, 1847. Sur. Booker Mullins.

Young, Armstead and Margaret Ferguson, Oct. 10, 1837. Sur. Jeremiah Ferguson.

Young, Berry and Nancy Standley, Mar. 1, 1823. Sur. John Young. 130.

Young, C. and Susan Simpson, Feb. 20, 1853. 80.

Young, David and Mary Cassell, dau. Elizabeth, May 23, 1812. Sur. John Cassell.

Young, Isaac, s. Peter, and Mary Walker, dau. Joel, Nov. 19, 1804. Sur. Geo. Walker.

Young Isaac and Sarah Cannaday, Nov. 27, 1824. Sur. Pleasant Cannaday.

Young, Jeremiah and Martha E. Frith, Nov. 2, 1858.

Young, Jeremiah and Elizabeth Gilbert, —, 1852. 132.

Young, Joel and Anna Lemon, dau. Isaac, May 19, 1821. Sur. Benj. Lemon.

Young, John and Susannah Harger, Oct. 3, 1811. Sur. Robt.
Scarborough.
Young, John and Elizabeth Standley, Jan. 27, 1808. Sur. Wm.
Standley. 122.
Young, John W. and Nancy E. Scott, Mar. 4, 1850. Sur. Wm.
Young. 97.
Young, John and Nancy Noe, dau. Nathaniel B., Dec. 11, 1833.
Sur. Nathaniel B. Noe.
Young, John and Elizabeth Crump, dau. Geo., Nov. 15, 1828.
Sur. Wm. Crump. 3.
Young, Joseph and Frances Fuller, dau. Briton, Mar. 6, 1839.
Sur. John M. Hanks. 3.
Young, Joshua and Nancy Walker, Nov. 14, 1798. Sur. John
Walker.
Young, Jubal and Martha Akers. Jan. ...., 1852. 132.
Young, Lewis and Sally Goode, dau. David Cooper, Nov. 10,
1841. Sur. Wiley Ferguson. 132.
Young, Milen and Polly Brock, dau. John, Oct. 14, 1790. Sur.
David Shockley.
Young, Mordecia, s. Peter, and Nancy Campbell, Mar. 21, 1840.
Sur. Marshall Waid. 132.
Young, Peter, Jr., and Elizabeth Glasspy, Sept. 13, 1844. Sur.
Wm. Gallaspy. 134.
Young, Peter and Malinda Mosley, dau. Velinder, Mar. 3, 1817.
Sur. Peter Fisher.
Young, Robt. and Chloe Kinsey, dau. Cloe A., Mar. 7, 1789.
Sur. Jacob Mollendon. 52.
Young, Saunders and Hetty A. Key, Jan. 11, 1843. Sur. Elizabeth
Keys. 132.
Young, Thos. and Elizabeth Marrs, Jan. 16, 1829.
Young, Thos. S. and Elizabeth A. Meador, Nov. 16, 1858.
Young, Thos. and Susannah Price, Sept. 7, 1818. Sur. John
Price. 130.
Young, Wiley and Nancy Clarkson, 1797.
Young, Wm. and Patsy Watson, Jan. 13, 1817. Sur. Wm.
Walden. 44.
Young, Wm. and Peggy Holcomb, Feb. 28, 1828. Sur. John
Young.

Young, Wm. and Jane Guerrant, Sept. 25, 1819. Sur. John R. Guerrant.

Zeigler, John and Mary Ann Brock, in 1800 package. Sur. Joshua Brock. 37. Bond given to Gov. James Monore, 1799-01.

Zeigler, Joram and Esther Zeigler, Nov. 4, 1832. Sur. Benj. Semones. 3.

Zeigler, Joshua and Eveline White, Nov. 4, 1839. Sur. James M. White.

Zeigler, Michael and Lucy Woody, July 3, 1826. Sur. Randolph Woody.

Zeigler, Michael and Sarah Woody, Feb. 7, 1842. Sur. Allen Woody.

Zeigler, Wm. and Rebecca Stewart, dau. David, Sept. 29, 1804. Sur. .... Pitcher.

Zink, Elias and Nancy Laprade, Oct. 17, 1842. Sur. Andrew Laprade.

Zink, Joseph and Barbary Fisher, Dec. 29, 1853. 18.

FRANKLIN COUNTY MINISTERS 1786-1858

1. Joshua Adams
2. Zechariah Angell
3. Abner Anthony
4. Albert Anthony
5. Mosby Arnold
6. Henry Ashworth
7. Joel Ashworth
8. John Ashworth
9. Thomas Ashworth
10. Garlard A. Austin
11. Abraham Barnhart
12. Richard B. Beck
13. William W. Bennett
14. Robert P. Bibb
15. Luke Bird
16. George Bowman
17. Isaac Bowman
18. John Bowman
19. Pleasant Brown
20. Jeremiah Burnett
21. Horatio Burns
22. Jeremiah Burns
23. Jesse Burns
24. Robert Burwell
25. Edwin A. Cabaniss
26. Edwin G. Cabaniss
27. William Class
28. R. A. Claughton (Clayton)
29. Nicholas H. Cobbs
30. John Comer, Sr.
31. John Conner
32. J. W. Conner
33. William Crump
34. James M. Darden
35. William Davis
36. Alex Doniphan
37. Thomas Douglas
38. Arthur W. Eames
39. Joseph H. Eames
40. John Eller
41. Jesse Fears
42. John W. Floyd
43. John R. Forbes
44. Lewis Foster
45. Thomas C. Goggins
46. Joseph Goodman
47. Robert Gray
48. Moses Greer
49. Moses Greer, Jr.
50. Rice Haggard
51. Robert Hairston
52. Randolph Hall
53. John Hank
54. William Hankins
55. A. F. Harris
56. W. M. Hash
57. Joseph Hatchett
58. Nathan A. Hooker.
59. Peter Howard
60. Michael Howry
61. Stephen Hubbard
62. Mathew W. Jackson
63. J. H. Jeffesron
64. James M. Jefferson
65. Jesse Jones
66. Robert Jones
67. William M. Jordon

68. George W. Kelly
69. William W. Kelly
70. Benjamin Kidd
71. John King
72. Samuel King
73. Thomas Lacy
74. John R. Lee
75. John W. Lewis
76. William Lovell
77. Jeremiah Lumsden
78. Nehemiah Lumsden
79. James Luster
80. John R. Martin
81. Orson Martin
82. William P. Martin
83. William H. Matthews
84. Bennett Maxey
85. David M. Mayo
86. Benjamin Meador
87. Joel W. Meador
88. Ford Miller
89. Jacob Miller
90. Othneil Minter
91. Silas Minter
92. James Mitchell
93. Jeptha Moore
94. Jubal A. Morgan
95. Jacob McEnally
96. Abraham Nafe
97. Alfred Normon
98. Joseph Payne
99. Urias Powers
100. Sam Regester
101. James Reid
102. Isaac Rentfro
103. Jesse Rentfro
104. Samuel D. Rice
105. T. M. Sanderson
106. John Saunders
107. Joseph Saunders
108. Samuel Sayford
109. G. Scherer
110. William M. Schoolfield
111. Thomas G. Shelor
112. Reuben Short
113. John Showalter
114. Daniel Shrewsbrry
115. Daniel Southall
116. William Smith
117. William Roy Smith
118. John T. St. Clair
119. William H. Starr
120. Robert Stockton
121. Owen Sumner
122. Benjamin Sweeny
123. Happy Talley
124. John T. Taylor
125. W. Thompson
126. John A. Taylor
127. Bird S. Turner
128. Elkanah B. Turner
129. John Turner
130. Wilson Turner
131. Henry VanOver
132. Arnold Walker
133. Charles A. Weatherford
134. Theo. F. Webb
135. Peyton Welch
136. Benjamin S. West, Sr.
137. William W. Wildman
138. Benjamin M. Williams
139. Henry Wise
140. Stephen Wood.
141. John Wyatt
142. W. M. Walker
143. William W. Albea
144. Jehu Hank

www.ingramcontent.com/pod-product-compliance
Lightning Source LLC
Chambersburg PA
CBHW061439300426
44114CB00014B/1749